More Praise for *Blended*

"The interest in leveraging technology in schools is growing at a rapid pace. That means district leadership is critical in order to harness these innovative tools as effectively as possible. This book provides superintendents with a blueprint to ensure that blending learning boosts student achievement."

—Daniel A. Domenech, executive director, American Association of School Administrators

"*Blended* not only describes what various blended learning models look like, it carefully lays out a blueprint that school administrators, teachers, and parents can use to make blended learning a reality in their schools. As Horn and Staker clearly state in this book, what we need more than anything in education today is a culture of iteration and innovation to think through and take advantage of this dynamic shift in potential learning models. This important book is a tremendous resource for anyone who wants to take on the significant change we need to make in education. I am going to make sure everyone on my team reads it from cover to cover. Highly recommended!"

—Jaime Casap, global education evangelist, Google

"Our schools need to improve, and technology, if used smartly, can help them do that. This book, building on the authors' previous groundbreaking work in *Disrupting Class*, provides a step-by-step guide for how to do blended learning right. It is a must-read for school officials and educators who want to get good results for their students."

—Joel Klein, CEO, Amplify; former chancellor, New York City Department of Education

"This book takes the innovative work in *Disrupting Class* to the next level. *Blended* unleashes the unprecedented opportunities for teachers and students to design personalized learning pathways for each learner, instead of a one-size-fits all approach. This blueprint propels educators and administrators, policymakers and community leaders to help break down America's traditional education silos by developing innovative teaching and learning environments that will help students succeed in a technology-driven global economy."

—*Bev Perdue, founder and chair, DigiLEARN; former governor, North Carolina*

"Michael Horn and Heather Staker, in *Blended*, have perfectly captured the tensions and optimism surrounding the inexorable move toward digital resources in American classrooms. This book will prove an invaluable resource to teachers, administrators and entrepreneurs who have a common mission: to leverage technology as a tool to provide excellence for every child in our country."

—*Jane Swift, CEO, Middlebury Interactive Languages; former governor, Massachusetts*

"The digital revolution is upon us, and teachers are hungering for ways to better connect with kids where they are, to give them an exceptional education, and to prepare them to succeed in an increasingly fast-paced world. As administrators we must ensure that our teachers are as ready as their students to make the most of a 21st-century classroom. While *Disrupting Class* offered a vision of the emerging digital landscape in education, *Blended* takes things a step further. In reading it we start to see just how, as educators, we're going to exist in this new world and how we can utilize blended-learning strategies to offer our students the education they deserve."

—*Terry B. Grier, superintendent of schools, Houston Independent School District*

"*Blended* offers a thoughtful and comprehensive examination of the blended learning landscape. While the authors make a strong case for the power of online learning to individualize instruction, they also reveal a yet untapped potential for online learning to empower students to own their education. With *Blended*'s contribution to the conversation, I am optimistic we can move past education that is customized to one that is genuinely personalized—that focuses less on education as delivery and more as discovery."

—*JoAnn Bartoletti, executive director, National Association of Secondary School Principals*

"With all the calls to reform, improve, or use technology to enhance education, Horn and Staker's approach is refreshing and pragmatic. They succinctly capture the three great advantages of blended learning: personalization, access, and cost, and support them with examples of what works and how. The authors illustrate how students are eager to take the initiative, to engage and discover resources that build on what they know and guide them to what they should know. Teachers can concentrate on students who need more attention. With this approach, mastery of content is possible for every student. *Blended* charts a course to substantially increase college and career readiness. A great read for education leaders and policymakers alike!"

— *Jim Geringer, vice chair, DigiLearn; former governor, Wyoming*

blended

Using Disruptive Innovation to Improve Schools

Michael B. Horn and Heather Staker

Foreword by Clayton M. Christensen

JOSSEY-BASS™
A Wiley Brand

Cover Design: Wiley
Cover Image: © hakkiarslan | by Thinkstock

Published by Jossey-Bass
A Wiley Brand
One Montgomery Street, Suite 1200, San Francisco, CA 94104-4594—www.wiley.com,
www.josseybass.com/highereducation

Jossey-Bass books and products are available through most bookstores. To contact Jossey-Bass directly call our Customer Care Department within the U.S. at 800-956-7739, outside the U.S. at 317-572-3986, or fax 317-572-4002.

Wiley publishes in a variety of print and electronic formats and by print-on-demand. Some material included with standard print versions of this book may not be included in e-books or in print-on-demand. If this book refers to media such as a CD or DVD that is not included in the version you purchased, you may download this material at http://booksupport.wiley.com. For more information about Wiley products, visit www.wiley.com.

Library of Congress Cataloging-in-Publication Data

Library of Congress Cataloging-in-Publication Data has been applied for and is on file with the Library of Congress.
ISBN 9781118955154 (hardcover);
ISBN 9781118955178 (ebk.);
ISBN 9781118955161 (ebk.).

Printed in the United States of America
FIRST EDITION
HC Printing   SKY10020661_090320

Contents

List of Videos

Foreword: When Disruptive Innovation and Paradigms Collide

We stand at the vanguard of a shift in education. For a long time, people have shouted back and forth about what ails our schools and have offered differing solutions. Yet there is no panacea. Each camp holds a piece of the solution, but because of the way our schools work, each piece is often diametrically opposed to another. With the emergence of blended learning in our nation's K–12 schools, we now have the opportunity to move beyond what have previously been trade-offs. Allow me to explain by illuminating how the concepts of *paradigm* and *disruption* relate to each other.

Thomas Kuhn's *The Structure of Scientific Revolutions,* which introduced us to the concept of paradigms, is one of the most useful books I've ever read. It summarizes a simple and general model of how bodies of understanding emerge and improve, based on Kuhn's lifetime of studying the history of science. The emphasis of Kuhn's model isn't the initial *starting* of a body of understanding per se. Rather, it focuses on how bodies of understanding improve.

A body of understanding typically starts with a hypothesis about a pattern between one thing and another. The method of improving understanding almost always is an *anomaly*—a discovery of something for which the original pattern cannot account. Anomalies force researchers to revisit the original explanation of causality and adjust it so that it accounts for the new observation as well as the original ones. Through this process of confronting and resolving anomalies that previously could not be accounted for, a body of understanding becomes more and more capable of explaining more and more things.

At some point in some bodies of understanding, causality becomes so broadly understood and accepted that the work of researchers in that field instinctively builds on that understanding. Kuhn called such a body of understanding of causality a "paradigm." It is a model that articulates what is to be observed and scrutinized; the kind of questions that should be asked and how these questions are to be structured and answered; and how the results of investigations should be interpreted.

Researchers rarely question a paradigm because it is so helpful in understanding what is happening in a field. They therefore assume that it is valid and engage in *normal science.* This entails learning how to measure things, defining and characterizing the phenomena, and probing for the boundaries of application of the paradigm. Much of this work entails grouping and comparing. This is how researchers continue to discover anomalies. When they observe an anomaly, they work to adjust and restate the paradigm to accommodate the outlying observation—or they rule that the anomaly occurs outside the boundaries of what the paradigm applies to.

On occasion, however, researchers discover an anomaly for which the paradigm simply cannot account. Researchers often then put it on a shelf somewhere—the academic equivalent of a "cold case." When researchers discover another anomaly the paradigm simply cannot account, it too is similarly put aside for the time being on the cold case shelf. When enough cold cases have accumulated, an enterprising researcher will then study them together and announce, "Hey guys! Look at all of these cold cases! Can you see the pattern across all of them? The paradigm simply cannot be true!"

Often, only a theory that is used in another branch of science in which the original and deepest believers of the paradigm have little background can help reveal the pattern across these anomalies. Because of this, the devout defend the validity of the original paradigm, often to their graves. Indeed, their instinctive toolkit that they used for learning in their branch of science renders many of them unable to see the anomalies that put the paradigm into question. For this reason, Kuhn observed that new researchers, whose training and disciplines are different, typically initiate the toppling of a paradigm and the development of the new knowledge that takes its place.

This process of developing, testing, and toppling paradigms is at work 24×7. It is not an event. Often it takes decades to build and then discredit paradigms.

As an aside, many people use the term "paradigm" for many purposes. Most of them have never read Kuhn's book. They use it in a speech to coronate their opinion into a "paradigm shift," to bolster the stature of an aggressor's intellectual fight with an academic foe, and so on. In my little corner of the world, the term "disruptive innovation" is similarly overused and overapplied by uninformed people who seek justification for anything they want to do anyway.

THE RELATIONSHIP BETWEEN STRATEGY AND INNOVATION

Much of the energy expended in normal science entails studying trade-offs, which typically can be displayed as a two-dimensional graph: to get more of one thing, on the vertical axis, you get less of the other, measured on the horizontal axis. The relationship between trade-offs, called an "efficiency frontier," can be linear, convex, or concave. Putting a satellite into orbit entails trade-offs, for example. Lifting it into a low orbit makes it faster in telecommunications, but the satellite needs to be small, lightweight, and focused on a single mission; a satellite in a high orbit can be bigger and have multiple missions, but it is much more expensive; and so on.

A decision to position one's company or products on a point on an efficiency frontier between trade-offs such as these is what my friends Michael Raynor and Michael Porter call "strategy." Strategy entails trade-offs. In education, a few of these trade-offs might be: Should the model of teaching be one-way (lecture) or two-way (discussion)? Should our model be based on personal tutors or teaching students by the batch? Should we build large schools to take advantage of economies of scale, or should we prefer smaller schools with fewer students per teacher? These are strategic choices along a theoretical frontier. After a strategic choice has been made, the types of innovations that educators focus on are what we call "sustaining innovations." These types of innovations make good products better. They help you to more effectively deliver the strategic choices you have selected.

Paradigms, such as those in satellite design and placement, don't dictate an optimal spot on the trade-off frontier. Rather, they define the trade-offs to be discussed and the metrics to be used in evaluating answers. In education, the paradigm frames things like the student-to-teacher ratio or the trade-offs between project-based learning (engagement) and lecture-based learning (knowledge absorption). Normal science rarely questions the existence of these trade-offs.

Disruptive innovation occurs when an entrepreneur or technologist figures out how to break a trade-off by giving more of one without requiring us to accept less of the other. Often, breaking a trade-off initiates the toppling of a paradigm. A key reason why disruptive innovations are so adept at toppling paradigms — and industry leaders — is that sustaining innovations are static. They make the best of trade-offs that were decided in the past.

Those with the perspective of a disruptive innovator initially accept the established trade-offs in the old paradigm. But they see that the trajectory of technological improvement is faster than what customers are able to use. As the performance of technology moves from "not good enough" to "more than good enough," the trade-offs are broken. The intersection of the trajectories in the theory of disruption dynamically releases the constraints that create trade-offs.

The trajectory that becomes disruptive always begins among undemanding customers at the bottom of sectors. In the vein of education, most teachers like me conceded early on, at least verbally, that the delivery of lectures online would, over time, disruptively surmount traditional in-class lectures. But we have collectively believed that it would be impossible for online learning to emulate the discussion in a senior research seminar in high school or college or case-based teaching at the Harvard Business School. In the onslaught of disruption, we have seen these as safe havens for traditional teaching.

Now, however, enter my friend Espen Anderson, professor at the Norwegian School of Management in Oslo. Espen is breaking trade-offs in classroom learning. The arrangement is disruptive and ongoing. Espen needs to be in Boston for medical reasons as I write this, even as his students need to learn through the case method in Oslo. Espen's solution? He tied his signature bow tie onto a robot in the Oslo classroom, taped his Apple iPad on top of the robot's neck, and brought his wireless joystick for the robot to Boston. Espen's students sit in assigned seats in Oslo, and each seat has three buttons. One signals to Espen, "I want to make a comment in support of the last comment." Another signals, "I disagree with that last comment." The third signals, "I have a comment on a different topic." This allows Espen to call on a student who has figuratively raised his hand in the air and guide the direction of the discussion. Espen can then figuratively walk to the whiteboard to summarize what the students are saying, as well as move to a student he has called upon and respond not just verbally, but with body language, to what the student says.

I tell his story not to say that K–12 education will look the way his classroom looks in the future, but to illustrate how because the process of technological improvement improves at a faster rate than people can use the improvement, Espen is showing us that trade-offs that historically were implicit in some of the paradigms of education are now being broken.

Here is a way to frame the process: Time is a way of preventing everything from happening at once. The future and the past both exist in the present, but they are not evenly distributed around the world. (William Gibson, Sean Carroll, and others have had similar thoughts.) Is Espen Anderson's classroom in the future or the present?

If we simply wait for the future to become the present—that is, if we wait until data about new ways to teach and learn arrive on the scene—data will continue to joust with other data, and little will change. This is so because without a compelling theory as a foundation, your data will not have a louder voice, nor more compelling logic, than my data will have. The basis of action and change is theory, not data.

Many elements of the paradigm about teaching and learning have served portions of society well in the past. Now we have a theory—disruptive innovation—that gives meaning to the data that are emerging. The data from classrooms, including Espen's, in many parts of the world are declaring that trade-offs in education are being broken.

I can see that in my past as a teacher, I was constrained by trade-offs. My innovations were sustaining ones. I have been a good teacher for students who thought as I did or had experiences like mine. I am mediocre, at best, in teaching students who frame the world differently. Online learning offers the chance to custom-deliver learning opportunities matched to each student. To have intellectually stimulating discussions with my students, I had to keep enrollment down. I always thought that the teacher taught and the students listened. No longer. Stimulating discussions among large numbers of students in widely differing locations is now possible. Students can teach one another in addition to teachers teaching students. We are all learning how to learn and teaching how to teach. And thank goodness. As Eric Hoffer remarked, "In a time of drastic change it is the learners who inherit the future. The learned usually find themselves beautifully equipped to live in a world that no longer exists."

This book, by my colleagues Michael Horn and Heather Staker, is a marvelous description of how many of the trade-offs in teaching and learning are being broken. Instead of our needing to accept less of one thing in order to get more of another, we can now expect with confidence that we actually can achieve more, period. As the capability of online learning moves up the trajectory of improvement and obviates more and more trade-offs, blended learning preserves access to the best of in-person teaching and learning as we navigate disruption. Blended learning makes the best of the old and new paradigms available to all of us who want to learn. And this book is designed to help teachers, school leaders, superintendents, and parents learn how to implement blended learning today and not stand on the sidelines waiting for the future to emerge somewhere else.

Clayton M. Christensen
Harvard Business School

Acknowledgments

After the publication of *Disrupting Class*, a fortunate thing happened. Teachers, school leaders, policymakers, parents, entrepreneurs, funders, philanthropists, technologists, corporate leaders, college professors, and many others reached out to us. We all shared one common goal: to transform our education system into a student-centered one that allows all children to fulfill their human potential.

Many of these people worked in education; many did not. Many agreed with our vision and wanted to connect with our growing network of innovators; others did not agree and wanted to teach me. Thanks to their outreach—and the thousands of phone calls, meetings, and school visits I've been privileged to partake in with people around the world—I've learned a tremendous amount. I'm inspired daily by the passions of people who work to make education better for students worldwide.

In our work at the Clayton Christensen Institute, a nonprofit and nonpartisan think tank dedicated to improving the world through disruptive innovation that I cofounded, we've been able to leverage this access to document what we've learned through our case studies, white papers, articles, blogs, speeches, workshops, and our Blended Learning Universe, a database of blended-learning school profiles. None of this research would be possible without our generous donors. In this book, we bring together all that we've seen and learned with our theories of innovation to help you design blended-learning environments that move our education system toward a student-centered one.

After *Disrupting Class*, I always wondered how one writes a second book. The answer for me has been to have an amazing coauthor and thought partner. Heather Staker is brilliant, passionate, and perhaps the most productive person

I have ever known. Had it not been for her skillful writing, vision, and research, this book would not have happened.

We have been fortunate to have an amazing team at the Christensen Institute over the past seven years who contributed to this book. Katherine Mackey was our first employee and wrote several of the case studies that galvanized this work. Meg Evans illuminated challenges on the ground that schools adopting blended learning experienced and made our theory-based work more tangible. Anna Gu dug deep to check our facts and pinpoint sources. Cathleen Calice carved out the time for the thousands of meetings that inspired this book, as well as the time to write it. Tom Arnett, Charity Eyre, Julia Freeland, and Mike Lemaire's research all helped shape this volume. My dear friend and Christensen Institute board chair Gisele Huff has been an instrumental sounding board and guiding light through the years and helped bring this to fruition. Ann Christensen and Hayden Hill make our work more impactful. Michelle R. Weise helps connect our work to the evolving reality of higher education. And I remain indebted to and inspired by my mentor, Clayton Christensen, who continues to teach me in ways big and small.

I'm lucky to have a lifelong partner in my wife, Tracy, who feels as passionately about my work as I do and who just as earnestly wants us to succeed in transforming schools around the world into student-centered ones that can personalize for each student's distinct learning needs. As we welcome our daughters into this world, her pushing and prodding, editing, cheerleading, and love propel me forward. I dedicate this book to her.

Michael B. Horn
Lexington, Massachusetts

In 2010 I began researching the emergence of blended learning in American schools. At the time I had no idea that what was then a small project—a joint effort between the Clayton Christensen Institute and Alex Hernandez and Eric Chan from the Charter School Growth Fund—would change my personal life in a big way. A few months into the research, I stumbled upon Acton Academy, a blended school that Jeff and Laura Sandefer founded in Austin, Texas. I was so impressed with the school that I persuaded my husband to move from Honolulu, Hawaii, to the heart of Central Texas so our five young children could enroll.

Today, each time that I visit a blended school, I have one question in my mind: Is this another school to which we would want to send our *own* children? I am hopeful that over the next decade, the answer will increasingly be yes.

I am grateful to Michael Horn, whose development of *Disrupting Class* sparked a far-reaching conversation about how to recenter learning around individual student needs. He is widely acclaimed for his intellect and eloquence, but those who work on his team know that he is equally gifted as a manager and mentor of people.

Several individuals opened doors for me that have led to opportunities to live up to the desire I feel to help improve schools and the education system. These people include Clayton Christensen, Pete Wilson, Salem Abraham, Beth Ann Bryan, Sari Factor, Francie Alexander, Roger Porter, Richard Wallace, Leilani Williams, and the Brain Chase team.

Many teachers and child whisperers were an invaluable support to our family this year. Special thanks to Miranda Livingston, Andrea Hall, Carley Clayton, Monica Fisher, Caroline Rudolph, Kaylie Dienelt Reed, Anna Blabey Smith, Samantha Simpson, Terri Dove, DeeAnne Paulson, Debra Wissman, and Janelle Black, who teach, guide, and love many Austin children, including my own.

I am inspired by my parents, who regard teaching as among the highest of vocations. L. Whitney Clayton, my father, gave up his successful law practice to become a minister and teacher. Kathy Clayton, my mother, served for thirty years as a school teacher, facilitated student-centered learning in her classrooms well before the concept was familiar, and in her poetic style wrote a beautiful book about it that inspired my thinking for this one.

Tate, Savannah, Audrey, Henry, and Grayson Staker are responsible for the passion and urgency I feel in helping to articulate the case for making schools not only more effective by society's standards, but also more joyful and nurturing from a child's point of view. Mothering them is the greatest opportunity of my life. Allan Staker is my forever companion and love. He continuously strengthens me, encourages me, and reminds me that there is no shortcut to adventure. I dedicate this book to him.

Heather Staker
Austin, Texas

This book would not have been possible without the support of numerous other individuals and organizations over the last several years. Thank you to Rich Crandall, Scott Ellis, Dick Peller, Emily Snyder, and Tom Vander Ark for their thoughtful reading and reviewing of the manuscript; Russ Altenburg, Scott Benson, Stacey Childress, and Luis de la Fuentes for their counsel and support; John Bailey, Andy Calkins, Brian Greenberg, Kevin Hall, Susan Patrick, Chip Slaven, Diane Tavenner, John Watson, Bob Wise, and Caitrin Wright for their thought partnership; Marjorie McAneny, Kristi Hein, Tracy Gallagher, Cathy Mallon, and the rest of the Wiley team for their guidance and masterful editing; our literary agents Danny Stern and Kristen Karp for their wisdom; and Ashley Glowinski, Jen Heady, Anjelica Sena, and Ned Ward of Stern+Associates for helping spread awareness.

About the Authors

Michael B. Horn is a cofounder of the Clayton Christensen Institute for Disruptive Innovation and serves as the executive director of its education program. He leads a team that educates policymakers and community leaders on the power of disruptive innovation in the K–12 and higher education spheres through its research. His team aims to transform monolithic, factory-model education systems into student-centered designs that educate successfully every student and enable each to realize his or her fullest potential.

In 2008, Horn coauthored the award-winning book *Disrupting Class: How Disruptive Innovation Will Change the Way the World Learns* with Harvard Business School Professor Clayton M. Christensen and Curtis W. Johnson. *Newsweek* ranked the book fourteenth on its list of "Fifty Books for Our Times." Horn has written several white papers about blended learning and, with Frederick Hess, is coeditor of the book *Private Enterprise and Public Education*. He has also written articles for leading publications such as *Forbes, Washington Post, Economist, Huffington Post*, and *Education Week* and, along with Brian Greenberg of the Silicon Schools Fund, leads "Blended Learning 101," a five-part series of free online content in partnership with the Khan Academy.

Horn testifies regularly at state legislative sessions and is a frequent keynote speaker at education conferences and planning sessions around the United States. *Tech & Learning* magazine named him to its list of the one hundred most important people in the creation and advancement of the use of technology in education.

In addition, Horn serves on a variety of boards, including as an executive editor of *Education Next*, a journal of opinion and research about education policy, and on the boards of Fidelis Education and the Silicon Schools Fund. Horn is also a member of the Education Innovation Advisory Board at Arizona State University, the Digital Learning Advisory Council to the Board of Education in Massachusetts, and the advisory committee for the Hechinger Institute on Education and the Media at Teachers College, Columbia University. Horn holds a BA in history from Yale University and an MBA from the Harvard Business School. He was also a 2014 Eisenhower Fellow and studied the education systems in Vietnam and Korea.

Heather Staker is a senior research fellow for education practice at the Clayton Christensen Institute for Disruptive Innovation. She has appeared on radio and television and in legislative hearings nationwide as a spokesperson for blended learning, competency-based learning, and student-centered design. Major publications Staker has authored or coauthored include "The Rise of K–12 Blended Learning," "Classifying K–12 Blended Learning," and "Is K–12 Blended Learning Disruptive?"

Named by Scholastic as one of the Five People to Watch in Education in 2012, Staker has written articles for *Education Next, Deseret News,* and *THE Journal,* as well as appeared frequently as the keynote speaker at education and innovation conferences across the country. Staker is also the co-producer of Brain Chase, a 6-week worldwide learning adventure disguised as a massive treasure hunt for K–8 students during summer vacation.

Prior to the Christensen Institute, Staker worked as a strategy consultant for McKinsey & Company, served as a member of the California State Board of Education during Governor Pete Wilson's administration, taught U.S. history as a teaching fellow at Harvard University, started a co-op preschool, and marketed Oil of Olay for Proctor & Gamble. She holds a BA in government from Harvard University and an MBA from the Harvard Business School. She is happily married to Allan Staker, and together they are raising five spirited children.

Introduction

You walk into a school that is clean and painted brightly. Student artwork hangs from the walls, and the library is well stocked. The teaching staff works hard, and administrators keep the school running in an orderly way. The school provides students with computers, sports, and field trips. Yes, many schools in the world struggle mightily, particularly in the inner city; documentaries such as *Waiting for Superman* and *A Right Denied* have highlighted heartbreaking public school blight. But certainly some schools are good. And if you're like most parents, you believe that the schools your own children attend—whether public or private; urban, suburban, or rural—are preparing your children well.[1]

This book is about the blending of online learning into schools. It is intended to be not only a resource for those wanting to make significant changes to their schools or who are already thinking about blended learning, but also an eye-opener for people who feel content with what they have. Schools are approaching the tipping point in a digital transformation that will forever change the way the world learns. If online learning has not already rocked your local schools, then it will soon. The authors of *Disrupting Class* (including Michael B. Horn, a coauthor of this book) made that prediction in 2008, when they forecasted that by 2019, 50 percent of high school courses would be online in some form or fashion.

Years later that prediction continues to appear accurate—some would even say conservative.[2] People may debate the timing, but we believe the more interesting question is whether the indisputable emergence of online learning across elementary, middle, and high schools is a good thing. Is our system devolving into a hopelessly impersonal, sci-fi-type automation, or is the surge of students learning online a positive thing? And how can we ensure the latter?

PATTERN OF DISRUPTIVE INNOVATION

Asking whether online learning is a good thing is much like asking whether email, Target, and TurboTax are good things. The U.S. Postal Service may not be a fan of email, but most everyone else has found that email makes communication faster, more convenient, and more affordable than mailing a letter with stamps. Macy's may not love Target, but countless consumers enjoy improved standards of living because of the affordability of discount retailers. H&R Block and other tax accounting firms rue the day TurboTax was born, but many individuals and small businesses consider TurboTax a godsend.

Email, discount retailers, and TurboTax are all examples of what Professor Clayton M. Christensen of the Harvard Business School calls "disruptive innovation." Although disruptive innovation may not sound, on first hearing, like something educators would want to embrace, it offers many benefits. The term refers to products and services that start in simple applications at the bottom of the market for those without the wealth or expertise to participate otherwise in the market.[3] For example, before TurboTax came along, most people struggled with a pencil and calculator to file their own returns because they could not afford to pay a professional tax accounting firm to do it for them. But Intuit's TurboTax software is "disrupting" the current, or incumbent, system made up of professional tax firms. It gives millions of people who cannot afford a professional tax firm a simple, affordable way to prepare their returns accurately with professional guidance.

Disruptive innovations compete according to a new definition of performance. That means they define quality completely differently from how the incumbent system does. Usually their new definition of quality centers on a benefit such as affordability, convenience, accessibility, or simplicity. In the case of tax preparation, with TurboTax, individuals who cannot afford H&R Block's one-on-one personal tax preparation or live too far away to visit one of its branches have gained a tax preparation service literally at their fingertips.

Not only that, but millions of individuals and small businesses who previously were customers of H&R Block have replaced the professional firm with TurboTax. This illustrates how disruptive innovations move relentlessly upmarket, as they strive to win the business of increasingly demanding customers. To do so, they must get better and better according to the *incumbent* definition of performance while remaining more affordable, convenient, accessible, or simple. In the case of tax accounting, the incumbent system competed based on its ability to help with complicated tax situations and navigate gray areas for which people needed to consult an expert. Initially TurboTax had limited ability to serve customers in these situations. It simply offered convenience and affordability for those grateful for any assistance at all. But over time, in an attempt to entice more demanding customers from the incumbent system, TurboTax software became capable of handling increasingly sophisticated problems. It also added features such as "Live Chat" and "Ask an Expert" to provide real-time help. Today, it provides enough sophisticated assistance and expert advice that many are abandoning the professional firms for TurboTax. These switchers receive double benefits — adequate expertise *plus* increased convenience and affordability. Sure, it may never be quite as good as the best in-person expert, but it's plenty good enough for countless individuals.

DISRUPTIVE INNOVATION AND ONLINE LEARNING

The pattern of disruptive innovation helps answer the question of whether the blending of online learning into K–12 schools is a blessing or a curse. For one thing, disruption explains why online learning began mostly outside the core classroom, *not* as an immediate solution for teaching math and reading to mainstream students (although in many schools it is now doing just that, as we discuss later). Similar to other disruptions, online learning began in simple applications to serve students in circumstances where there was no alternative for learning. We call these circumstances "nonconsumption" because they are occasions when the alternative to the disruptive technology is nothing at all. In K–12 schools, online learning began in the advanced courses that many schools struggle to offer in-house; in small, rural, and urban schools that cannot offer a broad set of courses with highly qualified teachers in certain subject areas; in remedial courses for students who need to recover credits to graduate; and with home-schooled and homebound students. Initially, even a plain vanilla online course was superior to those students' alternative—nothing.

But just as other successful disruptions march upmarket to attract more demanding customers, online learning has improved dramatically since its arrival. This pattern of disruptive innovation can be comforting because it offers assurance that low-end disruptive technologies improve over time. Internet access across the country is faster and more reliable than it was ten years ago. Virtual communications tools such as Skype and Google Hangouts make synchronous online communication simple and inexpensive. Online content is becoming more engaging. And most students now have an internet device within reach, whether as a laptop, a tablet, or a mobile smartphone.[4]

Furthermore, an increasing number of students are experiencing online learning while continuing to attend their traditional brick-and-mortar schools—a phenomenon called "blended learning." The emergence of blended learning is one way online learning is marching upmarket. By adding a brick-and-mortar component, online learning can offer more supervision, face-to-face mentors, and in-person fun with friends for the vast majority of students who need school for these purposes just as much as they need it to help them gain knowledge and skills. This book focuses on the rise of blended learning in K–12 schools and on the striking implications for students, educators, and schools as it gains momentum.

So back to the original question: Is the growth of online learning a good thing, or should we fight to protect the traditional classroom?

For one group, the answer is clear. For students who need more than their schools can provide for them today, online learning is a good thing, as it is certainly better than nothing. It offers a credit-recovery solution for millions of students who otherwise do not have a realistic way to repeat failed courses in time for graduation. It provides the opportunity for students to take Advanced Placement (AP) courses if their high schools do not offer them, which is the case in roughly 40 percent of high schools today.[5] It provides a potential curriculum backbone for the roughly 2.35 million students who learn at home each year.[6] And for untold numbers of students, online learning offers access to the courses—advanced and basic—required for college admission that their schools lack the resources to provide.

The incidence of nonconsumption, particularly at the high school level, is surprisingly high. In fact, nearly every high school student misses out on a desirable learning opportunity in some form and could benefit from an online alternative. In 2007, 26 percent of students attended a high school that did not offer *any* advanced courses—anything above geometry, so no algebra II, let alone calculus; anything above biology, so no chemistry and physics; nor any honors English class at all.[7]

But what about those students who attend public schools—either district or charter—and private schools, which offer a more comprehensive suite of courses and options? Are they missing out by dismissing the online-learning disruption as a low-end fad? To answer that question, we need to step back and look at the big picture of why the traditional classroom model, even in the best schools, is not up to speed with what students need to succeed in today's world and why we can do better.

THE FACTORY-BASED MODEL OF SCHOOLING

At Santa Rita Elementary School in the Los Altos School District in California, a suburban school in an affluent area of California, a scene unfolded in 2010 not too different from scenes in schools around the country. A fifth-grade student, Jack, started the year at the bottom of his class in math. He struggled to keep up and considered himself one of those kids who would just never quite "get it." In a typical school, he would have been tracked and placed in the bottom math group. That would have meant that he would not have taken algebra until high school, which would have negatively impacted his college and career choices.

But Jack's story took a less familiar turn. His school transformed his class into a blended-learning environment. After seventy days of using Khan Academy's online math tutorials and exercises for a portion of his math three to four days a week, rather than remaining tracked in the bottom math group, Jack rose to become one of the top four students in his class. He was working on material well above grade level.

Jack's rapid progress sounds like the stuff of movies or magic, but it isn't. It's an example of online learning's power to help teachers differentiate and customize learning to fit a student's needs.[8]

The Origins of Today's Schools

Today's schools were designed over a century ago to do just the opposite of differentiation and customization. They were designed to standardize the way they teach and test. The one-room schoolhouses that dotted the country at the turn of the twentieth century were by necessity good at customizing an education for each student, but they were not an economically efficient way to educate large numbers of students. Only 50 percent of five- to nineteen-year-olds in the United States were enrolled in school in 1900.[9] In order to create a universal education system that could accommodate large numbers of students, educators looked to the efficient factory system that had emerged in industrial America. This resulted in batching students by age into grades, placing them in a classroom with one teacher, and standardizing teaching and testing.[10] The theory went that with students grouped by grade level and then batched in classrooms, teachers could teach "the same subjects, in the same way, and at the same pace"—a standardized, or monolithic, process—so that schools could enroll a far greater number of students.[11]

This age-graded, classroom-based factory model worked spectacularly well. By 1930, over 75 percent of all students were entering high school. Forty-five percent graduated.[12] The factory-model schools prepared students for the economy of that era and helped lift millions into the middle class.[13] In 1900, the majority of students would take industrial jobs and did not need a deep education; only 17 percent of all jobs at the time required knowledge workers.[14] The fact that many students dropped out of high school, did not attend or complete college, or—more to the point—did not learn much academically[15] did not cripple students when they left for the workforce nor did it significantly hurt the American economy. If Thomas Jefferson were alive today, he might have even considered such a school system—one that sorted students out at various intervals—a success. In his proposed design of the ideal school system, Jefferson sketched a vision of a three-tiered school system that would sort students out at various intervals based on merit. In Jefferson's vision, only an elite group of students would receive further education so that they could lead wisely in elected office.[16] In other words, the dropouts that we bemoan today would have been celebrated as a sign of success, as the school system was designed to sort students into different careers.

Why Factory-Model Schools Fall Short Today

The challenge is that in today's world—in which over 60 percent of jobs require knowledge workers, and we expect schools to educate all children so that they can realize their fullest human potential—this design falls short.[17] And it doesn't just fall short for those students who start life with the most disadvantages, as we saw with Jack in Los Altos.

Here's why. As educators and parents know, just because two children are the same age, it does not mean that they learn at the same pace and have the same needs. Each child has different learning needs at different times. Although academics, including cognitive scientists, neuroscientists, and education researchers, have waged fierce debates about what these different needs are—some talk about multiple intelligences and learning styles, while others point to research that undermines these notions[18]—what no one disputes is that each student learns at a different pace. Some students learn quickly. Others learn more slowly. And each student's pace tends to vary based on the subject or even the concept. The reason for these differences, in short, is twofold. First, we all have different aptitudes—or what cognitive scientists refer to as "working memory" capacity, meaning the ability to absorb and work actively with a given amount of information from a variety of sources, including visual and auditory. Second, we all have different levels of background knowledge—or what cognitive scientists refer to as "long-term memory." This means people bring different experiences, or prior knowledge, into each learning experience, which impacts how they will learn a concept. If a teacher assumes that everyone in a class is familiar with an example from history that is only ancillary to the point of a particular lesson, for instance, but the teacher uses that example to illustrate a particular point, then the students who are unfamiliar with the example or who have misconceptions about it may develop misconceptions about the point of the lesson or miss the point altogether.[19]

Understanding this helps us understand why nearly all of us have had an experience of being stuck in a class in which no matter how many times the teacher explained a concept, we just couldn't grasp it. The class whisked along, we fell further behind, and frustration mounted. Many of us have also experienced the reverse. Sometimes we understood things before our classmates. We grew bored when the class repeatedly drilled a concept for those who struggled to understand. A stunning number of students — nearly half, according to one report — drop out of school not because they are struggling, but because they are bored.[20]

This means that if we hope to have all children succeed in school and life, then we need to be able to customize — or personalize — an education for each student's distinct learning needs. The challenge, though, is that because our education system is built to standardize the way we teach and test, despite the heroic efforts of many teachers who try painstakingly to differentiate instruction, tailoring the lesson to each child is nearly impossible in a typical classroom with twenty to thirty-five students and only one teacher.[21] With a system that mandates the amount of time students spend in class but does not expect each child to master the content, most students are forced to move on to the next concept when the whole class moves on, not when they are ready. This creates learning gaps that haunt them later in their schooling.[22] When students who might love a given subject — math, for example — fall behind and have no opportunity to catch up, they assume math just "isn't their thing" and drop the pursuit. The system shortchanges all too many students — just as Jack in suburban Los Altos could have experienced — before they have a real shot. It also shortchanges teachers, as it expects them to help each child be successful without adequate time for one-on-one instruction.

In sum, today's factory model of education, in which we batch students in classes and teach the same thing on the same day, is an ineffective way for most children to learn. This was not a problem for a long time because we had different goals for our school system, but it has become one now that the world — and our hopes for our children — have changed and our schools have not.

STUDENT-CENTERED LEARNING

Today's students are entering a world in which they need a student-centered schooling system. Student-centered learning is essentially the combination of two related ideas: personalized learning (what some call "individualized learning") and competency-based learning (also called "mastery-based learning," "mastery learning," "proficiency-based learning," or sometimes "standards-based learning").

Personalized Learning

There are several notions of what personalized learning is,[23] but when we say it, we mean learning that is tailored to an individual student's particular needs — in other words, it is customized or individualized to help each individual succeed. The power of personalized learning, understood in this way, is intuitive. When students receive one-on-one help from a tutor instead of mass-group instruction, the results are generally far superior. This makes sense, given that tutors can do everything from adjusting their pace if they are going too fast or too slow to rephrasing an explanation or providing a new example or approach to make a topic come to life for a student. Also, tutors usually persist until their students fully comprehend the material. A personalized approach also implies that students can receive a one-on-one learning experience when they need it, but can also partake in group projects and activities when that would be best for their learning.

Studies show the power of this kind of personalized learning for maximizing student success. One of the first studies to draw attention to personalized learning was Benjamin Bloom's classic "2 Sigma Problem" study, published in 1984, which measured the effects of students learning with a tutor to deliver just-in-time, customized help. The striking finding was that by the end of three weeks, the average student under tutoring was about two standard deviations above the average of the control class. That means that the average tutored student scored higher than 98 percent of the students in the control class.[24] A more recent meta-analysis by Kurt VanLehn, which revisits Bloom's conclusion, suggests that the effect size of human tutoring seems to be more around 0.79 standard deviations than the widely publicized 2-standard-deviation figure.[25] Even with this revision, however, the impact is hugely significant.

Competency-Based Learning

The second critical element of student-centered learning is competency-based learning,[26] that is, the idea that students must demonstrate mastery of a given subject — including the possession, application, or creation of knowledge, a skill, or a disposition — before moving on to the next one. Students don't move on from a concept based on the average pace of the class or within a preset, fixed amount of time.[27] Competency-based learning entails aspects of perseverance and grit because students have to work at problems until they are successful in order to progress; they can't just wait it out until the unit is over.

If students move on to a concept without fully understanding a prior one, it creates holes in their learning. It is unsurprising, then, that in study after study, competency-based learning produces better results than does time-based learning.[28] One researcher found that "students in mastery-learning programs at all levels showed increased gains in achievement over those in traditional instruction programs."[29] Another study found that "mastery learning reduced the academic spread between the slower and faster students without slowing down the faster students."[30] Yet another found that "teachers who [used] mastery learning … began to feel better about teaching and their roles as teachers."[31]

Blended Learning as the Enabler

Personalized and competency-based learning, implemented well and jointly, form the basis of a student-centered learning system. An important part of student-centered learning is that students develop a sense of agency and ownership for their progress and a subsequent ability to guide their learning. This translates into an ability to become a lifelong learner, which is necessary in today's rapidly changing world, in which knowledge and skills become outdated quickly.

The challenge, though, is how to implement student-centered learning at scale. Paying for a private tutor for every student would of course be wonderful, but it's prohibitively expensive. Differentiating instruction for each child—a step toward personalizing learning that teachers across America try valiantly to do—is difficult in today's factory-model education system. Similarly, allowing all students to progress in their learning as they master material may be possible in a school with a small student-to-teacher ratio and flexible groupings, but it is taxing on an individual teacher who has to provide new learning experiences for students who move beyond the scope of a course, and it therefore strains the resources of most schools.

This is why blended learning is so important. Blended learning is the engine that can power personalized and competency-based learning. Just as technology enables mass customization in so many sectors to meet the diverse needs of so many people, online learning can allow students to learn any time, in any place, on any path, and at any pace at scale. At its most basic level, it lets students fast-forward if they have already mastered a concept, pause if they need to digest something, or rewind and slow something down if they need to review. It provides a simple way for students to take different paths toward a common destination.

It can free up teachers to become learning designers, mentors, facilitators, tutors, evaluators, and counselors to reach each student in ways never before possible.

Of course, just because a school adopts online learning does not guarantee that learning will be personalized or competency-based; we wrote this book to help educators and students around the world realize these benefits. But the blend of online learning into schools marks the most powerful opportunity the world has known to make student-centered learning a widespread reality.

WHY SCHOOLS ARE REACHING A TIPPING POINT

Thousands of school districts across America—over 75 percent by some estimates—are starting to awaken to the possibilities of online learning.[32] Different needs are driving them to the tipping point. In 2010, we began collecting stories of schools, districts, charter management organizations, and other groups across the country that have chosen to replace the old system with a blended model. We talked to, and in many cases visited, over 150 of these programs.[33] When asked why they are making the change to blended learning, leaders most often say one of three things, which—no coincidence—reflects both the potential for student-centered learning and the challenges in achieving it that we have just discussed:

1. **Desire for personalization**. The leaders feel an urgency to prevent struggling students from falling through the cracks, while helping other advanced students move ahead. Student growth—the difference between what students know at the beginning of the year and at the end—is not high enough, and the leaders are desperate for a better way to tailor learning to each individual's needs.

2. **Desire for access.** The school is struggling to offer access to as broad a range of learning opportunities as their students and communities need. Families are starting to ask why, in a connected world, their students don't have the opportunity to earn credit for an MIT engineering course online or even have access to basic advanced courses. Geographical barriers are diminishing as a legitimate excuse for lack of opportunity in today's world.

3. **Desire to control costs.** Schools face budget shortages all the time. It's no surprise that leaders feel stretched. On top of that, communities want personalization. But having a human tutor for every child is prohibitively expensive, so leaders are eyeing blended learning as a big opportunity to achieve

the ideal of a tutor-like experience for every child without the added cost. Many schools are also looking for ways to pay teachers more.

These potential benefits of online learning—personalization, access, and cost control—are pulling people away from traditional education and toward the new opportunity of blended learning. Just as millions of individuals have abandoned traditional tax accounting firms in exchange for the affordability and convenience of TurboTax, millions are feeling drawn to the personalization, access, and cost control of online learning. These potential benefits are the energizing force driving the fulfillment of the prediction that at least 50 percent of high school courses will be online in some form by 2019.

Whether those benefits materialize as hoped depends on the implementation. In some cases, schools that intend to individualize instruction with online learning end up foisting technology onto busy teachers who have neither the time nor the know-how to reorient their classrooms around each student's personal needs. Other programs that seek to broaden access develop online courses that are no more effective than even their weakest face-to-face alternatives. And finally, many who hope to save money with online learning find that rather than eliminating any costs, their plans pile on new device and broadband expenses.

On the other hand, some programs are making progress. A few stories from the field offer a glimpse of how different leaders are using blended learning as the engine to power their shift away from the factory model. These leaders are harnessing online learning to bring students benefits related to personalization, access, and cost control that were previously out of reach.

Personalization

In the spring of 2008, Joel Rose, chief executive of human capital at the New York City Department of Education, was visiting a friend in Miami who ran employee-training centers. On the wall of one of the centers was a sign that read, "Choose Your Modality." The sign stopped Rose in his tracks. He realized that schools would work better if students could learn each concept in the way that best suited their personal needs, rather than in a one-size-fits-all classroom.

With the support of Joel Klein, then the chancellor of the New York City Department of Education, Rose secured funding and in the summer of 2009 opened the first "School of One" as a summer math program in a middle school in lower Manhattan. The students in that pilot soon discovered that their math program felt nothing like traditional summer school math. At the end of each day, the School of One tested each student to diagnose precisely what she knew. With this information in hand, overnight the School of One matched the student to a "learning playlist" for the next day—the precise set of activities and concepts on which each student would work based on her needs. The next morning, the school projected the daily station assignment for each student onto monitors on the wall, similar to the flight monitors at an airport. The playlists for students pulled from a menu of over one thousand math lessons; some of these used online software, whereas others were intended for small groups, virtual tutors, or face-to-face workshops. The key idea behind the model was to meet students exactly where they were academically and let them progress at their own paces and according to the modality that worked best for them for each concept.

 WATCH CLIP 1: Teach to One uses the Individual Rotation model to personalize learning by drawing on an assortment of learning modalities.

www.wiley.com/go/blended1

By the end of the summer, students in that pilot acquired math skills at a rate estimated to be seven times faster than their peers with similar demographics and pre-test scores.[34]

Buoyed by its early proof of concept, the School of One expanded beyond summer pilots into mainstream schools, and over the last several years it has gradually evolved in how it serves students, with an even greater number of possible math lessons. The extreme individualization has had a powerful effect. Rose said that it awakens in students an awareness of their strengths and weaknesses, which inspires them to conquer their daily online assessments and move on to master new skills. Furthermore, the model helps students feel less afraid to admit what they do not understand, because they are all working at their own pace. Meanwhile, teachers have detailed knowledge of how each student is doing every day, which allows them to respond more appropriately to struggling students. They spend less time grading assignments and more time analyzing student needs and delivering small-group or individual instruction.

In 2011, Rose moved on to found New Classrooms, a nonprofit with an offering called Teach to One, similar to the original School of One model. That model has since been scaled to serve several district schools outside of New York City, including in Washington, D.C., and Chicago. Results have been positive. According to a Columbia Teachers College study on the first-year impact of New Classrooms' Teach to One blended-learning model from the 2012–13 school year, 2,200 students in seven different schools experienced, on average, nearly 20 percent more growth than the national average in math on the Northwest Evaluation Association's (NWEA) Measures of Academic Progress (MAP) assessment.[35]

Access

During his tenure in office, former Alabama Governor Bob Riley felt discouraged about the lack of opportunity for many students in his state. Riley was born in Ashland, Alabama, a small town in Clay County where his family had ranched and farmed for six generations. Not surprisingly, when he was elected governor in 2002, he had a heart for the nearly 32 percent of Alabama public school students enrolled in rural schools. He wanted them to succeed. But Alabama simply could not provide a qualified teacher to offer the full range of advanced courses across all of its small rural schools. A year into his tenure, Riley learned that Alabama ranked fourteenth out of the sixteen southern states in availability of AP courses to high school students.[36]

In 2004, Riley realized that online learning offered a possible solution. He convened a task force to create the blueprint for the Alabama Connecting Classrooms, Educators, & Students Statewide (ACCESS) Distance Learning Program, with a mission to equalize education opportunities across the state.

The task force agreed to a basic plan to bring a wide variety of AP, foreign language, dual-credit, core, and elective courses to Alabama's high school students— and, eventually, several courses to middle school students as well—through the development of a statewide virtual school. It also worked with the Alabama Supercomputer Authority to upgrade and extend internet infrastructure across the state.

ACCESS licensed online courses from outside providers and created many of its own courses. By the end of 2012, it was the third-largest state virtual school in the country, with 44,332 course enrollments—a gain of 31 percent over the previous year. As a result, the number of AP test takers in Alabama public schools grew, as did the students' success rate. From 2004 to 2012, the number of AP test takers more than tripled; the number of African American AP test takers increased by over ten times; and the number of exam scores that qualified for college credits more than doubled.[37] ACCESS has helped bring advanced coursework and alternative education options to thousands of Alabama middle and high school students who previously had no such option.

Cost Control

The Knowledge Is Power Program (KIPP) is one of the largest charter networks in the United States. KIPP schools are famous for their "no excuses" mentality—the conviction that KIPP will not blame a failure for its students to learn on any excuse such as lack of health care or bad parenting.[38] The KIPP Empower Academy, one of 141 schools in the national KIPP network as of 2013–14, is based in South Los Angeles and serves students in kindergarten through fourth grade. Over 90 percent of students qualify under federal government rules for free or reduced-price lunch, and 10 percent qualify for special education.[39] All of the students are Black or Hispanic or identify as more than one race.[40]

When he signed on as the founding principal of KIPP Empower, Mike Kerr knew he wanted to base the school's instructional model on small-group instruction, a strategy that had produced strong results at his previous school in New York City. He planned to leverage funding from California's class-size reduction program to ensure that each of the five kindergarten classes that were to serve the first cohort of students had no more than twenty students per teacher. But only months before the new school's 2010 launch, Kerr and his team learned that as a result of the recession, California had slashed funding for the class-size reduction program. As a result, KIPP Empower was short of funding by over $100,000.[41]

Kerr and his team scrambled to find options. At first Kerr was skeptical about the suggestion to use technology to preserve the integrity of his small-group model. But after further research, the team decided to test whether a measured use of online learning for some of the instructional time could allow teachers to preserve a small-group strategy, despite the fact that class sizes had to increase from twenty to twenty-eight students per kindergarten and that the school could launch with only four classrooms instead of five.

When KIPP Empower opened its doors for the first day of school in the fall of 2010, 112 kindergarten students began what was to become a tremendously successful model for KIPP Empower, one that several other KIPP schools are replicating today. The kindergarteners began with a ninety-minute reading block, in which one third of the class met in small groups with the lead teacher, another third worked in small groups with an intervention teacher, and the other third worked independently on individual computers. Every thirty minutes the groups rotated to the next station. The children continued through the day with roughly the same rotational design for writing, math, and science. Although each class had twenty-eight students in total, the adult-to-student ratio was, at most, one-to-fourteen because the online stations freed up faculty to meet with smaller groups.[42]

 WATCH CLIP 2: KIPP Empower adopted the Station Rotation model to offer small-group instruction in the face of funding cuts.

www.wiley.com/go/blended2

Today, KIPP Empower serves roughly 550 students from kindergarten to fourth grade. Each year its results have been striking. Whereas 61 percent of students were "below basic" level on the Benchmark STEP Test in the fall of 2011, a full 91 percent were at the "proficient or advanced" level by the spring of 2012.[43] The following school year, in 2012–13, the students continued to produce results that were as astounding as the gap they had faced. California's Academic Performance Index (API) rates the academic growth of schools based on results from statewide testing,[44] with 1000 being the highest score and 800 being the targeted score. KIPP Empower tested at 991.

The nonprofit consulting firm FSG published a study in 2012 to explain how KIPP Empower achieved these results in the wake of a significant loss of state funding. The school launched with two fewer full-time teachers than anticipated, which saved money. Because of its blended rotational model, it maintained small-group instruction while also increasing enrollment from an originally anticipated 200 students in its second year of operations to 231 students, which brought in extra funds. In total, the financial benefit equated to roughly $1,467 per pupil.[45] Supporting a blended model did entail some extra hardware, software, and personnel costs that total approximately $502 per pupil—roughly $965 less than the financial benefit.[46] As a result of the savings, KIPP Empower's team is optimistic that it can be sustainable on public financing alone by its fifth year, which means that it will neither need to raise outside funds nor compromise its small-group strategy or its founding ideals for students.

BUILDING A FIELD OF EXPERTS

Educators and parents cannot afford to wait and hope that someone else will eventually figure out how to leverage online learning to help their schools capture the benefits of personalization, access, and cost control. Hundreds of proof points similar to those previously mentioned show that with online learning, society finally has a scalable, systematic way to bring these virtues to K–12 schools. For a trouble-ridden, resource-constrained, increasingly antiquated system, this is good news.

That is not to say that online and blended learning are in any way a panacea for all that ails schools. But along the dimensions of personalization, access, and cost control, they offer the potential to beat the establishment in a large-scale way when implemented well.

Several years after the first publication of *Disrupting Class,* much has changed in education. This book is a guide for anyone who wants to make the benefits of blended learning a reality for students and schools. It moves beyond the "whats" that the authors of *Disrupting Class* identified to give educators a way to see the "hows" more clearly. By the end, every reader should be a blended-learning expert. What do we ask in return? With this knowledge and expertise in hand, become the blended-learning leaders in your community and take action for the benefit of all children.

WHAT YOU'LL FIND IN THIS BOOK

The first part of the book provides some important background on blended learning and draws substantially from four research reports about blended learning that we published online from 2011 to 2013.[47] Chapter One presents an overview of blended learning—what it is and the different ways it is unfolding in schools. Chapter Two predicts how blended learning is likely to evolve in the future and what that means for the future of schools.

The next part of the book helps educators start on the blended-learning path before beginning to design their own solution. Chapter Three explains the importance of identifying a concrete learning problem to solve or a goal to achieve before creating and implementing a blended-learning solution. It offers educators a framework to help think through how to pickup this rallying cry. Chapter Four offers guidance on assembling the right team to design the solution.

The third part of the book helps educators design their blended-learning solution. Chapter Five introduces the jobs-to-be-done theory to help educators design the ideal student experience to serve their particular students. Chapter Six focuses on how to design an ideal experience for teachers. It isn't until Chapter Seven that we address the technology: how to pick the content, software, and hardware and design the learning environment itself. The placement of this chapter is intentionally later in the book, as a big mistake that many educators make is to start with the technology before identifying what they want to do with it. Chapter Eight ties the chapters together to help educators pick and customize the blended-learning model that best suits their needs. For educators anxious to put blended learning into action, this chapter brings together the previous strands to help them create a tangible plan.

In the fourth and final part of the book, Chapter Nine helps educators think through the culture they must create for their blended-learning model to be successful. Finally, in Chapter Ten, we introduce a theory called "discovery-driven planning" to help improve educators' odds of success with implementing innovations such as blended learning.

So with that as a prelude, it's time to roll up our sleeves and start building the future of learning.

NOTES

1. Over and over Americans give high grades of approval to the schools in their local communities. For example, in 2013, 71 percent of parents gave the school their oldest child attends a grade of A or B. See "The 45th annual PDK/Gallup Poll of the Public's Attitudes Toward the Public Schools," *Phi Delta Kappan,* September 2013, V95 N1, p. 21 (http://pdkintl.org/noindex/2013_PDKGallup.pdf).

2. Tom Vander Ark, the author of *Getting Smart,* stated at a Hoover Institution conference that the *Disrupting Class* prediction that 50 percent of high school classes would be online or blended before the end of the decade seemed crazy five years ago, but that he believes the prediction will be achieved before the stated date. See Tom Vander Ark, "Blended Learning in K–12 Education," Hoover Institution, Stanford University, January 17, 2014, Policy Panel.

3. Clayton M. Christensen, *The Innovator's Dilemma* (Boston: Harvard Business School Press, 1997).

4. Pew Internet Teens and Privacy Management Survey, July 26–September 30, 2012, http://www.pewinternet.org/data-trend/teens/internet-user-demographics/ (accessed March 25, 2014). In addition, according to the Speak Up 2013 National Research Project, 89 percent of high school students report having access to a smartphone. See http://www.tomorrow.org/speakup/pdfs/SU2013_MobileLearning.pdf

5. College Board 2013 public schools database and AP Program data.

6. This figure was derived from a combination of statistics on the number of families that homeschool their children — 2.04 million — and the number of students who are enrolled in full-time virtual schools — 310,000. Students in these full-time virtual schools are technically not home-schooled

students because their education is funded by public dollars, but the majority of these students are still learning at home. See Brian D. Ray, "2.04 Million Homeschool Students in the United States in 2010," National Home Education Research Institute, January 3, 2011 (http://www.nheri.org/Homeschool PopulationReport2010.pdf) and John Watson, Amy Murin, Lauren Vashaw, Butch Gemin, and Chris Rapp, *Keeping Pace with K–12 Online & Blended Learning: An Annual Review of Policy and Practice, 2013,* Evergreen Education Group, http://kpk12.com/cms/wp-content/uploads/ EEG_KP2013-lr.pdf

7. *Connecting Students to Advanced Courses Online: Innovations in Education,* prepared by WestEd for U.S. Department of Education Office of Innovation and Improvement, 2007, pp. 3–4. Indeed, less stark but no less damaging, thousands of California students today attend a school that does not offer the full suite of courses required to gain admission to a college in the University of California or California State University systems.

8. Michael B. Horn and Meg Evans, "Creating a Personalized Learning Experience," AdvancED Source, Spring 2013, p. 2.

9. Clayton M. Christensen, Michael B. Horn, and Curtis W. Johnson, *Disrupting Class: How Disruptive Innovation Will Change the Way the World Learns,* Expanded Edition (New York: McGraw-Hill, 2010), p. 54.

10. Educators in the United States began instituting the concept of grade levels, which had first emerged in Prussia, in the mid-1800s in Quincy, Massachusetts (*Disrupting Class,* p. 53). The practice accelerated at the turn of the twentieth century so that teachers could focus on just one set of students who were roughly the same age.

11. David Tyack and Larry Cuban, *Tinkering Toward Utopia: A Century of Public School Reform* (Cambridge, Massachusetts: Harvard University Press, 1995), p. 89.

12. James Bryant Conant, *The Revolutionary Transformation of the American High School* (Cambridge, MA: Harvard University Press, 1959), p. 3.

13. Sal Khan, *The One World Schoolhouse* (New York: Hachette Book Group, 2012), p. 77. Many have painted a bleak and more pernicious picture of the factory model of education. As mentioned in a previous endnote, the

first manifestations of what we now consider traditional K–12 instruction arose in eighteenth-century Prussia. The ruling class there hoped that compulsory, tax-supported public education would produce loyal citizens willing to submit to authority—particularly to the king. Johann Gottlieb Fichte, a Prussian philosopher and key figure in the development of the system, outright admitted that "if you want to influence a person, you must do more than merely talk to him; you must fashion him in such a way that he simply cannot will otherwise than what you wish him to will." Certainly not everyone subscribes to the idea that traditional classrooms contain the same authoritarian DNA as their Prussian progenitors. Those who do, however, offer a troubling interpretation. According to former New York State Teacher of the Year John Taylor Gatto, the notion of the "class period" was put in place "so that self-motivation to learn would be muted by careless interruptions." His argument is that the intermittent clang of the school bell, which divides learning into brief, stand-alone "subjects," prevents students from having time to form deep cross-disciplinary connections, explore "possibly heterodox or dangerous ideas among themselves," or engage in any real inquiry. As such, the classic school schedule is a tool to reinforce subjugation to the ruling class (Khan, pp. 76–77).

14. Patrick Butler et al., "A Revolution in Interaction," *McKinsey Quarterly*, 1:8, 1997 as cited in Michael E. Echols, *ROI on Human Capital Investment*, 2nd ed. (Arlington, VA: Tapestry Press, 2005), p. 3.

15. Eric A. Hanushek, Paul E. Peterson, and Ludger Woessmann, *Endangering Prosperity: A Global View of the American School* (Washington, DC: Brookings Institution Press, 2013), Ch. 1.

16. See Thomas Jefferson's proposed legislation in Virginia, a "Bill for the More General Diffusion of Knowledge" (http://etext.virginia.edu/etcbin/toccer-new2?id=JefPapr.sgm&images=images/modeng&data=/texts/english/modeng/parsed&tag=public&part=5&division=div1 (accessed April 10, 2014).

17. Butler et al., as cited in Echols, p. 3 (see n. 14). In the early 1900s, most nonagricultural labor involved extracting raw materials and converting them into finished goods—jobs such as coal mining, running heavy machinery, or operating production lines. By the turn of the twenty-first

century, however, only 15 percent of employees in the United States did this type of work. The majority now hold jobs in the knowledge economy, where workers spend most of their time interacting, whether as managers, nurses, salespeople, financial advisors, lawyers, judges, or mediators. These jobs require workers to deal with higher levels of knowledge, skill, and ambiguity as well as to make difficult judgment calls in ways that simply do not apply in most industrial jobs. And the need for these complex skills is growing; 70 percent of all U.S. jobs created between 1998 and 2005—4.5 million jobs in total—required judgment and experience. Bradford C. Johnson, James M. Manyika, and Lareina A. Yee, "The Next Revolution in Interactions," *McKinsey Quarterly*, November 2005, http://www.mckinsey.com/insights/organization/the_next_revolution_in_ interactions (accessed March 7, 2014). The authors point out that most developed countries are experiencing this trend. Other McKinsey analysts indicated that another skill that's vital for today's workers is the ability to learn on the job. The number of skill sets needed in the workforce has increased rapidly, from 178 in September 2009 to 924 in June 2012. See John Mills, David Crean, Danielle Ranshaw, and Kaye Bowman, "Workforce Skills Development and Engagement in Training through Skill Sets," *DCVER Monograph Series*, November 2012, http://files.eric.ed.gov/fulltext/ ED538262.pdf, p. 13. As Sir Michael Barber puts it, "Learning and work are becoming inseparable. Indeed, one could argue that this is precisely what it means to have a knowledge economy or a learning society." See Michael Barber, Katelyn Donnelly, and Saad Rivzi, "An Avalanche Is Coming: Higher Education and the Revolution Ahead," *IPPR*, March 2013, p. 51, http://www .ippr.org/images/media/files/publication/2013/04/avalanche-is-coming_ Mar2013_10432.pdf. The result of this problem on a worldwide scale is that seventy-five million people are unemployed, but businesses can't find enough so-called knowledge workers to fill job vacancies. See "Tackling Youth Unemployment" McKinsey & Company website, http://mckinseyon society.com/education-to-employment/ (accessed March 7, 2014).

18. For a fuller summary of some of the debates here, we recommend the following pieces. Jose Ferreira, "Rebooting 'Learning Styles,'" http://www .knewton.com/blog/ceo-jose-ferreira/rebooting-learning-styles/, March 25,

2014; Mark Bauerlein, "A Concluded Battle in the Curriculum Wars," http://www.edexcellence.net/commentary/education-gadfly-daily/common-core-watch/a-concluded-battle-in-the-curriculum-wars, March 25, 2014; Michael B. Horn, "Differentiating Learning by 'Learning Style' Might Not Be So Wise," http://www.christenseninstitute.org/differentiating-learning-by-learning-style-might-not-be-so-wise/, June 17, 2010.

19. Ruth Colvin Clark and Richard E. Mayer, *e-Learning and the Science of Instruction: Proven Guidelines for Consumers and Designers of Multimedia Learning* (San Francisco: Wiley, 2008), Ch. 2. This is one reason why building students' knowledge base in an intentional way is so important, but assuming that all students have the same knowledge base and treating them all the same is a mistake.

20. John M. Bridgeland, John J. Dilulio, Jr., Karen Burke Morison, "The Silent Epidemic: Perspectives of High School Dropouts," A Report by Civic Enterprises in association with Peter D. Hart Research Associates for the Bill & Melinda Gates Foundation, March 2006, p. iii.

21. For a fuller discussion of this phenomenon, see *Disrupting Class,* Ch. 1. In addition, as former teacher and current CEO of the Silicon Schools Fund Brian Greenberg said, personalization "is getting at that concept of every student gets what they need exactly when they need it. And in education speak we call that differentiation. But I think that differentiation is a word that was invented to make teachers feel bad about ourselves because in reality we just can't do it manually. And this is where technology holds some promise to maybe give teachers the potential to do more personalization." See Brian Greenberg, Rob Schwartz, and Michael Horn, "Blended Learning: Personalizing Education for Students," *Coursera,* Week 2, Video 2: Key Elements of the Student Experience, https://class.coursera.org/blendedlearning-001.

22. Educators often refer to these gaps as the "Swiss cheese" problem because of the resemblance to the holes in Swiss cheese. The challenge for a teacher in the traditional factory model is that it's hard to know where the holes in each student's learning are.

23. There are many definitions of personalized learning in the literature, which makes it difficult to evaluate the research on the effectiveness of personalized

learning approaches, as many people in the field use the term to refer to everything from interest-based learning to using "learning styles," meaning teaching people based on a notion of their being a visual or auditory learner, for example. As our explanation states, this is not what we mean by the term. That said, some of the definitions based on the literature follow in this note, but it's important to clarify that we believe personalized learning means students will both learn a basic set of competencies—knowledge, skills, and dispositions—common to all students *and* branch out into different areas of study to follow their passions. Although we are not experts, there are certain concepts and standards that are worth learning and being exposed to for all students, which are likely fewer in number, clearer to teachers and students, and higher in rigor and conceptual quality than what most U.S. students have confronted historically.

To create a set of common working definitions for the online and blended learning fields, iNACOL, the K–12 international online learning association, defines personalized learning as "tailoring learning for each student's strengths, needs and interests—including enabling student voice and choice in what, how, when, and where they learn—to provide flexibility and supports to ensure mastery of the highest standards possible." Susan Patrick, Kathryn Kennedy, and Allison Powell, "Mean What You Say: Defining and Integrating Personalized, Blended, and Competency Education," iNACOL, October 2013.

The U.S. Department of Education's 2010 National Education Technology Plan distinguishes among individualized, personalized, and differentiated instruction:

> Individualization, differentiation, and personalization have become buzzwords in education, but little agreement exists on what exactly they mean beyond the broad concept that each is an alternative to the one-size-fits-all model of teaching and learning. For example, some education professionals use personalization to mean that students are given the choice of what and how they learn according to their interests, and others use it to suggest that instruction is paced differently for

different students. Throughout this plan, we use the following definitions: Individualization refers to instruction that is paced to the learning needs of different learners. Learning goals are the same for all students, but students can progress through the material at different speeds according to their learning needs. For example, students might take longer to progress through a given topic, skip topics that cover information they already know, or repeat topics they need more help on. Differentiation refers to instruction that is tailored to the learning preferences of different learners. Learning goals are the same for all students, but the method or approach of instruction varies according to the preferences of each student or what research has found works best for students like them. Personalization refers to instruction that is paced to learning needs, tailored to learning preferences, and tailored to the specific interests of different learners. In an environment that is fully personalized, the learning objectives and content as well as the method and pace may all vary (so personalization encompasses differentiation and individualization) ("Transforming American Education: Learning Powered by Technology," National Education Technology Plan 2010, U.S. Department of Education Office of Educational Technology, November 2010).

24. Benjamin S. Bloom, "The 2 Sigma Problem: The Search for Methods of Group Instruction as Effective as One-to-One Tutoring," *Educational Researcher,* Vol. 13, No. 6 (Jun.—Jul., 1984), pp. 4–16, http://www.comp .dit.ie/dgordon/Courses/ILT/ILT0004/TheTwoSigmaProblem.pdf. In his study, students in one group each met with a good tutor. Students in a second group, the control group, learned in the conventional way in classes with roughly thirty students per teacher. Researchers assigned students randomly to both learning conditions. Each group had similar initial aptitude test scores and interests in the subject. In addition to the "2 Sigma" findings, 90 percent of the tutored students attained the level of summative achievement reached by only the highest 20 percent of the students under conventional instructional conditions.

25. Kurt VanLehn, "The Relative Effectiveness of Human Tutoring, Intelligent Tutoring Systems, and Other Tutoring Systems," *Educational Psychologist*, 46.4 (2011): 197–221 (http://www.tandfonline.com/doi/abs/10.1080/004615 20.2011.611369).

26. Competency Works, a collaborative initiative with iNACOL as its lead organization and MetisNet facilitating the project management, has worked with the field to create the following definition for high-quality competency-based learning (Chris Sturgis and Susan Patrick, "It's Not a Matter of Time: Highlights from the 2011 Competency-Based Learning Summit," iNACOL, 2011, http://www.inacol.org/cms/wp-content/uploads/ 2012/09/iNACOL_Its_Not_A_Matter_of_Time_full_report.pdf):

1. Students advance upon demonstrated mastery.

2. Competencies include explicit, measurable, transferable learning objectives that empower students.

3. Assessment is meaningful and a positive learning experience for students.

4. Students receive rapid, differentiated support based on their individual learning needs.

5. Learning outcomes emphasize competencies that include application and creation of knowledge along with the development of important skills and dispositions.

Built into many notions of competency-based learning is a sense of "minimum pace" or "teacher pace," which means that students can't just flail along, learn nothing, and remain stuck. More and more attention should be given to students who are lagging, so that they continue to progress at a minimum pace and not fall further behind.

27. Another way to articulate the differences between competency-based learning and the factory-model system is that in the factory-model system, time is fixed while learning is variable, but in a competency-based learning system, time is the variable and each student's learning is fixed.

28. We are indebted to Sal Khan for discussing the research base for mastery learning. Sal Khan, *The One World Schoolhouse: Education Reimagined* (New York: Hachette Book Group, 2012), pp. 40–41.

29. Daniel Levine, *Improving Student Achievement Through Mastery Learning Programs* (San Francisco: Jossey-Bass, 1985).

30. Denese Davis and Jackie Sorrell, "Mastery Learning in Public Schools," *Educational Psychology Interactive* (Valdosta, GA: Valdosta State University, December 1995).

31. T. Gusky and S. Gates, "Synthesis of Research on the Effects of Mastery Learning in Elementary and Secondary Classrooms," *Educational Leadership* 43, no. 8 (1986).

32. Watson et al., *Keeping Pace*, p. 17.

33. Summaries of many of these programs are available on the Blended Learning Universe (BLU) database at www.blendedlearning.org.

34. Heather Staker, "The Rise of K–12 Blended Learning: Profiles of Emerging Models," Clayton Christensen Institute and Charter School Growth Fund, May 2011 (http://www.christenseninstitute.org/publications/the-rise-of-k-12-blended-learning-profiles-of-emerging-models/), p. 139.

35. Douglas D. Ready, Ellen B. Meier, Dawn Horton, Caron M. Mineo, and Justin Yusaitis Pike, "Student Mathematics Performance in Year One Implementation of Teach to One: Math," New York: Center for Technology and School Change, November 2013.

36. This section is adapted from the following case study: Heather Staker and Andrew Trotter, "Providing Access to Alabama: Connecting Rural Classrooms through Distance and Online Learning," Clayton Christensen Institute, February 2011.

37. *The 10th Annual AP Report to the Nation,* Alabama Supplement, College Board, February 2014, http://media.collegeboard.com/digitalServices/pdf/ap/rtn/10th-annual/10th-annual-ap-report-state-supplement-alabama.pdf. "Alabama Still Gaining in Advanced Placement," Alabama Department of Education, February 2010, http://www.media.alabama.gov/Agency Templates/education/alsde_pr.aspx?id=2803

38. "How We Do It," KIPP website, http://www.kipp.org/our-approach/five-pillars (accessed September 10, 2013).

39. Brad Bernatek, Jeffrey Cohen, John Hanlon, and Matt Wilka, "Blended Learning in Practice: Case Studies from Leading Schools, Featuring Kipp

Empower Academy," Michael & Susan Dell Foundation, 2012, http://5a03f
68e230384a218e0–938ec019df699e606c950a5614b999bd.r33.cf2.rackcdn
.com/Blended_Learning_Kipp_083012.pdf.

40. "KIPP Empower Academy: Students & Teachers," Great Schools, http://
www.greatschools.org/california/los-angeles/25197-KIPP-Empower-
Academy/?tab=demographics (accessed September 10, 2013).

41. Bernatek, Cohen, Hanlon, and Wilka, "Blended Learning in Practice."

42. Ibid.

43. "KIPP Empower Academy Results," KIPP Empower, http://kipp2.innersync
.com/empower/results.cfm (accessed July 21, 2014).

44. "2012–13 Accountability Progress Reporting (APR): School Report — API
Growth and Targets Met: KIPP Empower Academy," California Department
of Education, http://api.cde.ca.gov/Acnt2013/2013GrowthSch.aspx?cYear=
2005–06&allcds=19–647330121699 (accessed September 10, 2013).

45. Bernatek, Cohen, Hanlon, and Wilka, "Blended Learning in Practice." Having two fewer teachers saved roughly $623 per pupil; increasing enrollment
from an originally anticipated 200 students in its second year of operations
to 231 students brought in an additional $844 in state and federal funds for
each student.

46. The extra personnel cost is in the form of an instructional technology assistant.

47. Chapters One and Two quote extensively from four papers we published
digitally in the years leading to the writing of this book. These reports include
"The Rise of K-12 Blended Learning," Clayton Christensen Institute,
Charter School Growth Fund, and Public Impact, January 2011, http://www
.christenseninstitute.org/wp-content/uploads/2013/04/The-rise-of-K-12-
blended-learning.pdf; Staker, "The Rise of K–12 Blended Learning"; "Classifying K–12 Blended Learning," Clayton Christensen Institute, May 2012,
http://www.christenseninstitute.org/wp-content/uploads/2013/04/
Classifying-K-12-blended-learning.pdf; and "Is K–12 Blended Learning
Disruptive?," Clayton Christensen Institute, May 2013, http://www
.christenseninstitute.org/wp-content/uploads/2013/05/Is-K-12-Blended-
Learning-Disruptive.pdf.

Part 1

Understanding

Chapter 1

What Is Blended Learning?

You can't go more than a few steps in education circles these days without hearing about blended learning. It's at the top of the list of trending topics related to changing education. Thanks in part to Sal Khan, founder of the Khan Academy — which serves more than ten million students per month in at least two hundred countries with its massive library of instructional videos and interactive exercises — the idea of blended learning is becoming commonplace.[1] But before the Khan Academy, and even before the term "blended learning" emerged, millions of students were experiencing the blend of online learning into their schools. Scholastic's READ 180 reading intervention program, which initially loaded on school computers through CD-ROMs and later migrated online, has been in classrooms since 1998, and today serves roughly 1.3 million students in over forty thousand classrooms.[2] Although the exact extent of blended learning at the K–12 level in America is unknown, experts at the Evergreen Education Group estimate that more than 75 percent of districts offer some online or blended options.[3]

But any fair look at education technology in U.S. K–12 schools must acknowledge that the nation has spent over $100 billion on computers in the past few decades with very little to show for it in the way of results.[4] So why all the hype about blended learning? What makes it any different from the long history of computers and technology in schools?

ONLINE LEARNING'S UPWARD MARCH

Blended learning has its roots in online learning. Like all disruptive innovations—from Amazon.com to TurboTax—online learning is improving steadily and predictably, as it seeks to serve more demanding users in tougher situations.

This pattern of disruptive innovations is critical to understanding what's ahead for online learning. When it emerged, online learning predictably had the reputation of being a low-end, second-string alternative to the traditional face-to-face classroom. Among the forty thousand or so K–12 students who were taking at least one online course in 2000, most used online coursework as a last-ditch effort to recover credits in time for graduation, avoid dropping out of school, or study independently in a homeschool or other distance-learning setting.[5] Online learning had little appeal for mainstream students.

But true to the pattern of disruptive innovations, online learning has marched steadily upward to reach a broader range of students and has even begun to replace traditional instruction in certain instances. In some schools, online foreign language courses were the first a viable substitute for attending a traditional face-to-face class. High Tech High, a charter school network based in San Diego, California, began using Rosetta Stone's foreign language program, for example, because of the software's reputation for helping students master languages faster than a lecture-style classroom can. "Rosetta Stone has spent millions in research and development, and it has a very clever way of interacting with its users," said Larry Rosenstock, CEO of High Tech High. He believes students can learn more in a year with Rosetta Stone than with even the best face-to-face teachers.[6]

One of the most significant ways that online learning improved was by leaning more heavily on in-person, brick-and-mortar experiences to provide support and scaffolding for students learning online. In the early days, online programs were largely indifferent to *where* students learned. The stand-alone, self-contained courses worked whether students were learning from home, a computer lab, or the library. Physical location simply didn't matter, provided that the learner had a good enough internet connection and a willing appetite for a fully virtual experience.

Those who provided the online courses soon discovered, however, that there is a limit to the number of students who can work without the explicit supervision and face-to-face mentoring of an adult. The same analysis in *Disrupting Class* that shows that 50 percent of all high school classes will be delivered online in some form by 2019 also reveals that homeschooling and full-time virtual schooling will *not* substitute for brick-and-mortar schooling, as their rapid growth flattens out at just under 10 percent of the U.S. K–12 student population.[7] That suggests that over 90 percent of students will continue to depend on adult supervision at brick-and-mortar schools.

This 90-percent estimate rings true. Most children need a safe place to be during the day outside of the home while their parents are busy. In fact, one of the main functions that schools perform is purely custodial—to watch over children and keep them safe. Most students also want a physical place to hang out together and have fun, as well as a place to receive help from their teachers, two other important aspects that can be separated from content delivery.

Eyeing the opportunity to harness the virtues of online learning for this 90 percent, innovative school leaders and teachers sought ways to weave online learning into the brick-and-mortar school experience. That effort produced the term "blended learning," which entered the K–12 education lexicon roughly at the turn of the twenty-first century. Because most parents and students need school to be more than purely virtual, the blend of online learning and K–12 campuses represents a major breakthrough in the integration of online learning into the mainstream.[8]

Outside of education, other purely virtual technologies have followed the same trail of adding a brick-and-mortar element to serve more people. For example, one way that some online retailers are gaining ground is by opening brick-and-mortar stores whose primary purpose is to serve as a showroom—a space where potential customers can test or try on inventory that was previously viewable only online—and then purchase from the online store. Bonobos, a men's apparel store that was once dogmatic about selling only online, opened six brick-and-mortar stores in 2012. The stores carry limited inventory and employ only a few salespeople. The retail "un-stores" are an example of disruption's upward march; after gaining a foothold by launching as a simple online solution, companies and organizations on a disruptive path pursue sustaining innovations—such as retail showrooms—to allow them to serve more demanding customers.[9]

WHAT BLENDED LEARNING IS—AND ISN'T

Blended learning is critically different from—but easily confused with—the much broader trend of equipping classrooms with devices and software. The common use of "blended learning" in education circles and the media suffers from a Goldilocks problem. People use the term either too broadly, to refer to all education technology ("edtech") crammed into a classroom, or too narrowly, to point to only the types of blended learning that they like best.

Beginning in 2010 we interviewed the educators behind over 150 blended-learning programs to arrive at a "just right" middle-ground definition that is broad enough to allow for variation but narrow enough to differentiate it from the bottomless category of the use of edtech in schools. It has three parts.

In Part through Online Learning

First, **blended learning is any formal education program in which a student learns at least in part through online learning, with some element of student control over time, place, path, and/or pace.**

The reference to a "formal education program" is important because it excludes instances when a student plays an educational Xbox game at home or browses a learning app in the grocery store line, independent of her formal school program. More critical to the definition, however, is "online learning, with some element of student control." In all blended-learning programs, students do some of their learning via the Internet. This does not mean using any digital tool, such as an online graphing calculator or Google Docs. Online learning means a bigger instructional shift from a face-to-face teacher to web-based content and instruction.[10]

Some element of student control is critical; otherwise, blended learning is no different from a teacher beaming online curriculum to a classroom of students through an electronic whiteboard. The technology used for the online learning must shift content and instruction to the control of the student in at least some way for it to qualify as blended learning from the student's perspective, rather than just the use of digital tools from the classroom teacher's perspective. It may be merely control of pace—the ability for students to pause, go back, or skip forward through online content as free agents. But often, online learning extends other types of control—in some cases students can choose the time at which they do their online learning, the path they want to take to learn a concept, or even the location from which they want to complete the online work—whether in a brick-and-mortar classroom or anywhere else.[11]

Bottom line: unless an education program includes online learning with at least some element of student control of time, place, path, and/or pace, it is not blended learning.

In Part in a Supervised Brick-and-Mortar Location

The second part of the definition is that **the student learns at least in part in a supervised brick-and-mortar location away from home**. In other words, the student attends a physical school with teachers or guides. Often it's the neighborhood school, but in other cases it's a learning center that could even be housed in a shopping mall space that has been converted into a drop-in computer lab. What about students studying online at Starbucks? That's not blended learning; the supervision of a Starbucks barista does not count. What about students learning full-time online at the kitchen table? Those are not blended learners either because they are not experiencing the "away from home" part. Blended learning means that students have at least some on-campus, away-from-home component built into their schedule.

An Integrated Learning Experience

The third part of the definition is that **the modalities along each student's learning path within a course or subject are connected to provide an integrated learning experience**. This means that if students are learning U.S. history in a blended way, the online and face-to-face components work together to deliver an integrated course. The opposite of this would be that the students learn some topics online and then return to their traditional classroom to repeat them in a face-to-face lecture. To prevent such lack of coordination, most blended-learning programs use a computer-based data system to track each student's progress and try to match the modality—whether it is online, one-on-one, or small group—to the appropriate level and topic. But in some schools, the teachers record progress the old-fashioned way and try to connect the modalities manually. Either way, the key idea is that blended learning involves an actual "blend" of whatever formats are within the course of study. Many blended programs today have yet to achieve the ideal of full integration across modalities, but the concept is nonetheless part of what most educators have in mind when they envision blended learning, and thus it is important to the definition.

Applying the Definition

Let's use this definition in a few hypothetical situations to see whether they are examples of blended learning.

> **Scenario 1**: Dominique's teacher posted all of his lesson plans, assignments, and quizzes on Blackboard's learning management system. Dominique can access this class page online from her brick-and-mortar classroom or from home using the tablet her school loaned her.

> **Scenario 2**: Matthew is a full-time student at Mountain Heights Academy, formerly known as the Open High School of Utah. He completes his work on his own off campus but connects with his online teachers live via webcam and Skype videoconferencing software. He also uses Skype to connect synchronously with the school's virtual chess club and virtual student government.

> **Scenario 3**: Angela enjoys playing online math games on the computer in the school library. She also takes algebra with a face-to-face teacher, who does not know about the online games but appreciates that Angela seems to be faster at recalling math facts.

If you concluded that none of these is an example of blended learning, you're correct. In the first scenario, the Internet is hosting information and tools for Dominique's class, but it is not managing the delivery of content and instruction; the face-to-face teacher is doing that. Thus Dominique does not have control over the time, place, path, or pace of her learning. The class is learning the same thing at the same time and moving through the curriculum as a single batch, or perhaps in a few groups, instead of using an online platform to serve each student the right level of content at each moment of instruction. Dominique is in a "technology-rich" classroom, but not a blended one.

The most common misnomer related to blended learning is to confuse blended learning with technology-rich instruction. Many schools are implementing one-to-one programs in which each student has access to a personal computing device. But the infusion of technology into schooling environments is not necessarily synonymous with blended learning. This confusion isn't confined to America; it seems just as common in places from Europe to Asia. Appendix 1.1 further discusses technology-rich instruction, as well as other terms that are related to, or mistaken for, blended learning.

In the second scenario, Matthew is not learning in a supervised brick-and-mortar location away from home. He is connecting with his classmates and teachers in real time, but not face-to-face on campus. Matthew is a full-time virtual school student, not a blended learner.

In the third scenario, Angela's math activities are not connected to create an integrated, unified algebra course. She learns math in the library, but no one is collecting those data and using them to update her learning plan back in the traditional math class. Angela is using online learning in the library, but not as part of a blended-learning program.

MODELS OF BLENDED LEARNING

So if none of these is an example of blended learning, what does blended learning look like on the ground? Because blended learning is still in the messy early stages of its development, schools are thinking about blended learning in hundreds of ways as they experiment to figure out what works best for them. As a result, at first glance many educators say that their programs defy categorization—that they are completely different from any other.

In our research, however, we have found that most blended courses fit somewhere within the broad parameters of four main models: Rotation, Flex, A La Carte, and Enriched Virtual. Figure 1.1 diagrams the relationships among these terms.

In many cases schools use multiple models and combine them in different ways to create a custom program. The purpose of these terms is to provide a language to describe the basic building blocks of the various combinations. The following sections describe each of these models and paint a picture of what they can look like in practice. The formal definition of each model and sample diagrams are in Appendix 1.2.

Rotation Model

The model that classroom teachers in particular gravitate toward first is the *Rotation* model. This category includes any course or subject in which students

Figure 1.1 Blended Learning Models

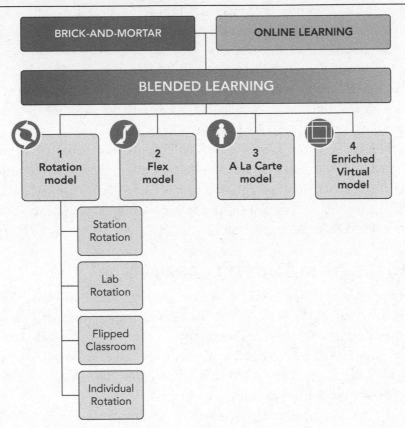

rotate—either on a fixed schedule or at the teacher's discretion—among learning modalities, at least one of which is online learning. Often students rotate among online learning, small-group instruction, and pencil-and-paper assignments at their desks. Or they may rotate between online learning and some type of whole-class discussion or project. The key is that the clock or the teacher announces that the time has arrived to rotate, and everyone shifts to their next assigned activity in the course.

The idea of rotating among stations is certainly not new to education. In fact, teachers have rotated groups of students among centers for decades, predominantly at the elementary school level. The new element is that online learning is now part of the cycle.

Station Rotation

In some cases, this rotation takes place within a classroom or set of classrooms. This is called a *Station Rotation*. The classic example is Scholastic's READ 180 program; it has been helping classrooms transition to a Station Rotation model since its start in 1998, and now, with over forty thousand classrooms using READ 180, it is one of the longest-lived and most widely distributed examples of the model.[12] The READ 180 system, which targets students from elementary through high school whose reading achievement is below proficiency, directs classroom teachers to begin and end each class session with a whole-group discussion that engages the entire class. In between, students break into groups and rotate through three stations:

1. **Small-group direct instruction**, in which the teacher uses resource books and works closely with individual students

2. **Individual learning**, using READ 180 software to practice reading skills

3. **Modeled and independent reading**, in which students use READ 180 paperbacks or audio books

According to the What Works Clearinghouse (WWC), a government-run database that provides research analysis about what works in education to improve student outcomes, the READ 180 program has resulted in an average gain of 12 percentile points for reading achievement and 4 points for reading comprehension among adolescent learners. Based on these results, WWC considers the extent of evidence for the program's potentially positive effects to be "medium to large," although no studies of READ 180 fall entirely within the scope of the review protocol for WWC evidence standards.[13] Apart from its effectiveness, however, its sheer size makes it a prominent example of a Station Rotation.

For those who want additional examples of Station Rotations, as well as of the other blended models, the Christensen Institute maintains the "Blended Learning Universe [BLU]" (available at www.blendedlearning.org), a database of blended-learning programs worldwide that is searchable by model and other features. The BLU lists several Station Rotation examples, including KIPP Empower, which was profiled in the introduction[14]; schools in California's Oakland Unified School District; several Pennsylvania districts involved in the Pennsylvania Hybrid Learning Initiative; the Alliance College-Ready Public Schools' network of charter schools; schools in the Aspire Public Schools network; Mission Dolores

Academy in San Francisco, an independent, K-8 Catholic school; The Avenues: World School, a high-end private school in New York City; and the Elia Sarwat High School and the Zaya Learning Center, both in Mumbai, India.

WATCH CLIP 3: Alliance College-Ready Public Schools uses a Station Rotation to provide the same material in three different ways.

www.wiley.com/go/blended3

WATCH CLIP 4: Aspire ERES Academy uses a Station Rotation to facilitate differentiated instruction.

www.wiley.com/go/blended4

WATCH CLIP 5: Mission Dolores Academy, a Catholic school in San Francisco, uses the Station Rotation model to meet individual needs in a financially sustainable way.

www.wiley.com/go/blended5

WATCH CLIP 6: The Avenues: World School provides students with laptops and an open learning environment to support its Station Rotation.

www.wiley.com/go/blended6

Lab Rotation

Lab Rotation is similar to Station Rotation, but students walk to a computer lab for the online-learning portion of the course. The idea is to free up teacher time and classroom space by using a computer lab and a different staffing structure for the online component. Schools have used computer labs for decades; the key difference today is that teachers are starting to integrate the computer time with the classroom time to create a seamless course.

Many people credit Rocketship Education in San Jose, California for putting Lab Rotation on the map. John Danner and Preston Smith launched the charter management organization in 2006 to help eliminate the achievement gap—the gap in academic performance between ethnic and socioeconomic groups. The goal was to help one million low-income, urban elementary students accelerate academically without depending on outside grants and fundraising to supplement the per-pupil funding their schools received from the government.[15]

To reach this goal, Danner and Smith set up a Lab Rotation model in which students spend 25 percent of their school day in a learning lab, where they practice core skills online. Monitors, rather than certified teachers, supervise students during lab time. During the other 75 percent of the day, students remain in their teacher-led classrooms for one block of math and science and two blocks of literacy and social studies. This model allows Rocketship to staff its schools with approximately 75 percent of the teachers that a traditional school would use, as well as 75 percent of the facility space that a typical elementary school would occupy. It also frees classroom teachers to focus on concept extension and critical-thinking skills, rather than on teaching and rehearsing basic skills.

WATCH CLIP 7: Rocketship Education relies on a strong culture and innovative staffing model to facilitate its Lab Rotation.

www.wiley.com/go/blended7

After its third year, Rocketship's first school ranked first in Santa Clara County and fifth in California when compared with similar schools—those with at least 70 percent low-income students. Rocketship's second school achieved similar acclaim. By the 2011–12 school year, the percentage of Rocketship students who scored "proficient" or "advanced" on the California standards for math was only five points lower than students in California's high-income districts—a notable step toward closing the achievement gap.[16] The Lab Rotation model helped the schools generate annual savings of approximately $500,000 in traditional expenditures per school. Rocketship doesn't actually "save" this money; it uses the spare funds to pay its teachers higher salaries (10 to 30 percent higher than surrounding districts), provide an extended school day and year, offer leadership training, and employ three or four school leaders who provide tailored professional development for its teachers.

Other places listed in the BLU as examples of Lab Rotation include the FirstLine schools in New Orleans, some elementary schools in California's Milpitas Unified Public School District, the middle and high schools in Kentucky's Danville Independent School District, and the Spark private schools in Johannesburg, South Africa.

Flipped Classroom

The third type of Rotation model, and the one that has received the most attention in the press to this point, is the Flipped Classroom, so named because it flips the typical function of the classroom on its head. In a classroom that's flipped, students consume online lessons or lectures independently, whether at home or during a homework period on campus. Time in the classroom, previously reserved for teacher instruction, is instead spent on what we used to call homework, with teachers providing assistance as needed.[17]

How can this improve student learning? Homework and lecture time have merely been switched. Students still learn through a lecture, and many online lectures are primitive videos.

Although there is truth in this characterization, it misses the key insight behind the Flipped Classroom. If some students don't understand what is presented in a real-time classroom lecture, they have little recourse. The teacher can try to slow down or speed up to adjust to differentiated needs, but inevitably what is too fast for one student is too slow for another. Moving the delivery of basic instruction to an online format gives students the opportunity to hit rewind or fast-forward according to their speed of mastery. Students decide what to watch and when, and this—theoretically at least—gives them greater ownership over their learning.

Viewing lectures online may not seem to differ much from the traditional homework reading assignment, but there is at least one critical difference: classroom time is no longer spent taking in raw content, a largely passive process. Instead, while at school, students do practice problems, discuss issues, or work on projects. Classroom time becomes a time for active learning, which thousands of research studies on learning indicate is far more effective than passive learning.[18] "From cognitive science, we hear that learning is a process of moving information from short-term to long-term memory," said Terry Aladjem of Harvard University's Bok Center for Teaching and Learning. "Assessment research has proven that active learning does that best."[19]

Jon Bergmann and Aaron Simms, science teachers at Woodland Park High School in Woodland Park, Colorado, began flipping their classrooms in 2007; many regard them as the pioneers of the Flipped Classroom at the high school level. "The key question," Bergmann says, "is what is the best use of your face-to-face class time? I would argue, at least in my case, that it was not me standing in front of my students yakking. That was not the correct answer; the correct answer was hands-on activities, inquiry- and project-based learning, and all those things that we have known that research has borne out to be effective and meaningful and important."[20]

WATCH CLIP 8: Aaron Sams discusses how and why he flips his Woodland Park High School classroom.

www.wiley.com/go/blended8

In 2013 the J. A. and Kathryn Albertson Foundation gave $1.5 million in grants to Idaho schools to try Khan Academy, mostly through a Flipped Classroom model. Forty-eight schools and twelve thousand Idaho students took part in the pilot project. Shelby Harris, a middle school math teacher at Kuna Middle School, says that as a result of this pilot, she no longer lectures in class. Instead, she works with students one-on-one or in small groups. "In some ways it feels less … teacher-ish," she said. "You almost have to redefine how you see yourself as a teacher." She regards herself now as a sideline coach, or even a cheerleader.[21]

Examples from the BLU of other schools that use the Flipped Classroom include those in the Stillwater Area Public School District in Minnesota, the Achievement First Charter Schools throughout New York and Connecticut, the Binah School for Jewish education in Massachusetts, the Catholic Schools Diocese of Phoenix, and the Dongpyeong Middle School in Busan, South Korea.[22]

WATCH CLIP 9: Some teachers at DongPyeong Middle School flipped their classrooms to engage their students and boost learning.

www.wiley.com/go/blended9

Individual Rotation

Individual Rotation is the fourth Rotation model. If this model were to wear a bumper sticker, it would be "Choose Your Modality"—the same motto that inspired Joel Rose to launch Teach to One, which we mention in the introduction to this book.[23] In an Individual Rotation, students rotate on an individually customized schedule among learning modalities. Either an algorithm or a teacher sets each student's schedule. Individual Rotations are different from the other rotation models because students do not necessarily rotate to each available station or modality; their daily schedules are customized according to individual playlists.

Students in the Teach to One program take a short assessment at the end of class each day. An algorithm analyzes the results to match students to lessons and resources that will best match their individual needs for the following day. The result is a unique daily schedule for each student and teacher. As it collects data, Teach to One learns more about students and ideally becomes even better at predicting the playlist that will be most effective for each student.

Carpe Diem Schools, which began in Yuma, Arizona, and now runs schools in several states, is another example of an Individual Rotation. The school's founder, Rick Ogston, began envisioning a whole-school blended model in 2003 (he was arguably one of the earliest blended-learning visionaries in that regard).[24] A large room filled with computers—similar in layout to a call center—is located in the middle of Carpe Diem's first blended school in Yuma (the design has evolved as it has expanded to new states). Students rotate every thirty-five minutes among different stations, which range from self-paced online learning using Edgenuity software in the large learning center to face-to-face learning experiences in breakout rooms along the periphery. Each student has an individualized playlist to guide him through the rotations. Paraprofessionals are on hand to assist students with Edgenuity. In the breakout rooms, a face-to-face teacher expands on the material introduced online and helps students apply it.

WATCH CLIP 10: The Individual Rotation model at Carpe Diem in Yuma, Arizona, relies on a unique facility and staffing design.

www.wiley.com/go/blended10

Charter schools in Arizona receive roughly $1,700 less per pupil each year than district schools. But because Carpe Diem's model requires fewer certified teachers, the Yuma school spends only $5,300 of the $6,300 per student the school receives. Most of the rest goes toward paying off the bond on the $2.6 million facility.[25] The facility itself represents a significant cost savings; with only five breakout rooms, it has fewer than half the classrooms that a traditional school requires for a similar enrollment level. A nearby traditional school building that accommodates only two hundred more students than the Yuma site cost roughly $12 million—over 2.5 times more expensive per student.

Four years after transitioning to an Individual Rotation, Carpe Diem's Yuma campus ranked first in its county in student performance for almost all grade levels and subjects on Arizona's statewide standardized test. *Bloomberg Businessweek* voted the school "Best Improved" on its 2009 America's Best High Schools List. The following year, the Yuma campus ranked first in its county in student performance in math and among the top 10 percent of Arizona charter schools. *U.S. News & World Report* named it a Bronze Medal School in its 2010 Best High Schools rankings.

Other schools listed in the BLU that use Individual Rotation include A. L. Holmes Elementary-Middle School in Detroit; Downtown College Prep Alum Rock in San Jose, California; Education Plus Academy in Wyncote, Pennsylvania; and Milan Village School in Milan, New Hampshire.

Flex Model

Even before many educators around the world were flipping their classrooms or adding online learning to their in-class stations, another group was pioneering a different model of blended learning outside of mainstream classrooms, primarily in credit recovery labs and alternative education centers. In south central Kansas, for example, Wichita Public Schools began contracting with Apex Learning during the 2007–08 school year to provide online courses to students who needed to recover credits or who had dropped out of school. It leased storefront spaces at local malls and converted them into large, open-space learning centers, where students could show up any time throughout the day to complete Apex courses under the supervision of credentialed, on-site teachers. Within a year, Wichita's program helped 449 students complete 931 courses—not a small number for that district.[26]

School systems began relying on online learning to deliver the backbone of student learning for other pockets of students, including those who wanted access to advanced courses, high school dropouts attracted to the idea of an "un-classroom" experience, and students in need of summer school. The programs required that students show up to a campus where they would access content and instruction primarily online. In contrast to the more rigid schedules of Rotation models, these alternative programs allowed students to learn via an individually customized, fluid schedule among learning modalities, which meant that they could alternate between online learning and face-to-face formats, such as tutoring or small-group discussion, when necessary and on a case-by-case basis.

The umbrella term for this type of schooling is the *Flex* model. The term refers to courses or subjects in which online learning is the backbone of student learning, even if it directs students to offline activities at times. The teacher of record is on-site, and students learn mostly on a brick-and-mortar campus, except for any homework. Students move through a Flex course according to their individual needs. Face-to-face teachers are on hand to offer help, and in many programs they initiate projects and discussions to enrich and deepen learning, although in other programs they are less involved.

Tom Vander Ark, the author of *Getting Smart*, identified a key difference between Rotation and Flex models when he said that, in general, "Rotation schools add some online learning to what otherwise may look like a traditional school, [whereas] Flex schools start with online learning and add physical supports and connections where valuable."[27] (The exception to this observation, we note, is Individual Rotation, which is more like the Flex model from this perspective.)

Although most Flex programs began by serving dropouts and other nonconsumers of mainstream education, the model is starting to arise within schools' core academic classes. The Education Achievement Authority (EAA) is

Michigan's school improvement district. It takes on the tough job of turning around the lowest 5 percent of persistently failing schools in the state. Its mission is to "disrupt traditional public schooling and provide a scalable prototype for 21st century teaching and learning." To do this, some EAA schools are relying on the Flex model.[28]

At Nolan Elementary-Middle School in Detroit, the EAA has replaced rows of desks with tables, floor pillows, and workstations. Furniture is modular to allow for flexible groupings, which is important because Nolan groups students by readiness, not by grade. The backbone of the model is Agilix's Buzz platform, a technology infrastructure that allows students to select and manage their own learning plans, demonstrate the ability to apply their knowledge in teacher-graded performance tasks and common assessments, and earn badges as they demonstrate citizenship and academic progress—all hallmarks of a competency-based system. Buzz also helps instructors monitor students so they can provide strategic intervention.[29] In 2013, at the end of its first year of turnaround, 71 percent of students at Nolan achieved one or more years of growth in reading and 61 percent in math. Nolan ranked third out of 124 Detroit schools in reading growth.[30]

Other examples from the BLU of Flex programs include Innovations High School in Salt Lake City; Lufkin High School in Lufkin, Texas; Flex Public Schools, managed historically by K12, Inc.; Nexus Academy, managed by Connections Education, which is part of Pearson; Buena Vista Elementary School in Nashville; Edison Learning's Dropout Solutions Centers; the network of AdvancePath schools; the network of SIATech schools; Algoma High School in Algoma, Wisconsin; and the Charles E. Smith Jewish Day School in Rockville, Maryland.

 WATCH CLIP 11: At San Francisco Flex Academy, students learn online and get help on a flexible basis from academic coaches and teachers.

www.wiley.com/go/blended11

A La Carte Model

The most common form of blended learning at the high school level is the *A La Carte* model.[31] This model includes any course that a student takes entirely online while also attending a brick-and-mortar school. Suppose the neighborhood high school does not offer Mandarin Chinese or physics, for example. Students can take those courses online during study hall or after school, in addition to the regular classes they are taking on campus. This is a form of blended learning because the students are experiencing a blend of online learning and brick-and-mortar schooling, despite that fact that the online courses themselves do not have a face-to-face component. A La Carte courses can have offline components, just as Flex courses do. But the key distinguishing feature between the two is that with A La Carte, the teacher of record is the online teacher, whereas with Flex, the teacher of record is the face-to-face teacher.

A La Carte is expanding, as more states require that students take an online course prior to graduation. As of April 2014, six states had some version of this requirement: Alabama, Arkansas, Florida, Idaho, Michigan, and Virginia. Other states are promoting A La Carte courses by funding student choice at the course level, which means that they guarantee funding for students to take a given number of online courses each year. Utah was one of the first states to offer course-level student choice. Starting in 2012, students in Utah could supplement their brick-and-mortar education with up to two approved online courses per year, which will expand to six by 2016.

The Abraham family in Canadian, Texas shows why A La Carte is gaining popularity. Canadian is a town of 2,649 people in the far north corner of the Texas panhandle. The place is so remote that a portion of the Tom Hanks movie *Cast Away,* about a man who is stranded on a deserted island, was filmed there. The Abrahams have eight children and are intent on giving their children the opportunity to attend top universities if they choose. The problem, however, is that Canadian High School, the only high school for miles, has a total of 206 students. It cannot afford to provide the full menu of Advanced Placement, foreign language, and elective courses that the Abraham children need to compete, or even qualify, for admission to top-tier colleges.

Salem Abraham, father to the eight children, sat on the local school board for twelve years and has fought hard to bring access to A La Carte courses not only to students in his town but also to all Texas students, particularly those in rural areas.

His strategy has paid off so far for his family at least; his oldest child was admitted to Harvard, his second to Notre Dame, and his third to Stanford—successes that the Abrahams attribute in part to the Spanish 4 and other advanced courses their teens took online because Canadian High School did not offer them.

Enriched Virtual

The fourth blended-learning model is *Enriched Virtual*. This model describes courses that offer required face-to-face learning sessions but allow students to do the rest of the work online from wherever they prefer. Some courses may meet in person on Tuesdays and Thursdays, for example, and allow the students to work independently on online lessons, whether on or off campus, on Mondays, Wednesdays, and Fridays. Others may customize the in-person meeting requirement based on student progress; if the student is falling behind, she must meet face-to-face more often.

The model differs from Flipped Classroom because in Enriched Virtual classes, students seldom meet face-to-face with the teacher every weekday. It differs from a fully online course because brick-and-mortar experiences are required; they're not merely optional office hours or social events.

Many Enriched Virtual programs began as full-time online schools and then, noticing that their students needed more support, developed blended programs to provide face-to-face enrichment and a safe, peaceful physical setting. One example is Commonwealth Connections Academy (CCA), a virtual charter school that Connections Education operates to serve more than 9,000 students across the state of Pennsylvania. CCA opened in 2003 as a full-time virtual school, but as enrollments increased, a subset of students struggled with their online work. Some had unreliable internet connections at home, despite the internet-access subsidy that CCA provided. Others felt too isolated. Many needed more face-to-face community and connection. CCA decided the solution was to create brick-and-mortar centers for students and teachers to congregate.[32]

In 2012, CCA opened the first teaching center in Downtown Philadelphia for anyone who wanted to learn in a blended setting and encouraged struggling students to take advantage of the opportunity. By the 2013–14 school year, roughly 150 students were enrolled at the Philadelphia center. At that location, students attend two to four days per week, either for the morning session (8:15 A.M.—11:30 A.M.) or the afternoon session (12:15 P.M.—3:30 P.M.), depending on their preferences. Every staff member in the facility oversees a homeroom of fifteen to seventeen students and works with those students as an advisor. The school is open Monday through Friday, but it closes early on Friday to give faculty time for a critical job: assigning student schedules for the upcoming week. During those Friday afternoon meetings, staff members review student data and discuss which students need a change. They communicate changes to homeroom teachers, who in turn email or phone their students to advise them of their schedule for the following week, including the days they need to be on campus and the teachers with whom they need to meet.

All CCA students have certified online teachers who serve as their teachers of record for each subject. Those who attend the teaching center, however, have additional layers of support. For math and English/Language Arts (ELA), a face-to-face certified teacher meets with groups of seven to eight students to reteach as necessary and then reset assignments and quizzes to test for mastery afterward. They also hold office hours on Friday mornings for students who want one-on-one help. Students work on other courses—science, social studies, foreign languages, and electives—from an on-site learning café, where "success coaches" are available to meet with them one-on-one and in small groups. Success coaches are subject-matter experts who have work experience and advanced degrees, but not traditional teacher certification. The staffing model is collaborative; although the virtual teachers are the teachers of record, the face-to-face teachers provide critical supplementation.

The Philadelphia center provides students with bus tokens to travel to the center using public transportation. Some travel from neighboring counties for the opportunity to be part of the face-to-face community. In many ways CCA's centers give form to the underlying motivation for an Enriched Virtual blend; typically such models offer support and a brick-and-mortar "home" for students who want to learn predominantly online, with the associated flexibility that that can offer, but need a place and community in which to do so.

Other examples in the BLU of Enriched Virtual programs include Impact Academy in Henry County Schools, Georgia; Arizona Virtual Academy; Chicago Virtual Charter School; Falcon Virtual Academy in Colorado Springs; Fairmont Preparatory Academy in Anaheim, California; Hawaii Technology Academy; New Mexico Virtual Academy; Rio Rancho Cyber Academy in New Mexico; and Riverside Virtual School in Riverside, California.

WATCH CLIP 12: Henry County Schools in Georgia provide a learning space and face-to-face teachers to enrich students who are taking online courses at Impact Academy.

www.wiley.com/go/blended12

MIXING OF BLENDED MODELS

We have amended the descriptions of the blended-learning models several times to make them as comprehensive as possible—that is, the set of models attempts to describe the entire range of existing blended-learning environments. But the categories are by no means mutually exclusive. Many programs mix and match the models. The result is a combination approach.

Some schools combine the Flipped Classroom with Lab Rotation. Students learn online at home and then rotate to a computer lab during a portion of their on-campus schedule. Other schools match Flex with Enriched Virtual. At the end of Chapter Eight we provide more detail about programs that combine models. Generally speaking, if it does not fit squarely within the Rotation, Flex, A La Carte, or Enriched Virtual definition, a blended-learning program is likely a combination of those models. Furthermore, some schools operate several models and combinations of models at the same time to serve different populations of students in different subjects under the same roof.

To Sum Up

- More than 90 percent of U.S. students need custodial supervision away from home during the day. Online learning is growing by blending into brick-and-mortar schools to serve these students.
- The definition of blended learning is a formal education program in which a student learns at least in part through online learning with some element of student control over time, place, path, and/or pace and at least in part at a supervised brick-and-mortar location away from home. The modalities along each student's learning path in a course or subject are connected to provide an integrated learning experience.
- Blended learning is different from technology-rich instruction. With the former, students have at least some control of the time, place, path, and/or pace of their learning, whereas with the latter, the learning activities are standardized across the class.
- Four models of K–12 blended learning are most common: Rotation (which includes the Station Rotation, Lab Rotation, Flipped Classroom, and Individual Rotation models), Flex, A La Carte, and Enriched Virtual.
- The Christensen Institute maintains the "Blended Learning Universe [BLU]," a database tool that organizes and presents data about blended programs, which are searchable by model and other features. You can access the BLU at www.blendedlearning.org.
- Many schools are mixing and matching models.

APPENDIX 1.1: DISCUSSION OF KEY TERMS

Online learning is education in which the Internet delivers content and instruction. Some online learning involves an *online teacher*—a real person who interacts with the students, reviews their assignments, and imparts instruction entirely over the Internet. Online learning may be *synchronous* (communication in which participants interact in real time, such as online video conferencing) or *asynchronous* (communication separated by time, such as email or online discussion forums).[33]

Traditional instruction resembles a factory system and is a remnant of the industrial era. The system groups students by age, promotes them from one grade to the next in batches, and offers all students in each cohort a single, unified curriculum that is delivered based on the time of the year. The instructional format is predominantly face-to-face, teacher-led lectures or demonstrations of the material (the general term for this format is *direct instruction*). Instructional materials are mainly textbooks, lectures, and written assignments. Courses and subjects are often individual and independent instead of integrated and interdisciplinary, particularly in secondary school. One of the main functions of the traditional classroom is to keep students learning in their seats for the prescribed number of minutes (this is called *seat time* in public-education code.)

Technology-rich instruction shares the features of traditional instruction, but has digital enhancements such as electronic whiteboards, broad access to internet devices, document cameras, digital textbooks, internet tools, Google docs, and online lesson plans. Despite the presence of digital tools, online learning does not generally replace face-to-face instruction for content delivery.

Blended learning is a formal education program in which a student learns at least in part through online learning with some element of student control over time, place, path, and/or pace *and* at least in part at a supervised brick-and-mortar location away from home. The modalities along each student's learning path in a course or subject are connected to provide an integrated learning experience. Blended learning is the engine that can make student-centered learning possible for students worldwide, rather than only for the privileged few. Because of its modular architecture, online learning is inherently suited to providing personalized, competency-based learning at an affordable cost, so these terms often go hand in hand.[34]

Project-based learning focuses on helping students explore real-world problems and challenges in a dynamic, engaged, active way. The intent is to inspire students to obtain a deeper understanding of the subjects they are studying.[35] Many blended-learning programs pair online learning with project-based learning to help students demonstrate that they can apply their knowledge and connect their understanding across disciplines. Project-based learning can take place online and offline.

APPENDIX 1.2: K–12 BLENDED-LEARNING TAXONOMY

The following taxonomy is imperfect and continues to evolve. It is a snapshot of the types of blended-learning programs that we see today across K–12 education in the United States and abroad.

1. **Rotation model**—a course or subject in which students rotate on a fixed schedule or at the teacher's discretion between learning modalities, at least one of which is online learning. Other modalities might include activities such as small-group or full-class instruction, group projects, individual tutoring, and pencil-and-paper assignments. Students learn mostly on the brick-and-mortar campus, except for any homework assignments.

   a. **Station Rotation**—a course or subject in which students experience the Rotation model within a contained classroom or group of classrooms. The Station Rotation model differs from the Individual Rotation model because students rotate through all of the stations, not only those on their custom schedules. (See Figure A1.1.)

   b. **Lab Rotation**—a course or subject in which students rotate to a computer lab for the online-learning station. (See Figure A1.2.)

   c. **Flipped Classroom**—a course or subject in which students participate in online learning off-site in place of traditional homework and then attend the brick-and-mortar school for face-to-face, teacher-guided practice or projects. The primary delivery of content and instruction is online, which differentiates a Flipped Classroom from students who are merely doing homework practice online at night. (See Figure A1.3.)

   d. **Individual Rotation**—a course or subject in which each student has an individualized playlist and does not necessarily rotate to each available

Figure A1.1 Station Rotation

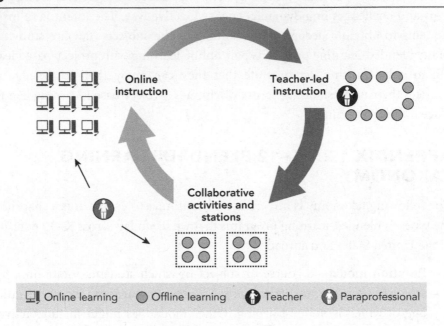

Online instruction

Teacher-led instruction

Collaborative activities and stations

🖳 Online learning ⬤ Offline learning 👤 Teacher 👤 Paraprofessional

station or modality. An algorithm or teacher(s) sets individual student schedules. (See Figure A1.4.)

2. **Flex model**—a course or subject in which online learning is the backbone of student learning, even if it directs students to offline activities at times. Students move on an individually customized, fluid schedule among learning modalities. The teacher of record is on-site, and students learn mostly on the brick-and-mortar campus, except for any homework assignments. The teacher of record or other adults provide face-to-face support on a flexible and adaptive as-needed basis through activities such as small-group instruction, group projects, and individual tutoring. Some implementations have substantial face-to-face support, whereas others have minimal support. For example, some Flex models may have face-to-face certified teachers who supplement the online learning on a daily basis, whereas others may provide little face-to-face enrichment. Still others may have different staffing combinations. These variations are useful modifiers to describe a particular Flex model. (See Figure A1.5.)

Figure A1.2 Lab Rotation

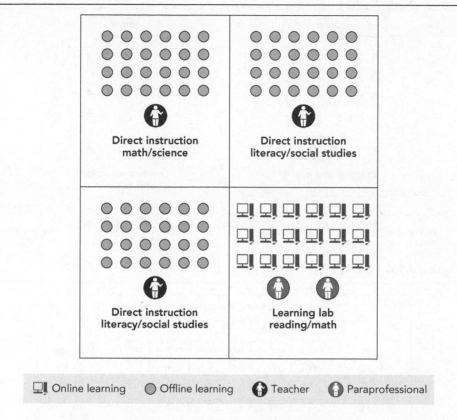

Direct instruction
math/science

Direct instruction
literacy/social studies

Direct instruction
literacy/social studies

Learning lab
reading/math

🖥 Online learning   ⬤ Offline learning   🧑 Teacher   🧑 Paraprofessional

3. **A La Carte model**—a course that a student takes entirely online to accompany other experiences that the student is having at a brick-and-mortar school or learning center. The teacher of record for the A La Carte course is the online teacher. Students may take the A La Carte course either on the brick-and-mortar campus or off-site. This differs from full-time online learning because it is not a whole-school experience. Students take some courses A La Carte and others face-to-face at a brick-and-mortar campus. (See Figure A1.6.)

4. **Enriched Virtual model**—a course or subject in which students have required face-to-face learning sessions with their teacher of record and then are free to complete their remaining coursework remote from the face-to-face teacher. Online learning is the backbone of student learning when the

Figure A1.3 Flipped Classroom

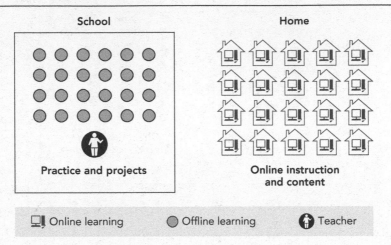

School

Practice and projects

Home

Online instruction and content

Online learning ⬤ Offline learning Teacher

Figure A1.4 Individual Rotation

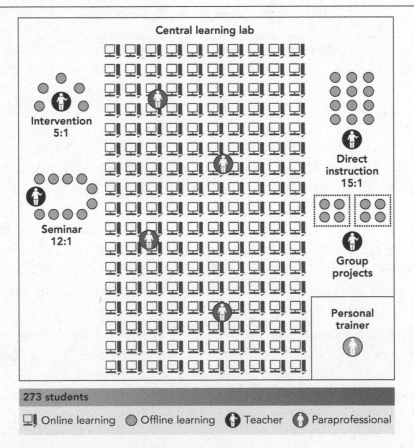

Central learning lab

Intervention
5:1

Seminar
12:1

Direct
instruction
15:1

Group
projects

Personal
trainer

273 students

Online learning ⬤ Offline learning Teacher Paraprofessional

Blended: Using Disruptive Innovation to Improve Schools

Figure A1.5 Flex Model

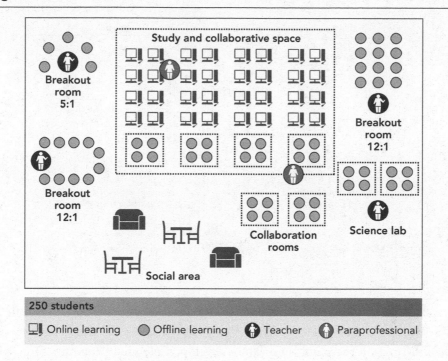

Figure A1.6 A La Carte Model

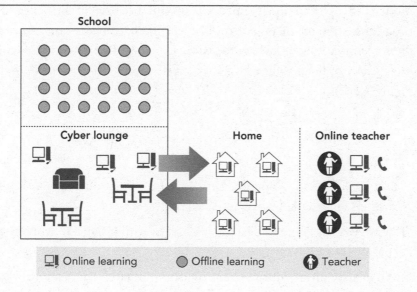

Figure A1.7   Enriched Virtual Model

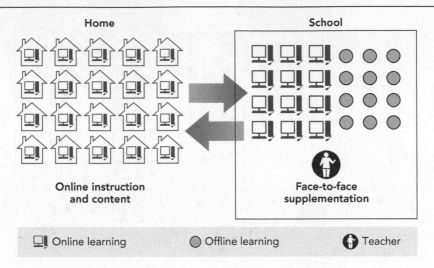

students are located remotely. The same person generally serves as both the online and face-to-face teacher. Many Enriched Virtual programs began as full-time online schools and then developed blended programs to provide students with brick-and-mortar school experiences. The Enriched Virtual model differs from the Flipped Classroom because in Enriched Virtual programs, students meet face-to-face with their teachers every weekday. It differs from a fully online course because face-to-face learning sessions are more than optional office hours or social events; they are required. (See Figure A1.7.)

NOTES

1.   "Fact Pack," Khan Academy, April 1, 2014, https://dl.dropboxusercontent .com/u/33330500/KAPressFactPack.pdf

2.   Interview with Francie Alexander, Chief Learning Officer, Scholastic, Inc., September 6, 2013.

3.   John Watson, Amy Murin, Lauren Vashaw, Butch Gemin, and Chris Rapp, *Keeping Pace with K–12 Online & Blended Learning: An Annual Review*

of Policy and Practice, 2013, Evergreen Education Group, http://kpk12
.com/cms/wp-content/uploads/EEG_KP2013-lr.pdf, p. 17.

4. *Disrupting Class* estimates that in the past couple of decades leading up
    to the book's publication in 2008, schools spent well over $60 billion in
    equipping classrooms with computers. See Clayton M. Christensen, Michael
    B. Horn, and Curtis W. Johnson, *Disrupting Class* (New York: McGraw
    Hill, 2011), p. 81. We are indebted to Sean Kennedy of the Lexington
    Institute for updating the number to $100 billion to take into account
    more recent expenditures. See Sean Kennedy, "School Tech Plan Unlikely
    to Help Blended Learning," Lexington Institute, May 9, 2013, http://
    www.lexingtoninstitute.org/school-tech-plan-unlikely-to-help-blended-
    learning/?a=1&c=1136 (accessed April 10, 2014).

5. Christensen, Horn, and Johnson, *Disrupting Class*, p. 98.

6. Heather Staker, *The Rise of K–12 Blended Learning: Profiles of Emerging
    Models,* Clayton Christensen Institute and Charter School Growth Fund,
    May 2011, http://www.christenseninstitute.org/wp-content/uploads/2013/
    04/The-rise-of-K-12-blended-learning.emerging-models.pdf, p. 93.

7. Michael B. Horn and Heather Staker, "The Rise of K–12 Blended Learning,"
    Clayton Christensen Institute, January 2011, http://www.christensen
    institute.org/wp-content/uploads/2013/04/The-rise-of-K-12-blended-
    learning.pdf, p. 2.

8. According to respondents to a California survey, K–12 blended learning is
    growing quickly. From 2012 to 2014, blended learning in traditional districts
    grew 43 percent, while charters experienced a whopping 287 percent
    increase. Overall, 74 percent more students were experiencing blended
    learning in 2014 than in 2012. Brian Bridges, "California eLearning Census:
    Increasing Depth and Breadth," California Learning Resource Network,
    April 2014, http://www.clrn.org/census/eLearning%20Census_Report_
    2014.pdf.

9. Other examples of enterprises that were once avowedly web-only and then
    later opened physical stores include online eyeglass retailer Warby Parker,
    the women's fashion retailer Piperlime, and the online beauty subscription
    company Birchbox. Hilary Stout, "Birchbox, Seller of Beauty Products,

Steps Out From Web With a Store," *The New York Times*, March 23, 2014, http://www.nytimes.com/2014/03/24/business/birchbox-seller-of-beauty-products-steps-out-from-web-with-a-store.html?_r=1 (accessed April 10, 2014).

10. We agree with Tom Vander Ark's characterization of blended learning: "Compared to high-access environments, which simply provide devices for every student, blended learning includes an intentional shift to online instructional delivery for a portion of the day in order to boost learning and productivity." Digital Learning Now!, Blended Learning Implementation Guide 2.0, September 2013, http://learningaccelerator.org/media/5965a4f8/DLNSS.BL2PDF.9.24.13.pdf, p. 3.

11. Florida Virtual School originated and trademarked the motto "Any Time, Any Place, Any Path, Any Pace" to reflect its philosophy that learning is an ongoing activity not confined solely to classrooms and class schedules. Its motto captures some of the inherent educational benefits of online learning for students. See Katherine Mackey and Michael B. Horn, "Florida Virtual School: Building the First Statewide, Internet-based Public High School," Clayton Christensen Institute, October 2009, http://www.christensen institute.org/wp-content/uploads/2013/04/Florida-Virtual-School.pdf, p. 3.

12. READ 180 was not technically blended learning until 2010 because before then students experienced the software through CD-ROM or a local server, not online. But students did rotate between READ 180 software and face-to-face stations from the start in 1998, so in practice the experience was similar to blended learning.

13. "READ 180," What Works Clearinghouse, Institute of Education Sciences, October 2009, http://ies.ed.gov/ncee/wwc/pdf/intervention_reports/wwc_read180_102009.pdf.

14. Ian Quillen, "Los Angeles Empower Academy First School in KIPP Network to Embrace Blended Learning," *Huffington Post*, November 20, 2012, http://www.huffingtonpost.com/2012/11/20/la-school-first-in-kipp_n_2166918.html (accessed September 10, 2012).

15. This section about Rocketship Education is based on the profile that Eric Chan of the Charter School Growth Fund contributed to the report by Heather Staker, *The Rise of K–12 Blended Learning* (see n. 6), pp. 131–133.

16. Sharon Kebschull and Joe Ableidinger, "Rocketship Education: Pioneering Charter Network Innovates Again, Bringing Tech Closer to Teachers," Opportunity Culture, Spring 2013, http://opportunityculture.org/wp-content/uploads/2013/07/Rocketship_Education_An_Opportunity_Culture_Case_Study-Public_Impact.pdf?utm_content=mhorn%40in nosightinstitute.org&utm_source=VerticalResponse&utm_medium=Email&utm_term=Rocketship%20Education%3A%20Pioneering%20Charter%20Network%20Innovates%20Again%2C%20Bringing%20Tech%20Closer%20to%20Teachers&utm_campaign=Rocketship%20Education%3A%20Bringing%20tech%20closer%20to%20teacherscontent (accessed July 31, 2013).

17. This section about the Flipped Classroom is adapted from Michael B. Horn's article entitled "The Transformational Potential of Flipped Classrooms," *Education Next,* Summer 2013, Vol. 13, No. 3, http://educationnext.org/the-transformational-potential-of-flipped-classrooms/ (accessed September 10, 2013).

18. Craig Lambert, "Twilight of the Lecture," *Harvard Magazine*, March-April 2012, http://harvardmagazine.com/2012/03/twilight-of-the-lecture (accessed September 10, 2012).

19. Ibid. The article also highlights Eric Mazur, a physics professor at Harvard University, who has been an advocate for flipping the classroom at the higher-education level since he first tried it in 1990. He sees education as a two-step process: information transfer, and then making sense of and assimilating the information. "In the standard approach, the emphasis in class is on the first, and the second is left to the student on his or her own outside the classroom," he said. "If you think about this rationally, you have to flip that, and put the first one outside the classroom, and the second inside." In addition, cognitive science research shows that "active processing" is a key ingredient in learning. Its importance is explained as follows: "learning occurs when people engage in appropriate cognitive processing during learning, such as attending to relevant material, organizing the material into

a coherent structure, and integrating it with what they already know." See also Ruth Colvin Clark and Richard E. Mayer, *e-Learning and the Science of Instruction: Proven Guidelines for Consumers and Designers of Multimedia Learning* (San Francisco: Wiley, 2008), p. 36. We also recommend Susan A. Ambrose, Michael W. Bridges, Michele DiPietro, Marsha C. Lovett, and Marie K. Norman, *How Learning Works: Seven Research-Based Principles for Smart Teaching* (San Francisco: Wiley, 2010), p. 132. The section describes the research on the importance of using active reading strategies.

20. Stephen Noonoo, "Flipped Learning Founders Set the Record Straight," *THE Journal*, Jun. 20, 2012, http://thejournal.com/Articles/2012/06/20/Flipped-learning-founders-q-and-a.aspx?Page=1 (accessed September 10, 2013). For more information about how to flip the classroom, see Jonathan Bergmann and Aaron Sams, *Flip Your Classroom: Reach Every Student in Every Class Every Day* (Washington, DC: International Society for Technology in Education, 2012).

21. Adam Cotterell, "48 Idaho Schools 'Flip the Classroom' and Pilot Khan Academy Online Learning," September 3, 2013, http://boisestatepublic radio.org/post/48-idaho-schools-flip-classroom-and-pilot-khan-academy-online-learning (accessed September 10, 2013).

22. For more about Flipped Classrooms in South Korea, see Michael B. Horn, "Busan Schools Flip Korea's Society, Classrooms," *Forbes,* March 25, 2014, http://www.forbes.com/sites/michaelhorn/2014/03/25/busan-schools-flip-koreas-society-classrooms/ (accessed April 10, 2014).

23. The story of Joel Rose riffing off this motto for School of One (later renamed Teach to One) is available in Staker, *The Rise of K–12 Blended Learning* (see n. 6), p. 140.

24. "Carpe Diem: Seize the Digital Revolution," Education Nation, http://www.educationnation.com/casestudies/carpediem/ (accessed September 10, 2013).

25. Nick Pandolfo, "In Arizona Desert, A Charter School Computes," NBC News.com, Sep. 22, 2012, http://www.nbcnews.com/id/48912833/ns/us_news-education_nation/t/arizona-desert-charter-school-computes/#.Ui_XjcakqYw (accessed September 10, 2013).

26. Katherine Mackey, "Wichita Public Schools' Learning Centers: Creating a New Educational Model to Serve Dropouts and At-Risk Students," Clayton Christensen Institute, March 2010, http://www.christenseninstitute.org/wp-content/uploads/2013/04/Wichita-Public-Schools-Learning-Centers.pdf.

27. Tom Vander Ark, "Flex Schools Personalize, Enhance and Accelerate Learning," Huffington Post, February 9, 2012, http://www.huffingtonpost.com/tom-vander-ark/flex-schools-personalize-_b_1264829.html (accessed September 11, 2013).

28. Next Generation Learning Challenges, "Grantee: Education Achievement Authority of Michigan," http://nextgenlearning.org/grantee/education-achievement-authority-michigan (accessed April 10, 2014).

29. Agilix, "Educational Achievement Authority (EAA) of Michigan: Disrupting Education in Persistently Low Achieving Schools," case study, http://agilix.com/case-study-buzz-eaa/ (accessed April 10, 2014).

30. Next Generation Learning Challenges (see n. 28).

31. This is based on California data, so it depends on the assumption that the distribution of blended models in California is typical of that in other states. The finding in California is that 59 percent of districts and charters who responded to a 2014 survey reported using A La Carte at the high school level. Fifty-three percent used Enriched Virtual, 32 percent used Flex, and 29 percent used Rotation. Brian Bridges, "California eLearning Census: Increasing Depth and Breadth," California Learning Resource Network, April 2014, http://www.clrn.org/census/eLearning%20Census_Report_2014.pdf. Based on our own observations of the evolution of online learning and the theory of disruptive innovation, we feel confident that these data hold more or less true across most of the United States.

32. The story about CCA is from an interview with Dawna Thornton, director of Commonwealth Connections Academy Philadelphia Center, Connections Learning, May 30, 2014.

33. International Association for K–12 Online Learning, "The Online Learning Definitions Project," October 2011, http://www.inacol.org/cms/wp-content/uploads/2013/04/iNACOL_DefinitionsProject.pdf, p. 7; Watson et al., *Keeping Pace with K–12 Online & Blended Learning* (see n. 3), p. 8.

34. It is important to note that the definition of blended learning is from the perspective of an individual student—in keeping with the notion of moving toward a student-centered learning design—not from the perspective of a school. What would the definition of a blended-learning school be? The annual *Keeping Pace* report offers one definition: stand-alone schools with a school code (as opposed to programs within a school) that deliver much of their curriculum in a blended format and require students to show up at a physical site for more than just state assessments. See Watson et al., *Keeping Pace with K–12 Online & Blended Learning* (see n. 3), p. 9.

35. "What Is Project-Based Learning?," Edutopia, http://www.edutopia.org/project-based-learning/.

Chapter 2

Are All Classrooms Going to Blend?

Blended learning may sound like an interesting option, but is it for everyone? At the end of an education discussion we were leading with principals and administrators in upstate New York, a superintendent from an affluent suburb confided to us that blended learning makes a lot of sense for struggling students in underresourced schools. But why should he risk his reputation and professional capital advocating for a new way of teaching and learning when the traditional approach worked great in his highly ranked schools?

History is full of examples of executives in other industries who felt the same way. When the first commercially successful steamship traveled on the Hudson River in 1807, it underperformed transoceanic sailing ships in nearly every way. It cost more per mile to operate, it was slower, and it was prone to frequent breakdowns. Sea-weary sailors who heard about steam technology when they came ashore undoubtedly dismissed the idea that steam could ever be as good as the classic, dependable sail. Steam seemed appropriate only for modest journeys along narrow lakes and rivers, where the ability to move against the wind—or when there was no wind at all—was important. But the vast reach of the Atlantic Ocean—surely that demanded sails.

Executives at Digital Equipment Corporation (DEC) must have felt the same way in the mid-1980s when they saw the first personal computers appear. They assumed that those simple, cheap personal computers were fine for children and hobbyists but could never serve their demanding customers—sophisticated corporations and universities—who depended on much more serious mini-computers and mainframe computers to get the job done. In fact, the first personal computers underperformed DEC's minicomputers in nearly every way. Their processing speeds were dramatically slower, and they had limited memory capacity and could not multitask. Personal computers were irrelevant for DEC's customers.

Looking back, it is now clear that both steam-powered engines and personal computers are examples of disruptive innovations. Like all disruptive innovations, both steam engines and personal computers improved over time until they became good enough to replace the incumbent systems for the vast majority of people. If they could have glimpsed the future, sailing ship manufacturers and DEC executives would have seen the impending disruption of their industries and perhaps taken steps to stay on top.

It turns out that understanding innovation theory is like putting on a pair of lenses that can help people see into the future and predict the trajectory of any innovation. With the lenses on, one can foresee that some innovations are sustaining to the incumbent system; such innovations help get the job done even better for existing customers or users according to the time-honored way that existing customers have judged things to be of high quality. Batteries that last longer, jumbo jets that fly farther, televisions with sharper resolution—all are examples of sustaining innovations. Other innovations are disruptive to the incumbent system; they start among consumers who either have very simple performance needs or have no alternative; then, over time, they march upmarket. The key finding is that disruptive innovations are destined to one day replace the vast majority of the incumbent system.

Let's put on these lenses to foresee the future of blended learning. Is blended learning a sustaining innovation that offers an important enhancement and improvement to the traditional classroom? Or is it a disruptive innovation that will fundamentally transform the classroom in the future?

The answer affects countless issues related to the future of schooling. First, it affects blended-learning implementations: successful organizations deploy sustaining initiatives substantially differently from disruptive ones. Second, it affects design: sustaining initiatives lead to improvements to the established design, whereas disruptive initiatives lead to an entirely new way of thinking about teachers, facilities, and the student experience. Third, it affects impact: sustaining innovations will improve the traditional classroom, whereas disruptive innovations are more likely to transform schooling into a system that is personalized, competency-based, accessible, and affordable. Finally, it affects strategy: by definition, disruptive innovations are on a path to replace the incumbent system. If blended learning is on that type of path, wouldn't that be nice to know?

THE THEORY OF HYBRIDS

A couple hundred years ago, shipbuilders faced a similar question. Back then people crossed the oceans on sailing ships that harnessed the power of the wind. When steam power was invented, it was a primitive technology. It was more expensive and less reliable than sails, and it couldn't power a ship all the way across the ocean because the ships couldn't carry enough fuel, given that the steam engine was then relatively inefficient. But it was immediately attractive to boaters traveling in narrow rivers and lakes, who appreciated its ability to provide power in the absence of wind. As a result, steam power got its disruptive foothold in the inland waterway market. Soon steamboats dotted the rivers and lakes of America.[1]

Meanwhile, seeing steam's potential, the old sailing-ship companies that specialized in wind-powered transoceanic travel did not completely ignore the new technology. The only place they could even think about using steam power, however, was in their mainstream market — to help them build ships that would cross entire oceans even more efficiently. They had little motivation to refocus on inland waterway customers, given that they had the opportunity to continue to build bigger, more profitable ships to cross the oceans. Not wanting to dismiss steam power entirely, however, sailing-ship companies searched for a middle ground. They ultimately pioneered a *hybrid* solution, one that combined both steam and sails. In 1819, the hybrid vessel *Savannah* made the first Atlantic crossing powered by a combination approach; in truth, only 80 hours of the 633-hour voyage were by steam rather than sail.[2] Steam power imparted some important advantages when the wind died down or blew the wrong way, but because it was incapable of being the primary source of power for such long distances, having sails as well was critical.

The wind-powered ship companies never made a true attempt at entering the pure disruptive steamship market—and ultimately they paid the price. By the early 1900s, the steam-powered ships, which had started in those inland waterways that looked unattractive to the wind-powered ship companies, became good enough for transoceanic travel. Customers migrated from sailing ships to steam-powered ships, and every single sailing ship company went out of business.

This story illustrates the theory of hybrids, a companion theory to the theory of disruptive innovation. The theory says that whenever a disruptive technology emerges, the leading firms in the field typically want to make use of it. But it is not yet good enough for their customers, so they develop a hybrid. The hybrid solution marries the old technology with the new to create a "best of both worlds" combination that they can offer to their customers at premium prices.

In the end, however, the hybrid solution does not disrupt the industry; rather, it sustains the leading firms by allowing them to serve their existing customers better and more profitably. *Because of this, a hybrid innovation is a type of sustaining innovation.* Meanwhile, the pure disruption starts at the low end or among nonconsumers, becomes better and better as it seeks to serve more demanding users in more complicated situations, and eventually displaces the hybrid, as it becomes good enough while retaining the values that made it disruptive—affordability, convenience, accessibility, or simplicity.

The important point to note about the theory of hybrids is that hybrid technologies are not on a disruptive path, despite their having some features of the disruptive technology on board.

Hybrids and Automobiles

The theory of hybrids helps us predict the future of many sectors, such as automobiles. Electric engines represent a disruptive innovation relative to gasoline-powered engines. Electric-powered cars travel a shorter range on a single charge, and they can't accelerate as fast as their gasoline-powered counterparts. Despite the hype generated by expensive pure-electric cars at the high-end of the market,[3] the theory of disruptive innovation suggests that the best place to launch pure electric vehicles to achieve transformation will be in places of nonconsumption[4] where their limitations are valued — such as in senior citizen communities or as a product for teenagers whose parents don't want them driving fast or far. Indeed, electric cars are emerging in both of these areas.[5]

But the electric engine has already had a more significant impact on the industry — as a hybrid. Toyota's hot-selling Prius, which combines a gasoline-powered engine with a battery-powered one, was among the first hybrid cars in the market. Mainstream drivers flocked to it because of its superior gas mileage. Although one might predict that pure electric vehicles will ultimately disrupt the car industry, hybrid vehicles will likely sustain gasoline-powered cars — and the companies that build them — for some time to come.

Delaying Disruption

The theory of hybrids helps explain the evolution of numerous industries, from photography to retailing.[6] There is one important caveat, though, illustrated well by the evolution of consumer banking. The disruptive innovation here is for consumers to do all their financial transactions through mobile wallets and online banking.[7] But established branch banks are offering a hybrid solution that combines online banking with traditional brick-and-mortar branch banks for exchanging paper currency and depositing and cashing checks. Some might wonder why ATMs, online banking, and mobile wallets have not completely wiped out branch banking. It turns out that branch banks perform valuable functions related to handling paper currency and coins, which are still very much a part of the established commercial system. ATMs and mobile wallets cannot yet get all of these functions done. Disruptive innovation theory predicts that in the long term, if pure digital currency substitutes for physical money, then at that point most branch banks — or at least the bank teller aspect of them — will become obsolete. As we'll see, the ability for branch banks to hang on, despite the arrival of disruptive technologies, provides a powerful analogue for what is happening to K–12 classrooms.

IS BLENDED LEARNING DISRUPTIVE?

The hundreds of blended-learning programs now in progress across the country, coupled with the theory of hybrids, have left a trail of clues to whether they are disruptive or sustaining. So far, the evidence suggests that the answer is both. Some models of blended learning have all the signs of a hybrid sustaining innovation. They offer promising improvements to the traditional classroom, but they do not disrupt it. Meanwhile, other models have the characteristics of pure disruptions; although the evidence, which we discuss later in this chapter, suggests that these models will not disrupt schools, the models are disruptive relative to the traditional classrooms *within* schools.

Figure 2.1 draws a line between models of blended learning that are taking shape as hybrids and those that appear disruptive. The hybrid models are sustaining to the traditional classroom, whereas the disruptive models are poised to replace it with something altogether different.

For those who want to anticipate the future of blended learning, understanding this distinction is the key.

Figure 2.1   The Hybrid and Disruptive Zones of Blended Learning

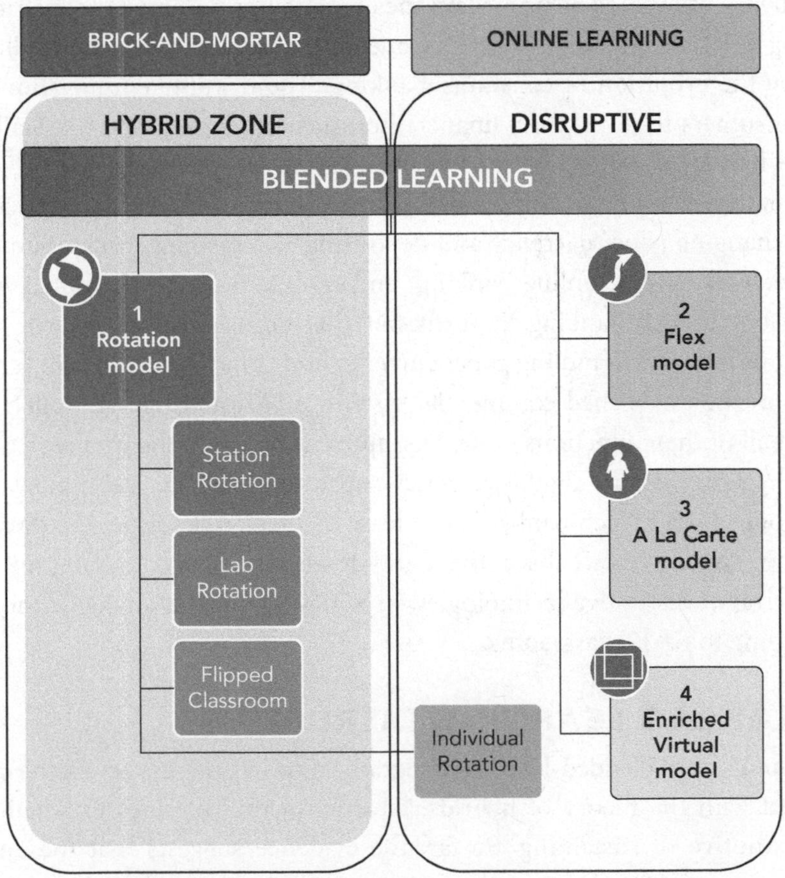

HYBRID MODELS OF BLENDED LEARNING

Educators who manage traditional classrooms are in some ways similar to the executives at sailing-ship manufacturers, Toyota, and branch banks. Traditional educators see the emergence of online learning but are hesitant to adopt it in its pure form because it does not meet the needs of their mainstream students as well as the traditional classroom does. So they develop a hybrid solution, which promises the "best of both worlds"—the advantages of the traditional classroom, combined with the benefits of online learning. In education as in other sectors, the model in which a technology is adopted is often more impactful than the technology in and of itself.

Educators are generally deploying three models of blended learning—the Station Rotation, Lab Rotation, and Flipped Classroom models—according to a pattern that resembles the ways in which hybrids are deployed in other sectors. The pattern has four principal characteristics.

1. ***Hybrid innovations include both the old and new technology,*** *whereas pure disruptions do not offer the old technology in its full form.*

The hybrid steamship *Savannah* had both sails and a steam engine. The Toyota Prius uses both gasoline and electricity. Hybrid banking allows consumers to conduct transactions in both physical branch banks and online.

In a similar vein, the Station Rotation, Lab Rotation, and Flipped Classroom variants of blended learning represent a combination of the old and the new. They preserve the rough contours of a traditional classroom—the facilities, staffing, and basic operations—and at the same time introduce an element of online learning. People often describe them as "best of both worlds" blends.

For example, KIPP Empower relies on both the traditional classroom model and online learning for its Station Rotation. The hybrid design is traditional in the sense that it does not tear down walls, shift away from face-to-face teacher-led instruction, or dramatically change the flow of the student's schedule. At the same time, it's new because it uses online learning as a part of its core instruction.[8]

The Station Rotation, Lab Rotation, and Flipped Classrooms all feature this combination. They seek to add online learning onto the traditional classroom in an effort to preserve the virtues of both approaches. Pure disruptions, on the other hand, disband with the traditional approach altogether, as this chapter addresses later.

2. *Hybrid innovations target existing customers* rather than nonconsumers.

Sailing ship makers designed the *Savannah* for their existing customers, transoceanic shippers, not to transport cargo on inland waterways. The Toyota Prius serves mainstream highway drivers, whereas pure electric vehicles that appear to be disruptive have been most successful initially with senior citizens. The general rule is that people design hybrids to make current customers happier, not to serve those whose alternative is nothing. It's one of the sure signs that hybrids are a type of sustaining innovation.

The hybrid models of blended learning are no different. They have largely been designed and implemented for existing students taking core subjects in mainstream classrooms.[9] In fact, as we've noted, rotations have been a classic feature of mainstream classroom design for decades, particularly at the elementary school level. The blended-learning version merely adds an online component to the rotation. Furthermore, most of these programs are using rotations for core subjects such as math and reading, not to provide access to otherwise unavailable subjects.

3. *Customers want hybrids to outperform the existing system according to the old rules of the game,* whereas disruptions compete on different terms and offer an alternative set of benefits.

The designers of the hybrid *Savannah* used steam power to try to make transoceanic passage even more successful. In contrast, the first pure steamship manufacturers changed the focus away from performance on the open ocean. They said that what really matters is the ability to make progress along an inland waterway when the wind isn't working in your favor. Successful disruptive innovations do not challenge the incumbent system head on; instead, they find an alternative market that values them for what they are.

Hybrid models of blended learning are similar to hybrids in other industries in this respect. They preserve the function of the traditional classroom, including keeping students in their seats in the classroom for the prescribed number of minutes. They bring sustaining improvements that help the classroom perform better based on traditional metrics.

In the typical Flipped Classroom, for example, students use connected devices after school—usually from home—to watch asynchronous instructional videos and complete comprehension questions. At school they practice and apply their learning with a face-to-face teacher. This model does not define performance in a new way, such as simplicity or convenience. Instead, it harnesses online learning as a sustaining innovation to help stretch the traditional classroom to perform its old job even better.

Pure disruptions, in contrast, are not focused on the job of keeping students in their seats for the prescribed number of minutes.[10] The opposite is true. Disruptive models of blended learning excel at allowing students to move through content at their own pace and making time-in-seat completely variable. They compete, ideally, on completely different terms from those of the traditional classroom—although, given an antiquated set of policies focused on seat time, sometimes they have to retrofit themselves or add convoluted features to remain compatible with the traditional regulatory structures.[11] Their natural strength is in the way they maximize personalization, access, and cost control.

4. *Hybrid innovations tend to be more complicated to operate* than disruptive *innovations.*

The example of the hybrid *Savannah* illustrates this fourth rule for spotting a hybrid. Whether a sailing ship or steamship is more complicated to operate is a matter of debate. But the *Savannah* was the most complicated of them all because it required expertise in both.

In the same way, hybrid models of blended learning are not noticeably simpler for teachers than the existing system. On the contrary, in many cases they appear to require all the expertise of the traditional model *plus* new expertise in managing digital devices and in integrating data across all the supplemental online experiences in the teacher-directed rotation.

Disruptive innovations, on the other hand, stand out for their simplicity, and the disruptive models of blended learning are no different. As long as students have connected devices, they can access tutorials and courses, even if they are stuck at a bus stop. Nurturing, face-to-face adults are of course critical to children's success, but these models begin to encourage maturity and independence by allowing students to participate in the management of their own learning.

DISRUPTIVE MODELS OF BLENDED LEARNING

While traditional educators are implementing hybrids, another set of school leaders are at the forefront of transforming the learning environment by implementing disruptive models of blended learning. The Individual Rotation, Flex, A La Carte, and Enriched Virtual models all have disruptive potential.

There is a simple rule of thumb for spotting a disruptive model of blended learning: *if students are learning in a blended setting, and you can't figure out where the front of the classroom is, then it's probably a disruptive model.* This guideline is not ironclad, but it generally works. Online learning is so central to managing and tracking student learning that most of the old constructs that define the traditional classroom—such as a chalkboard or whiteboard at the front of the room—are no longer relevant. Ideally, the teacher role pivots from being the "sage on the stage" to still being an active member—or even designer—of the learning process but in a very different role, often in the form of a tutor, discussion facilitator, hands-on project leader, or counselor. And with a disruptive model, usually the building architecture, furniture, and operations all look substantially different from anything traditional. The Flex and Individual Rotation models generally operate in wide open learning environments that might better be called learning studios than classrooms. Many Flex models even operate in storefront spaces that typically are reserved for retail stores. The teachers in these models don't spend their time delivering lesson plans based on a given day on the calendar. The A La Carte model dispenses with the physical classroom altogether, as the teacher of record is remote from her students. In the Enriched Virtual model, the facilities have been added to complement the virtual learning, in much the same way that Bonobos added physical stores that carry no inventory. As a result, the physical spaces in Enriched Virtual models tend to look much more like the learning studios featured in the Flex and Individual Rotation models. In general, the disruptive models of blended learning feel much more like this—online learning improving by adding a brick-and-mortar component that is distinct from the traditional classroom, as opposed to the sustaining, hybrid models in which the traditional classroom has added an online-learning feature.

Similar to other disruptions, most of the earliest disruptive blended-learning implementations began by serving pockets of nonconsumption. Many of the first Flex programs were focused initially on dropout and credit recovery and summer school. Most A La Carte programs came about to serve students who otherwise did not have access to courses such as Advanced Placement and foreign language offerings. The various Enriched Virtual programs emerged mostly to provide more support for students enrolled in full-time virtual schools—as well as to accommodate families who wanted full-time virtual schools but lived in states that prohibited them. Individual Rotation programs are still rare, but they will likely gain scale outside the mainstream classrooms of district schools.

Disruptive models compete on different terms and offer different benefits from the traditional classroom. They excel at allowing students to move through content at their own pace and making time-in-seat completely variable. They attract a following because of their special ability to bring the benefits of personalization, access, and cost control to the system. Instead of requiring face-to-face adults to manage both online learning and traditional instruction, they delegate the job of managing instruction to the Internet, thereby freeing up face-to-face adults to focus wholeheartedly on the many other important jobs that they should be doing to support, enrich, and mentor students.

FORESEEING THE K–12 EDUCATION REVOLUTION

The bottom line from this discussion of hybrids is that some varieties of blended learning are hybrids of the old and new, and as such they are sustaining innovations. That means they are poised to build on and offer sustaining enhancements to, but not fundamentally re-architect, the factory-style classroom.

One common misperception is that sustaining innovations are bad and disruptive innovations are good. This is false. Sustaining innovations are vital to a healthy and robust sector, as organizations strive to make better products or deliver better services to their best customers. The forces that propel well-managed organizations upmarket are always at work and are a crucial part of any successful organization. Schools that are struggling with flat or deteriorating test scores and strained budgets can find relief by harnessing the efficiencies that models such as the Station Rotation, Lab Rotation, and Flipped Classroom bring to the system.

But disruptive models of blended learning are on a different trajectory from those within the hybrid zone. They are carrying online learning on the march upward by helping it improve to intersect with the needs of more and more students and educators who feel enticed by the prospect of newfound opportunities for personalization, access, and cost control. As disruptive models progress, they are on track to gain dominance over the traditional system over time. Any hybrid variety of blended learning will eventually fall by the wayside as the pure disruption becomes good enough over the long term, just as steam engines eventually replaced sails for transoceanic voyages, and photo sharing on social-media sites is replacing print photography.

There are two important caveats to this prediction. One is that the disruption is likely to affect high school and, to some extent, middle school classrooms much more than elementary school classrooms. At high schools, as well as many middle schools, there is widespread nonconsumption in areas such as advanced courses, foreign languages, and credit recovery; at the elementary school level, such pockets of unmet demand are not as prevalent or as voiced. Furthermore, high school and middle school design typically features course-by-course modular architecture, which allows for modular online courses to be substituted into the system more readily.

In contrast, the future of elementary schools at this point is likely to be largely, but not exclusively, one of sustaining innovation for the classroom.[12] The closest that elementary schools come to presenting a disruptive path for blended learning is in the area of extended school hours and after-school programs. For example, Chicago Public Schools implemented a Flex model after-school program, called the Additional Learning Opportunities Initiative, to extend the school day using laptops and paraprofessionals for some students in grades one through eight.[13] If elementary schools continue to face budget cuts and need to reduce the number of traditional minutes in the school day, then this could create a sizable nonconsumption opportunity and a foothold for disruptive innovation. But this scenario has not played out to this point, so for now the future at the elementary level is uncertain. Tutoring—in everything from speech therapy to English language learning as well as foreign-language learning—presents other areas of nonconsumption that could drive the disruption of elementary school classrooms.[14]

The second caveat is that the long term may be quite long. Because the disruption is emerging, to a large extent, within the physical architecture of existing "egg crate–shaped" schools, the disruptive models simply lack physical space to take root in many cases, unless administrators literally tear down walls (which some are doing) or make do with suboptimal floor space. As with branch banking, given the constrained system within which schooling occurs, the disruption could take longer than it might otherwise.

Despite these caveats, the overall prognosis for the disruption of the classroom at the high school and middle school levels strains conventional wisdom, and predictably so. Whenever a disruptive innovation arrives, the established system usually views entrants in the emerging disruptive market as irrelevant to its well-being. The K−12 education sector is following suit. Flex, A La Carte, and other disruptive blended-learning models appear as only small line items on a long list of education trends and possibilities. But the pattern of disruptive innovation can take the guesswork out of anticipating the eventual size and scope of the rise of blended learning. It indicates that the future learning environments of high school and middle school, and to some extent elementary school, will be substantially different from the typical classrooms of today.

WHAT IS TO BECOME OF SCHOOLS?

In many ways education is the final frontier of the Internet, which has touched nearly every other sector of the economy (short of mining and massage parlors, perhaps). It is quickly making its way into every school in America at every grade level. Oftentimes schools are using computers to create technology-rich classrooms or to implement hybrid models of blended learning. In the fall of 2012, fifteen schools in five school districts across Pennsylvania launched the Pennsylvania Hybrid Learning Initiative to pilot mostly Rotation models of blended learning. Similar initiatives are underway in Washington, DC Public Schools, the Los Angeles Unified School District, and other districts across the country, as well as among independent and charter school networks.[15]

These efforts to outfit traditional classrooms with computers vary in their impact. On the one hand, *Disrupting Class* points out that computers have been around for several decades and schools are well populated with them, but the basic design of classrooms looks largely the same as it did before the personal computer revolution. The teaching and learning processes are similar to what they were in the days before computers, and, as a result, student learning has improved only marginally at best. When schools cram computers into traditional classrooms, at best they sustain or only slightly improve the way they already teach and run the schools.[16]

On the other hand, some high-quality implementations of sustaining blended-learning programs are leading to breakthrough improvements for traditional classrooms. In one of the largest studies to date, the RAND corporation and the Department of Education conducted a two-year, large-scale, randomized controlled trial to measure the effectiveness of students rotating between online Algebra I instruction — using Carnegie Learning, Inc.'s Cognitive Tutor Algebra I (CTAI) program — and traditional face-to-face classroom instruction. RAND selected a diverse population of more than 18,000 students in 147 schools in seven states for the study. Half the students experienced the CTAI rotation, while the other half learned without the online component. By design, the trial was explicitly sustaining to the classroom. RAND made an effort "to design the study so that it minimized the disruption to normal school operations such as the assignment of students and teachers to curriculum and classes."[17]

RAND's report concluded that the Rotation blended-learning model boosted the average high school student's performance by eight percentile points by year two, which equates roughly to doubling math learning in a year for those students.[18] At a time when thousands of schools are struggling to close the achievement gap or to boost overall learning, results such as these are significant. Every stakeholder with an interest in improving education should take online learning and squeeze from it every possible sustaining improvement it can bring to the traditional classroom. This effort is already well underway — and has been for years. The next chapters of this book offer recommendations for how to realize the full potential of blended learning — not only in disruptive ways, but also in ways that sustain and improve the traditional approach.

Meanwhile, a proportionately small but steady transformation is underway at the margins of mainstream schooling, and it is on course to replace the traditional classroom altogether at the high school level, as well as in many middle schools and perhaps some elementary schools. But the emergence of online learning and some models of blended learning as disruptive technologies does not in any way spell the doom of America's public schools. Notably, the disruption is taking place at the classroom level, not at the school level. In that way, Christensen, Horn, and Johnson got it right when they titled their book *Disrupting Class,* not *Disrupting School.*[19]

What, then, is the future role of schools? Rather than being destined to deteriorate or disappear, brick-and-mortar schools have an opportunity to shift some of their focus in response to the disruption. We suspect that schools will no longer have to be the primary source for content and instruction but can instead focus their capabilities on other core services. We return to Jon Bergmann's question from Chapter One: "What's the best use of face-to-face class time, given the migration of content and instruction to the Internet?"[20]

As content and instruction shift online, schools can focus more on activities that they have tried to do historically but all too often lacked the time, space, and resources to do well—from the application of knowledge and skills to drive deeper learning to the provision of nonacademic services that are critical to the success of children.

Deeper Learning

U.S. schools and teachers have for a long time sought to help students engage not just in learning knowledge, but also applying knowledge in deeper ways that invite exploration and creativity, as well as help students master critical thinking, collaboration, and communication skills in different domains. Historically this has too often involved a tradeoff between making sure students had the core knowledge necessary for these critical activities versus engaging in these activities and hoping students would be able to fill in their knowledge gaps. With the migration of content and instruction online, some schools are starting to find systematic ways to help students apply their knowledge and skills in a physical context. Acton Academy, an independent-school network that began in Austin, Texas, and employs a Flex model of blended learning, pairs individual, self-directed learning that is often online with Socratic discussion and project-based learning. The Socratic discussions teach students to talk, listen, and challenge ideas in a face-to-face circle of peers and guides. The projects require the students to work in face-to-face teams to apply the concepts they learn during individual work time and Socratic discussions. They also foster a "need to know" to motivate the online learning and provide a public, portfolio-based way for students to demonstrate achievement. Several other blended schools use brick-and-mortar experiences, including group discussions, wet labs, and hands-on projects, to help students dig deep and apply skills—or engage in what many refer to as deeper learning.[21] As online learning helps students *to know,* schools should be able to focus increasingly on helping students *to do* and *to be.*

WATCH CLIP 13: At Acton Academy, the Flex model in the elementary studio features online learning followed by group projects and Socratic discussions.

www.wiley.com/go/blended13

Safe Care

Society, including families and the democracy at large, asks schools to perform a number of functions, only one of which is to impart learning to students. Another central job is custodial—to care for children and keep them safe while parents are at work or otherwise unavailable. Many schools could certainly afford to improve in this regard. During the 2011 to 2012 time span, 35 percent of Chicago's 681 schools failed food inspection at least once for reasons such as no hot water in bathroom sinks, food kept at unsafe temperatures, and more than two hundred rodent droppings found in food service areas.[22] Such deficiencies in the basic care of children are horrifying to parents but often overlooked, as educators are compelled to prioritize the job of imparting content and instruction. As schools shift more of the management of content and instruction to the Internet, they will have the opportunity to refocus and devote more time and resources to providing world-class physical care.

Wraparound Services

In addition to their custodial role, schools already provide important social services for many students, which range from counseling and mentoring to health services and free meals. In the years ahead, schools will likely have to provide even more of these services for some students. Some have speculated that technology creates an opportunity to place on overdrive the counseling services that schools have long provided and rethink how schools do everything from academic monitoring to the development of self-direction in students, from college awareness and admissions applications to transcript management and course selection, all to help students be prepared for college, career, and life.[23]

Geoffrey Canada, creator of the ninety-seven-block Harlem Children's Zone in central Harlem, New York, led some of the groundbreaking work in addressing how schools that want to help low-income children must integrate practices not commonly thought of as the domain of schools, to help not only the students but also their neighborhoods and even the child-rearing practices of their parents.[24] In his book *Sweating the Small Stuff*, author David Whitman calls on schools to undertake a "new paternalism" for low-income, minority youth.[25] He cites examples of six "No Excuses" secondary schools that integrate services to fill essential needs that their families and others have neglected. Among the most important characteristics of these schools is that they are warm, caring places where teachers and principals form parental-like bonds with students.

Cincinnati Public School District developed a similar concept with its community-schools model, now in place in thirty-four of the fifty-five schools in the system. Community schools partner with a network of community-service providers to deliver a range of support, not only for students but also for the entire community. They serve dinner, subsidize transportation, help families apply for Medicaid—the list goes on. "What's the alternative?" former principal Craig Hockenberry asked a *New York Times* reporter writing about the program. "We should just sit back and watch these families deteriorate?"[26] Although doing these things alone *is not guaranteed to improve student outcomes,* if the schools don't do them, the majority of their students likely have little hope. As many have noted, if a student is hungry, the chances of her learning are slim. As more school leaders find that their children need broader social services to meet even basic prerequisites for learning, the simultaneous arrival of online learning could prove a welcome concurrence to carry some of schools' otherwise expanding burden and free up resources to focus on these important aspects of schooling.

Fun with Friends and Extracurricular Activities

From the perspective of children, having a place to have fun with friends is another vital role that brick-and-mortar schools play, as is having a place for extracurricular activities such as sports and the arts. One school in our research has developed several successful campuses with its blended-learning model. Its combination of online learning, face-to-face teachers, and innovative facilities has been effective in terms of raising math and reading scores on state standardized tests. But visitors to these schools sometimes say that the environments, with their rows of computers and cardboard partitions, can feel stark. Having figured out how to boost academics through online learning, perhaps these schools now have the capacity and resources to deliver in a world-class way on another function. They could develop the best dance programs, makerspaces (community-oriented workspaces where people come together to build things; more on this in Chapter Five),[27] or student philharmonic—or an assortment of these and other options across their campuses.

In many ways the arrival of online learning is welcome news for stressed-out schools that have long been asked to do too much with too little. Once online learning becomes good enough, schools will be able to rely on it to deliver consistently high-quality learning adapted to each student. That will free schools to focus on fulfilling the other functions. These other functions will likely include things such as guaranteeing clean and pleasing physical environments; the elimination of bullying; nutritious meals; excellent face-to-face mentoring, discussion, and enrichment; the fostering of knowledgeable citizens; the encouragement of good health and wellness; and a range of athletic, musical, and artistic programs. In addition, with students mastering knowledge online, schools should have a far greater capacity to help students focus on developing the skills required to become master creators and innovators—critical skills in the world they will inhabit after school.[28]

The biggest risk with this vision is that schools will not rise to the occasion as online learning expands. They will delegate much of student learning to the Internet, but they will not redirect face-to-face teachers and brick-and-mortar resources in ways that significantly enrich the online learning. In some blended-learning programs already underway, the on-site faculty sit back passively and let the online content providers do all the work. They feel like they have been "replaced" and offer little to enhance the learning or mentor the learners. These schools tend to be neither inspiring nor effective. One main purpose of the remaining chapters in this book is to help education leaders and influencers design higher-quality implementations that optimize the brick-and-mortar environment and the role of in-person teachers to prevent this foreseeable loss.

> ## To Sum Up
>
> - The Station Rotation, Lab Rotation, and Flipped Classroom models of blended learning generally match the pattern of hybrids, which combine the old with the new in pursuit of a "best of both worlds" solution. Hybrids are a form of sustaining innovation and are intended to serve mainstream students in traditional classrooms even better.
> - The Individual Rotation, Flex, A La Carte, and Enriched Virtual models of blended learning match the pattern of pure disruptions. As such, they are poised to disrupt most traditional classrooms in high schools, many in middle schools, and fewer in elementary schools.
> - High-quality implementations of sustaining varieties of blended learning bring vital improvements to the traditional classroom. Channeling sustaining models to their highest potential is an important and worthwhile priority across the system.
> - As online learning and the disruptive models of blended learning begin to overtake the traditional classroom, schools should shift resources to other important jobs, such as excellent face-to-face mentoring, role models, discussion, and enrichment; guaranteeing clean and pleasing physical environments; the elimination of bullying; nutritious meals; the fostering of knowledgeable citizens; the encouragement of good health and wellness; a range of athletic, musical, and artistic programs; and the development of students into master creators and innovators.

NOTES

1. The story about steamships is largely adapted from Clayton M. Christensen, *The Innovator's Dilemma: When New Technologies Cause Great Firms to Fail* (Boston: Harvard Business School Press, 1997), pp. 75–76.

2. The *Savannah* was wrecked off of Long Island in 1821. No other American-owned steamship would cross the Atlantic for nearly thirty years after the Savannah's historic voyage. John H. Morrison, *History of American Steam Navigation* (New York: W. F. Sametz & Co., 1903).

3. Even though Tesla has generated significant attention from its expensive pure electric automobiles and new distribution system, the theory of disruptive innovation predicts that the slow incremental improvement of

the old paradigm—through a variety of sustaining innovations, including a hybrid—will continue to outperform the pure disruption on the traditional metrics of performance. If Tesla manages to make a breakthrough in the battery technology to create cars that can go farther and faster for a competitive price, then the theory predicts that the incumbent car companies would be highly motivated to do whatever it takes to adopt those innovations to hang on to their market share—and that we shouldn't underestimate the power of that motivation. This does not mean that Tesla cannot be successful per se; for example, by modularizing and becoming a supplier of components to help low-end, disruptive electric car companies starting in areas of nonconsumption improve and move upmarket. Similarly, Tesla could potentially be successful through the ongoing use of exorbitant subsidies—either through its founder's willingness to finance a loss or from the government—but there are many risks to this strategy that raise doubt as to its longer-term viability. We discuss Tesla in Chapter Four as well.

4. If an organization tries to deploy a pure disruption in the mainstream market, it can survive only if it receives eternal subsidies. The venture capital firm Kleiner Perkins Caufield Byers (KPCB) provides a case in point. In 2008, with much fanfare, it established its Green Growth Fund as a $1 billion initiative to invest in and support later-stage greentech ventures. Many of the companies in which it invested that deployed pure disruptions in established markets appeared to be profitable—but the top line was filled largely with subsidies. As the subsidies have fallen away, piece by piece, so too have several of the companies in which it invested. It's important to note that where there is no nonconsumption in a market, a hybrid solution is the only viable option for a new technology that underperforms the old based on the original definition of performance. That means that in markets with full consumption, hybrid innovations tend to dominate, rather than pure disruptions. See Clayton M. Christensen, Michael B. Horn, and Heather Staker, "Is K–12 Blended Learning Disruptive? An Introduction to the Theory of Hybrids," Clayton Christensen Institute, May 2013.

5. The prediction that electric cars will find a disruptive foothold in the teenage market is already proving true. In Peachtree City, a suburb forty minutes south of Atlanta, it's legal for teens with learners' permits to drive golf carts

unsupervised. Hence thousands of whirring electric golf carts dart around town. Emily Bunker, a sixteen-year-old who drives a beige cart with a disco ball hanging in the rearview mirror, said that although her cart tops out at 19 mph, "it feels so good not to have to take the bus." Her fellow junior Nancy Mullen said that parents are willing to let their kids drive golf carts because they're "good practice for real cars, kind of like bumper cars." Allison Entrekin, "Life in the Slow Lane: In the Atlanta Suburb of Peachtree City, the Hottest Set of Wheels Goes 19 mph," *Hemispheres Magazine*, February 2014, p. 20, http://www.hemispheresmagazine.com/2014/02/01/dispatches-18/ (accessed February 18, 2014).

6. Digital photography represents a disruptive innovation relative to film-based technologies. The top firms from the days of film have not transitioned to digital completely, nor have they ignored it entirely. Instead, they market a hybrid solution, which is to snap photos using a digital camera and then print out the photos on expensive Kodak, HP, or Canon photographic printer paper. In contrast, upstart firms such as Facebook and Instagram, which Facebook acquired, are peddling the purely disruptive form of photography, which is to snap photos using a digital camera and then share them entirely digitally. It is also worth noting that single-lens reflex (SLR) cameras have incorporated digital in a sustaining hybrid format as well, as the shutters in these cameras still operate by a mechanical mechanism, not an electric one as do "camera phones." Given that relatively few people use SLRs, as the equipment serves the niche of serious hobbyists and professional photographers, this may be a place where a hybrid solution prevails for some time to come.

Online shopping represents a disruptive innovation relative to traditional brick-and-mortar retailing. Traditional brick-and-mortar stores, such as Nordstrom, Target, and Costco, have of course not switched to purely digital storefronts. Instead, they have developed the hybrid solution of offering customers both traditional brick-and-mortar stores as well as an online option. Some call this "bricks-and-clicks" retail—a classic hybrid strategy designed to sustain and improve how traditional stores operate. The purely disruptive online retailers, however, are steadily gaining ground and making the online experience better and better, such that more customers are turning to sites such as Amazon.com, which does not have brick-and-mortar stores. As mentioned in Chapter One, an interesting way that some online retailers are improving and gaining ground is by opening brick-and-mortar stores whose primary purpose is to serve as showrooms for online items and therefore carry limited inventory. The example from Chapter One is Bonobos, a men's apparel store that was once dogmatic about only selling online, but then opened six brick-and-mortar stores in 2012. The stores carry limited inventory and employ only a few salespeople. This phenomenon of a pure disruption incorporating an element of an old technology—but not the old technology in its full form—is an example of disruption's upward march; after getting a foothold by launching among nonconsumers and those with the lowest performance needs, companies on a disruptive path pursue sustaining innovations—such as retail showrooms—to allow them to climb upmarket to serve more demanding customers.

7. Millions of poor people in developing countries who do not have access to traditional branch banks use clunky early-model mobile phones to make payments as a practical alternative to cash and bank accounts. Disruptive mobile wallet providers are meeting this need; Tagattitude and Turkcell are two examples. For a fuller discussion of the disruption of banking, we also recommend Fiona Maharg-Bravo, "The Online Challenge for Banking," *New York Times*, February 21, 2014 (http://mobile.nytimes.com/blogs/dealbook/2014/02/21/the-online-challenge-for-banking/?nl=business&emc=edit_dlbkam_20140224).

8. Brad Bernatek, Jeffrey Cohen, John Hanlon, and Matthew Wilka, "Blended Learning in Practice: Case Studies from Leading Schools, featuring KIPP Empower Academy," Michael & Susan Dell Foundation, September 2012, http://5a03f68e230384a218e0–938ec019df699e606c950a5614b999bd.r33.cf2.rackcdn.com/Blended_Learning_Kipp_083012.pdf

9. Disruptive innovation is a relative phenomenon. When the disruptive models of blended learning are deployed to serve existing students in core subjects in traditional classrooms, they may in fact be sustaining innovations. And when the hybrid models of blended learning are implemented in areas of nonconsumption, they may be disruptive.

10. The exception is the Individual Rotation model, which rotates students on fixed schedules and thus could be more compatible with a seat time–based system than the Flex, A La Carte, and Enriched Virtual models.

11. For example, full-time virtual schools have attendance tools calibrated to meet each state's seat-time — or attendance — requirements. But several choose not to do this by simply counting virtual heads logged online. Instead, they measure a combination of that plus verification by teachers of actual work completed, which is mapped back to the attendance requirements, be they measured in minutes, hours, or days. Similarly, competency-based blended-learning programs often must map their competency-based report cards to traditional ones to satisfy various college admissions expectations for students.

12. Although 46 percent of respondents in a 2013 California survey report having students participate in online or blended learning, just 19 percent of elementary districts and charters engage in online learning, whereas a whopping 73 percent of unified and high school districts and charters do. Furthermore, of those districts or charters that say they have students learning online, 78 percent indicated that high school students participate in online learning; 49 percent said middle-school students do; and 28 percent said elementary-school students are engaged in online learning. Not only that, but how schools are blending online learning differs starkly between elementary schools and secondary schools as well. According to the census, the top three blended models across all districts and charters are the Rotation model (47 percent), the A La Carte model (40 percent), and the Enriched Virtual model (33 percent). When these numbers are disaggregated by grade span, however, a different picture emerges. In elementary schools engaged in online learning, Rotation blended learning is the dominant model, accounting for 80 percent of the implementations; just 15 percent of elementary districts/charters use more than one blended model. In unified and high school districts/charters engaging in online learning, however, the top model is the A La Carte model (48 percent), and 38 percent employ more than one blended model. See Brian Bridges, "California eLearning

Census: Between the Tipping Point and Critical Mass," California Learning Resource Network, May 2013, http://www.clrn.org/census/eLearning_ Census_Report_2013.pdf

13. "Chicago Public Schools," Blended Learning Universe, Clayton Christensen Institute, http://www.christenseninstitute.org/chicago-public-schools/ (accessed August 14, 2013). The Additional Learning Opportunities (ALO) program was launched in 2010 to serve students in grades first through eighth at fifteen schools with ninety minutes of additional learning time after the school day. Although the program lost funding in 2012, its positive results helped Chicago Public Schools move toward its Full School Day initiative for full-day kindergarten and a longer school day. Budget Summary, Chicago Public Schools, 2013, http://www.cps.edu/FY13Budget/ Documents/Departments.pdf

14. When there isn't a lot of nonconsumption, there are two options for a new technology with disruptive characteristics: it can take root in a hybrid solution, or it can enter a market as a pure disruption dependent on eternal subsidy to be good enough to meet mainstream needs. The hybrid models of blended learning are more likely than the disruptive models to dominate at the elementary school level because of the lack of nonconsumption at that level. This lack of a disruptive foothold makes it hard for pure disruptive models to enter the system anywhere other than to serve mainstream elementary students in core areas. Consequently, most elementary school classroom models will be hybrids that offer a "best of both worlds" solution corresponding to the needs of the existing elementary school system.

15. Sean Kennedy and Don Soifer, "Why Blended Learning Can't Stand Still: A Commitment to Constant Innovation Is Needed to Realize the Potential of Individualized Learning," Lexington Institute, p. 11, http://www.lexington institute.org/library/resources/documents/Education/WhyBlended LearningCantStandStill.pdf

16. *Disrupting Class,* p. 72.

17. John F. Pane, Beth Ann Griffin, Daniel F. McCaffrey, and Rita Karam, "Effectiveness of Cognitive Tutor Algebra I at Scale," RAND Corporation, March

2013, http://www.rand.org/content/dam/rand/pubs/working_papers/
WR900/WR984/RAND_WR984.pdf, p. 7.

18. Ibid.

19. Although traditional and hybrid classrooms are poised for disruption, we do not see brick-and-mortar schools falling by the wayside any time soon. This is because although there are many areas of nonconsumption at the classroom level—particularly in secondary schools—there is little nonconsumption at the school level in the United States. Almost every student has access to a government-funded school of some sort, and, as we discussed in Chapter One, most students and families need access to schooling. We predict that hybrid schools, which combine existing schools with new classroom models, will be the dominant model of schooling in the United States in the future. But within secondary schools, the disruptive models of blended learning will substantially replace traditional classrooms over the long term.

20. Comment from Jon Bergmann during "Blended Learning, Flipped Classrooms, and Other Innovative Teaching Techniques," *U.S. News & World Report* STEM Conference, panel discussion, Austin, TX, June 18, 2013.

21. The William and Flora Hewlett Foundation has invested significantly in researching the idea of deeper learning and trying to have it implemented in schools across the world. See http://www.hewlett.org/programs/education/deeper-learning (accessed on April 14, 2014).

22. Pam Zekman, "2 Investigators: Chicago Schools Flunk Food Inspections," CBS 2 Chicago, October 29, 2012, http://chicago.cbslocal.com/2012/10/29/2-investigators-chicago-schools-flunk-food-inspections/ (accessed August 14, 2013).

23. Mary Ryerse, Carri Schneider, and Tom Vander Ark, "Core & More: Guiding and Personalizing College & Career Readiness," Digital Learning Now Smart Series, May 27, 2014.

24. Paul Tough, *Whatever It Takes: Geoffrey Canada's Quest to Change Harlem and America* (New York: Houghton Mifflin, 2008).

25. David Whitman, *Sweating the Small Stuff: Inner-City Schools and the New Paternalism* (Washington, D.C.: The Thomas B. Fordham Institute, 2008).

26.   Javier C. Hernandez, "Mayoral Candidates See Cincinnati as a Model for New York Schools," *New York Times,* August 11, 2013, http://www.nytimes .com/2013/08/12/nyregion/candidates-see-cincinnati-as-model-for-new-york-schools.html?pagewanted=all&_r=0 (accessed August 14, 2013).

27.   See Makerspace, http://makerspace.com/ (accessed May 27, 2014).

28.   For more on this idea, we recommend Tony Wagner, *Creating Innovators: The Making of Young People Who Will Change the World* (New York: Scribner, 2012).

Part 2

Mobilizing

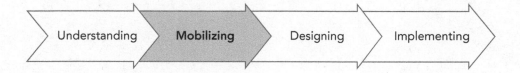

Understanding | **Mobilizing** | Designing | Implementing

Chapter 3

Start with the Rallying Cry

Students carry devices in their pockets and use them when and wherever they can. Teachers hear about new products and wonder if anything might help a struggling or disengaged child in their class. Administrators, who feel pressure to produce blue-ribbon results on a shoestring budget, understand that digital solutions have improved average worker productivity in the general economy by more than 2 percent a year over the past sixty years.[1] Many wonder if technology could give them a boost, too. Schools have no choice but to consider technology.

But the prospect of advocating for an investment in technology can feel intimidating. Who knows if the plan will pay off and lead to better results? Beyond proposing the investment, the job of designing and executing the implementation of a technology plan is even more daunting. Many people find it's hard to know where to start. The most common mistake is to set forth with an appetite for the dazzling technology, rather than with an interest in the relief it might bring when applied strategically to a frustrating problem. Regrettably, this leads only to the cramming of more devices, screens, gadgets, and software into students' and teachers' already noisy lives.

At one elementary school in Honolulu, Hawaii, we watched as the parents' organization labored to raise money for electronic whiteboards for every classroom. The intention was for these boards to be transformational. They would allow students to experience what in effect was a giant touchscreen in each room. Surely this investment would bolster student engagement and teacher effectiveness. Students sold gift wrap. Parents clipped Box Tops coupons. Even the kindergarteners did their part by saving for the coin drive. Eventually the school had enough funding to complete the project. But within a few months, many teachers used the boards for little more than taking attendance (students touched their names on the board when they arrived each morning, and the system automatically informed the front office) and projecting videos. A few sat in disrepair, and one teacher even taped a poster right on top of the electronic whiteboard in her classroom.

Despite the allure of that technology, little changed at the Honolulu school. The fancy whiteboards became a layer crammed on top of the already crowded, urban classrooms. Teachers lost precious instructional time and money trying to integrate a technology "solution" that produced little return on education.[2]

The size of this problem is significant. Personal computers have been around for four decades. Schools are well populated with them. Figure 3.1 shows a map of locations in the United States with a one-to-one computing program at the K–12 level. In each of these locations, schools are investing to ensure that absolutely every student has access to a computer. In 1981, there was a computer for every 125 students in schools. In 1991 there was one for every eighteen, and by 2009 it was one for every five students.[3]

Certainly some of these one-to-one programs are yielding a positive return on education; the One-to-One Institute, for example, focuses on using computers to create personalized-learning opportunities that boost student achievement. But overall, the unfortunate truth is that despite the massive investment, computers have had little effect on how teachers teach and students learn, except to increase costs and draw resources away from other school priorities.[4] In his book *Oversold and Underused: Computers in the Classroom,* Larry Cuban reported that across a large sample of schools in his study, computers had little or no impact on

Figure 3.1 Map of United States One-to-One Computer Programs at the K– 12 Level

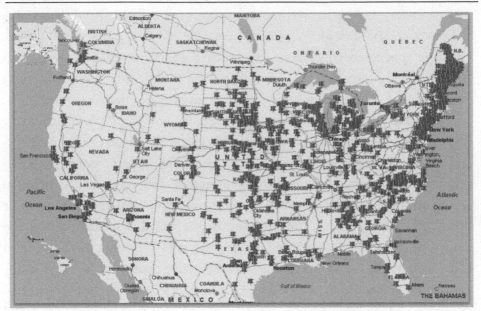

Source: Adapted with permission from the One-to-One Institute website (accessed on October 1, 2013).

the way students learned. Teachers still delivered the instruction. Students used computers for word processing, to search the Internet for research papers, and to play drill-and-kill games. "In the end," Cuban concluded, "both supporters and critics of school technology (including the researchers) have claimed that powerful software and hardware often get used in limited ways to simply maintain rather than transform prevailing instructional practices."[5]

Indeed, without the right strategy behind them, some well-intentioned one-to-one programs can run into serious problems. In 2013, Los Angeles Unified School District committed to a $1-billion effort to provide all its students with $678 Apple iPads. But the first wave of the deployment was chaotic at best. More than three hundred students evaded a security filter to access unauthorized content. "These are personal pornography devices," one parent said. Other parents worried whether they were liable for the countless iPads that students had lost or broken within the first few weeks of the rollout.[6]

THE ALTERNATIVE TO CRAMMING

The nightmarish deployment of devices in Los Angeles was newsworthy; more common is for schools to layer computers on top of whatever is already happening in classrooms and then pick up right where they left off, with business as usual. The quiet phenomenon of cramming occurs whenever school communities do not take the necessary steps to change the norm through an intentional transformation. The most successful blended-learning programs are much more deliberate and generally share a common starting point: *they begin by identifying the problem to solve or the goal to achieve. They start with a clear rallying cry.*

This idea of leading with the problem or goal might at first seem obvious, but a glance at major education purchases in recent years shows that the temptation to lead with the technology is pervasive. Blame Apple in part for launching a stream of must-have tablets and handhelds — devices that make everyone run to their desks to apply for school improvement grants. Lenovo, Dell, and most other computer makers employ dedicated marketing teams that focus on selling technology packages to the education sector. Google's Chromebooks, which retail for under $300, likewise feed the frenzy. None of these companies or devices in itself is bad, but the temptation of these slick interfaces and dazzling products can get people more excited about a product than about a solution to a problem. This temptation leads to schools investing big dollars in one-to-one programs without a clear statement of intent about what all that computing power will accomplish.

The best blended programs across the country differ from each other dramatically. One delivers math to sixth graders in New Orleans, another brings science courses to high school students in Nevada, and yet another caters to English language learners in California. But nearly without exception, those leading the most successful programs avoid the trap of "technology for technology's sake" by beginning with a clearly articulated problem or goal *that does not reference technology.* In other words, saying that a lack of devices or "twenty-first century tools" is the problem to be solved keeps the focus on technology for technology's sake and is a circular reference. The problem or goal must instead be rooted in improving educational effectiveness — by such means as boosting student outcomes or opportunities, doing more with less, or improving the ability of teachers to do their jobs.

DEFINING THE PROBLEM OR STATING THE GOAL

The most successful blended programs begin generally in response to a desire to (1) boost student achievement and quality of life through personalization, (2) provide access to out-of-reach courses and opportunities, (3) improve a school system's financial health, or (4) a combination of all three. Sometimes schools discover an immediate need or problem related to these areas that nudges them toward blended learning; in other cases, they spot an opportunity and decide to go for it.

Beginning with a Defined Problem

Quakertown Community School District, roughly forty-five miles north of Philadelphia, is an example of a district that embraced technology in response to a clear problem. One feature of Pennsylvania is that it has more than a dozen cyber charter schools across the state. These are full-time schools that students attend entirely virtually, without setting foot on a campus. When a student leaves a Pennsylvania district school for a cyber charter, the district must pay for that student's charter enrollment. Although the legislature debates the funding formula for cyber charters nearly every year, on average Pennsylvania districts lose roughly $9,200 for every non-special-education student and $19,200 for every special-education student who attends a cyber school.[7]

 WATCH CLIP 14: Quakertown Community School District produces A La Carte courses to provide students with flexibility.

www.wiley.com/go/blended14

Because districts have high fixed costs that are difficult to reduce from year to year, even though they are not on the hook for educating students who leave for cyber charters, districts across Pennsylvania feel the heat from the loss of per-pupil funding for each student who leaves. Quakertown is one such district. In 2007 its administrators came together to decide what to do about the financial problem this loss created. Their solution was to launch the Infinity Cyber Academy—the district's own online-learning program—as an in-house alternative to cyber charters. The district uses its own face-to-face teachers to develop and deliver over eighty types of online courses, thanks to the help of professional development. It renovated its high school and created a large open-learning space with a café, comfortable furniture, and charging stations. The district screens students before they enroll in the Infinity Cyber Academy to determine if they are likely to be successful. All students who enroll, whether part- or full-time, still are welcome at pep rallies, on sports teams, and at prom.[8]

The result is that Quakertown gives all of its sixth through twelfth grade students the opportunity to participate in an A La Carte model of blended learning (as well as in a full-time virtual school) without leaving the district. Lisa Andrejko, former superintendent of Quakertown, estimates that in the first four years of its operation, Infinity Cyber Academy helped the district retain over $2.5 million that would have left the district had students moved to or continued with cyber charter schools.

Beginning with an Aspirational Goal

For many schools and communities, the decision to consider blended learning is less abrupt. No major problem hits them in the face. Instead, leaders have educational goals they want to realize for their students—and online learning proves to be the answer.

FirstLine Schools is a charter management organization based in New Orleans that specializes in school turnarounds. It uses the Response-to-Intervention (RTI) method to provide early, systematic assistance to children who have difficulty learning—a prevalent problem in turnaround environments. When it opened Arthur Ashe Charter School in 2007, FirstLine led an effort to boost the test scores of entering students from the 25th percentile to the 50th or 60th—not a small feat at a school with the highest percentage of special-needs students in New Orleans.[9] But it could not seem to boost achievement much higher after that initial lift. Furthermore, in the past FirstLine had relied on a big team of paraprofessionals and interventionists to help teach small groups, but this was proving expensive to scale sustainably as FirstLine sought to turn around more schools.[10]

FirstLine saw blended learning as an opportunity to reach for a higher ideal in both respects. Its leaders set two goals: first, to raise student achievement on the School Performance Score, the state's metric for scoring schools based on standardized test results; and second, to accomplish the first goal in a financially sustainable and scalable way.

In August 2011, the FirstLine team piloted a Lab Rotation model at its Arthur Ashe Charter School. The design, now standard practice across the school, uses a computer lab with online software to bring students up to grade level faster without wasting time reteaching skills they already know. Students cycle through the computer lab for online learning and targeted remediation in small groups with a face-to-face teacher. Teachers make small-group assignments based on a review of math, medical, and behavior data to make evidence-based decisions on the right intervention.

By the end of the first year (2011–12), Arthur Ashe reduced its per-pupil funding deficit by 72 percent—from $2,148 per student down to $610 per student. The following year, students at Arthur Ashe experienced four times more growth in math than students attending FirstLine's nonblended schools, and Arthur Ashe had a twelve-point gain on its School Performance Score. This raised Arthur Ashe to one of the top three schools in the city for growth.

For those venturing forth to start a new school, the aspirational goals often look different from those at an organization like FirstLine, which is running an existing operation. New schools often start out with the ambition to bring a new vision, philosophy, or model to the community. Jeff and Laura Sandefer, who founded Acton Academy, which we introduced in Chapter Two, fit into the latter category. Their oldest daughter attended a top high school in Austin, Texas, while their younger sons were at a Montessori school that allowed its students broad freedom to direct their own learning. One day the Sandefers asked a high school teacher at their daughter's school if he thought they should transfer their sons from Montessori into a more traditional model. He told them to make the switch as soon as possible before the boys became too accustomed to the freedoms that the Montessori method allowed.

The Sandefers decided to do the opposite of the teacher's recommendation. They not only decided against enrolling their sons in a traditional school, but they also set a goal of opening thousands of micro-schools to expand learner-driven education worldwide.

Other leaders identify goals related to boosting student engagement, increasing access to mentors, improving teacher training, closing the achievement gap, reducing learning loss associated with absences, offering more career training, preparing students to complete college, and so forth.[11] The point is to go through the process of stating goals up front before embarking on blended learning—and certainly before investing in gadgets.

Say It SMART

Not all statements of problems and goals are created equal. Leaders can take their ideas a step further by defining them as SMART (specific, measurable, assignable, realistic, and time-related) objectives. According to George T. Duran, one of the first to write about SMART goals, organizations should consider the following criteria when designing objectives:

- **Specific**—Does it target a specific area for improvement?
- **Measurable**—Does it quantify or at least suggest an indicator of progress?
- **Assignable**—Who will be responsible?
- **Realistic**—Can results be achieved realistically, given available resources?
- **Time-related**—When can the results be achieved?[12]

FirstLine Schools came close to setting a SMART goal when it stated that it wanted to use blended learning to raise the School Performance Score at Arthur Ashe in a financially sustainable, scalable way. It could have written this objective even better by making a statement such as this one:

> Our goal is to use blended learning to raise the School Performance Score 10 points at Arthur Ashe while reducing our reliance on paraprofessionals and interventionists by 20 percent. Chris Liang-Vergara, our director of instructional technology for personalized learning, will lead the team. We will achieve these results by the end of the next school year.

Although the task of assigning the project to the right leader may need to wait until the next step of organizing the team (which we discuss in Chapter Four), the practice of setting a SMART rallying cry up front can help schools bring their blended-learning aspirations into sharper resolution. Down the road, some may find that their students also benefit from using the SMART framework when they reflect on their personal-learning goals as part of a student-centered environment.

SHOULD LEADERS FOCUS ON SUSTAINING OR DISRUPTIVE RALLYING CRIES?

In the previous chapter, we showed that some models of blended learning are generally sustaining innovations that improve traditional classrooms. Sustaining innovations begin among mainstream students in core classes and do the same job as the existing system, only better. On the other hand, other models of blended learning are starting to replace the factory model altogether, particularly at the high school level, and to some extent in middle school. Disruptive innovations bring new opportunities to nonconsumers—those whose alternative is nothing at all—and then improve over time to serve even those in the mainstream.

So which is best? Should leaders define problems and goals in areas of nonconsumption that disruptive models are best suited to attack, or is there value in launching sustaining innovations in core areas as well?

We think that both are essential.[13] The majority of K–12 students experience much of their core curriculum through the factory model and will continue to do so for years to come, particularly at the elementary school level. The growing body of evidence that blended learning is successfully tackling tough problems for core subjects such as math and reading suggests that leaders should pay close attention to the benefits it could bring to all traditional classrooms. Why ignore an opportunity to improve on what we have?

At the same time, the pattern of disruption is at work in K–12 education. Online learning is disrupting America's classrooms, particularly at the middle and high school levels. Leaders can either turn a blind eye to the arrival of this disruptive innovation or harness it to help shape the transformation, bring its benefits to their students, and shield their students from its downsides. Those who begin now to pilot and experiment will have the upper hand when demand for student-centered schooling expands. Furthermore, there is no reason to wait to offer disruptive models of blended learning for those whose alternative is nothing—such as students without access to advanced courses, homebound students, and those who need credit recovery. In some cases, such as for the Sandefers, the disruptive innovation is becoming good enough even for the mainstream.

To address both opportunities strategically and meaningfully, the key is to divide the two categories and brainstorm sustaining goals separate from disruptive goals. The broader reason to look at the categories separately is that sustaining and disruptive innovations serve different purposes and follow different patterns. Cobbling them together and evaluating them against each other distorts the ability to see each opportunity for what it is.

For these reasons, we recommend that leaders brainstorm their SMART objectives in two steps: first by identifying core problems and goals that are ripe for sustaining innovations, and then by identifying nonconsumption problems and goals, for which disruptive strategies are good bets.

HOW TO IDENTIFY CORE OPPORTUNITIES

Some problems and goals pertain to the needs of mainstream students and teachers in core courses and subjects. KIPP Empower, which we highlight in the introduction, faced a core problem in the months preceding its launch, when administrators learned that California had slashed funding for the class-size reduction program, and as a result the school lost $100,000 of expected revenue. This funding shortfall forced the team to consider using a Station Rotation model as a way to lower the cost of small student-teacher ratios during group-instruction time for mainstream students in writing, math, and science.

Oakland Unified School District, a large urban district east of San Francisco, also used blended learning to pursue a core opportunity. The Rogers Family Foundation approached Oakland Unified about forming a pilot group to demonstrate how to implement a technology investment in a way that would maximize results—higher student engagement, fewer absences, and, ultimately, higher academic achievement. Rogers selected four schools out of forty to be in its pilot group. All four schools chose a Station Rotation or Lab Rotation plan of attack. The hypothesis was that a Rotation model would allow teachers to focus on smaller groups while other students received personalized, adaptive content that the teacher did not have to create and that provided useful data about each student. This, in turn, would drive progress in solving the identified problems.[14]

Those are just two examples. Other core opportunities could include:

- Addressing the needs of kindergarteners and transfer students who enter the district with wide disparities in reading skills
- Providing high school teachers more time to give individual feedback on writing assignments
- Offering more science labs for high school students, despite budget shortfalls
- Helping middle school students who lack the family support to complete take-home projects

For all of these examples, most U.S. schools already have programs in place. But the classrooms could benefit from innovations that help them serve students better. Such circumstances present fertile opportunities for educators to implement sustaining innovations using blended learning. Already millions of students are enjoying the benefits of Station Rotations, Lab Rotations, Flipped Classrooms, and other blended combinations to help solve these core problems. In some cases, educators are even finding that disruptive models are becoming compelling solutions to core predicaments. Leaders should take careful inventory of core opportunities as they define the problem or state the goal that they want blended learning to solve.

HOW TO IDENTIFY NONCONSUMPTION OPPORTUNITIES

Nonconsumption opportunities are a separate and important consideration when identifying the target for a blended-learning program. Nonconsumption exists any time schools cannot provide a learning experience; they have no easy option other than to do without it. Miami-Dade County Public Schools (Miami-Dade), based on the southern tip of Florida and the nation's fourth-largest school district, faced such a moment in the summer of 2010. The district found itself short of the number of teachers it would need to ensure that eight thousand high school students had access to the courses they needed stay on track for on-time graduation. Unable to hire that many teachers itself, Miami-Dade invited Florida Virtual School (FLVS) to set up Virtual Learning Labs (nicknamed "Very Large Labs" by some) at dozens of school sites within just a few short summer months.

Each Virtual Learning Lab was to house at least fifty students in any open room available on campus, such as a library or computer lab. The labs offered students access to any of the over 120 courses in FLVS's catalog that they needed to get on track to graduate.

 WATCH CLIP 15: An online Florida Virtual School teacher is the teacher of record for A La Carte courses that Miami-Dade County Public Schools delivers in Virtual Learning Labs.

www.wiley.com/go/blended15

As of 2013, more than fifty-six schools—out of the 392 schools in the county[15]—were using in-school labs to offer FLVS courses to as many as ten thousand students in Miami-Dade. Other Florida districts followed suit. Suncoast Community High School in the Palm Beach County School District asked FLVS to provide an Advanced Placement course it was missing. Ponce de Leon High School in the Holmes County School District used FLVS to expand its foreign language options. The districts found that an A La Carte model offered a way to close their gaps.[16]

Other nonconsumption opportunities that schools have identified include:

- Serving students who have dropped out of school

- Helping students recover units and credits to stay on track for graduation

- Providing access to electives

- Offering speech or behavioral therapy

- Providing SAT/ACT test preparation

- Reducing the learning loss resulting from absences because of extracurricular activities

When they engage in this brainstorm, leaders are often surprised at the amount of nonconsumption their students experience. The gaps can be blessings in disguise, however, because they open opportunities for schools to experiment with disruptive innovation. Few people object to setting up a Flex lab for unit and credit recovery, offering an A La Carte course in Swahili to a student intent on learning that language, or giving eleventh graders access to an Enriched Virtual course that prepares them for the SAT test. These are entry points for experimenting with student-centered models without incurring much resistance from the established system. Solving these problems not only provides learning opportunities that students were missing but also gives schools a convenient way to experiment with how to move beyond the factory model.

Nonconsumption opportunities are an important and distinct consideration when choosing the rallying cry. Leaders should take on a two-pronged strategy of pursuing both core and nonconsumption opportunities as they embark on blended learning.[17]

THREATS VERSUS OPPORTUNITIES

We have observed that although many leaders believe that disruptive innovation is critical to transforming education from a factory model to a student-centered system, they are reluctant to commit to the two-pronged strategy we just described. Most choose to focus exclusively on core opportunities—sustaining-innovation opportunities. They are accountable for making adequate yearly progress on core standards, and they struggle to focus on areas of nonconsumption rather than the areas of consumption, which feel like the immediate priority. How can schools focus on disruptive innovation and transforming to a student-centered model when all of their resources, process, and priorities are focused on sustaining and improving their existing classrooms?

In an insightful stream of research, Clark Gilbert[18] pointed to a way for leaders to convince their organizations to invest resources in disruptive innovation.[19] He said that if one frames a phenomenon to an individual or a group as an external threat, then it elicits a far more intense and energetic response than if one frames the same phenomenon as an opportunity.[20] The implication is that leaders who want to transform factory-style classrooms should start by framing nonconsumption problems as external threats. A great example is that of Superintendent Andrejko of Quakertown, who was vocal about the fact that the district was losing hundreds of thousands of dollars each year to cyber charters. She was clear that if the district did not take action, jobs were at risk.

The second part of Gilbert's recommendation is that after the initial threat framing, the leader should reframe the problem as an opportunity. This is important because if an organization persists in seeing the problem as a threat, a response called "threat rigidity" sets in. The instinct is to cease being flexible and instead focus all resources on countering the threat by reinforcing and fortifying the old model all the more tenaciously. Some educators who are investing in one-to-one initiatives are following this fruitless pattern. They see how online learning threatens the established system, so they race to bring computers to mainstream students in core subjects. By so doing, they miss the disruption completely and instead end up with computers crammed into traditional classrooms.

A better strategy is to help the team that is handling the threat redefine it as an opportunity with limitless potential. Quakertown's team envisioned an in-house cyber academy that would give all teachers in the district the opportunity to teach online if they wanted, provide over eighty new online courses to students, and produce a significant ancillary revenue stream. By recasting the threat as an opportunity, the implementation team became creative about ways to expand the course catalog, serve students in other districts, and make the Infinity Cyber Academy a real point of pride.

Leaders who want to ensure that their schools are making the most of disruptive innovation to unlock the potential of student-centered learning should give some priority to defining and attacking nonconsumption opportunities. To secure community support and sufficient resources, they need to define these opportunities initially as potent threats. After securing support, the leaders should hand off the project to an independent team. This team should reframe the initiative as a pure opportunity, worthy of a flexible, opportunistic implementation plan.

To Sum Up

- The most common mistake schools make with technology is to fall in love with the technology itself. This leads to cramming—the layering of technology on top of the existing model in a way that adds costs but does not improve results.
- To maximize the impact of blended learning, start by identifying the problem to solve or the goal to achieve. This is the organization's rallying cry. State it in a SMART way—specific, measurable, assignable, realistic, and time-related.
- Look for opportunities to implement blended learning as a sustaining innovation to improve on the traditional system for mainstream students in core subjects. Why ignore an opportunity to improve on what already exists?
- Also brainstorm opportunities to fill gaps in areas of nonconsumption. Solving nonconsumption problems not only gives students learning opportunities that were previously unavailable but also offers schools a convenient way to experiment with how to move beyond the factory model.
- Leaders can secure support and protect resources for disruptive innovation by first framing nonconsumption problems as threats and then helping the implementation team reframe them as bright opportunities.

NOTES

1. Susan Fleck, John Glaser, and Shawn Sprague, "The Compensation-Productivity Gap: A Visual Essay," *Monthly Labor Review* 69(1) (2011): 57–69, http://www.bls.gov/opub/mlr/2011/01/art3full.pdf.

2. According to GSV Advisors, offerings should achieve one or all of the following to provide a return on education (ROE): (1) drive down costs for learners and/or institutions; (2) increase student and/or instructor access to education; (3) improve learning outcomes; and (4) increase "capacity" of instruction and instructors. Deborah H. Quazzo, Michael Cohn, Jason Horne, and Michael Moe, "Fall of the Wall: Capital Flows to Education

Innovation," July 2012, p. 25, http://gsvadvisors.com/wordpress/wp-content/themes/gsvadvisors/GSV%20Advisors_Fall%20of%20the%20Wall_2012–06–28.pdf. Analyzing ROE is critical to the financial health of the education sector, where big dollars are at stake. For example, in 2014, Miami-Dade County Public Schools signed a deal with Promethean for the company to be the exclusive supplier of interactive boards for over ten thousand classrooms. This fourth-largest district in the United States also has plans to deploy one hundred thousand HP and Lenovo Windows 8 devices. Funding for these big buys comes from a $63-million plan approved in June 2013. Morningstar, "Promethean Selected to Provide Interactive Board Technology & Teacher Training to Over 10,000 Miami-Dade Classrooms," http://news.morningstar.com/all/market-wired/MWR11G012603001/promethean-selected-to-provide-interactive-board-technology-teacher-training-to-over-10000-miami-dade-classrooms.aspx (accessed April 11, 2014).

3. Institute of Education Sciences, "Fast Facts: Educational Technology," http://nces.ed.gov/fastfacts/display.asp?id=46 (accessed April 11, 2014).

4. *Disrupting Class* discussed this problem in greater depth in Chapter Three, "Crammed Classroom Computers."

5. Larry Cuban, *Oversold and Underused: Computers in the Classroom* (Cambridge, MA: Harvard University Press, 2001), pp. 133–134.

6. Howard Blume and Stephen Ceasar, "L.A. Unified's iPad Rollout Marred by Chaos," *Los Angeles Times,* October 1, 2013, http://www.latimes.com/local/la-me-1002-lausd-ipads-20131002,0,6398146.story (October 18, 2013).

7. "Charter and Cyber Charter School Reform Update and Comprehensive Reform Legislation," March 2013, http://www.pahouse.com/PR/Charter_and_Cyber_Charter_School_Report.pdf

8. The profile about Quakertown is adapted from the Clayton Christensen Institute, "Quakertown Community School District," Blended Learning Universe, http://www.christenseninstitute.org/quakertown-community-school-district-2/ (accessed April 11, 2014).

9. Data provided by Rebekah Cain, director of development & communication, FirstLine Schools, April 14, 2014.

10. The profile about FirstLine Schools is adapted from the Clayton Christensen Institute, "Arthur Ashe Charter School," Blended Learning Universe, http://www.christenseninstitute.org/arthur-ashe-charter-school/ (accessed April 11, 2014).

11. A 2013 study by the Thomas B. Fordham Institute provides fodder for reflecting on several goals that could be worthy for schools to pursue. The study looked at the attributes that parents value most in schools. It found that although most parents seek schools with a solid core curriculum and an emphasis on science, technology, engineering, and math (STEM), beyond that parents have different values. Schools could set a goal to use online learning to offer opportunities that respond to the diversity of parental values reflected in their community. For example, some parents are pragmatists who assign value to schools that offer vocational classes and job-related programs. Others, whom the study labels as "Jeffersonians," prefer a school that emphasizes instruction in citizenship, democracy, and leadership. So-called "Multiculturalists" care about students learning to work with people of diverse backgrounds, whereas "Expressionists" want a school that emphasizes arts and music instruction and "Strivers" assign importance to their child's being accepted in a top-tier college. Dara Zeehandelaar and Amber M. Northern, "What Parents Want: Education Preferences and Trade-offs," Thomas B. Fordham Institute, August 26, 2013, http://www.edexcellence .net/sites/default/files/publication/pdfs/20130827_What_Parents_Want_ Education_Preferences_and_Trade_Offs_FINAL.pdf

12. George Doran, "There's a S.M.A.R.T. Way to Write Management's Goals and Objectives," *Management Review*, 1981, 70(11), pp. 35–36.

13. To some extent this idea echoes the ideas put forth in a new book: Ted Kolderie, *The Split Screen Strategy: Improvement + Innovation* (Edina, MN: Beaver's Pond Press, 2014).

14. Rogers Family Foundation, "Oakland Unified School District Blended Learning Pilot," http://www.rogersfoundation.org/system/resources/0000/ 0022/BlendedLearning_final.pdf; Sean Kennedy and Don Soifer, "Why Blended Learning Can't Stand Still: A Commitment to Constant Innovation Is Needed to Realize the Potential of Individualized Learning," April 2013,

pp. 7–12, http://www.lexingtoninstitute.org/wp-content/uploads/2013/11/WhyBlendedLearningCantStandStill.pdf

15. DadeSchools.net, http://www.dadeschools.net/ (accessed July 22, 2014).

16. "Models for Virtual Learning Labs across Florida," Florida Virtual School, http://www.flvs.net/educators/VLL/VLL%20Models.pdf

17. Leaders who want their schools to lead the pack as the most repeatedly successful innovators in education need to set up a "disruptive growth engine"—a process for consistently looking for opportunities to fill areas of nonconsumption and pioneer new models for student-centered schooling. The four-step process for building this engine is to: (1) start before you need to, (2) place a senior administrator with significant authority in charge, (3) staff the team with experts who can move and shape the plan, and (4) train the entire organization to be on the lookout for disruptive opportunities. Leaders should plan to repeat this process again and again on a set rhythm to establish a culture of growth and innovation. This idea is from the book *Innovator's Solution* by Clayton M. Christensen and Michael E. Raynor (Boston: Harvard Business School Publishing Corporation, 2003), pp. 267–284.

18. See Clark Gilbert and Joseph L. Bower, "Disruptive Change: When Trying Harder Is Part of the Problem," *Harvard Business Review*, May 2002, 94–101; Clark Gilbert, "Can Competing Frames Co-exist? The Paradox of Threatened Response," working paper 02–056, Harvard Business School, 202.

19. This section is adapted from Clayton M. Christensen and Michael E. Raynor (2003), *The Innovator's Solution: Creating and Sustaining Successful Growth* (Boston, MA: Harvard Business School Press), pp. 112–116.

20. Daniel Kahneman and Amos Tversky, "Choice, Values, and Frames," *American Psychologist*, 39 (1984), pp. 341–350.

Chapter 4

Organize to Innovate

The previous chapter helps leaders take the first step toward blended learning by defining a set of sustaining and disruptive problems and goals that serve as the organization's rallying cries. This chapter covers the next step: organizing the right team to turn a rallying cry into a concrete, high-impact initiative.

The importance of organizing the right team came into focus for us during a phone conversation with a team of district technology leaders from a suburban district outside of one of America's large cities. The U.S. Department of Education had awarded the district millions of dollars in 2010 as part of the Investing in Innovation (i3) grant competition. The district pledged to use the funds to personalize learning—a compelling starting point for a rallying cry. To achieve that purpose, it developed a state-of-the-art information system that integrated standards-based learner plans, a content recommendation and management tool, and an engaging user interface that students, teachers, and parents could access. But a few years later and knee deep in implementation, the leaders were uncertain.

One participant in the call told us that despite ample teacher training and district support to help deploy the new system, few teachers were using the tools to bring about the far-reaching transformations in their classrooms that the district leaders had hoped to see. "What more can we do?" she asked.

The district had tripped on the second step of developing a successful blended-learning strategy—the phase that comes after setting the rallying cries. Because many of the changes needed to create a student-centered education system are not all contained within a single classroom—for example, as we saw in Chapter Two, many of the blended-learning models that lead to fully personalized and competency-based learning at scale[1] do away with the classroom entirely—there are limitations to how much any single teacher can do. Giving teachers full autonomy to solve problems within their classrooms can be important to solve certain problems, but that approach also has its limits when teachers cannot change certain school architectures or district processes. What was holding the district back was the lack of a more sound strategy for involving the right team of people to move its innovation forward. By the same token, for teachers and schools just looking to get started on the road toward student-centered learning, there are many concrete and immediate steps an individual teacher can take to enhance her classroom. The trick is diagnosing the desired level of change, which then determines what type of team is necessary and ultimately who needs to be at the table.

A FRAMEWORK FOR TEAM DESIGN

With a set of important problems and the desire to use blended learning to attack them, whom do you bring to the table to create a solution? Should classroom teachers embark on blended learning on their own? How involved should the principal—or even the superintendent—be? What about other members of the community? Are we talking about a simpler operation, or does establishing blended learning require bringing in the equivalent of the Navy SEALs? The following framework helps answer these questions. It begins with the premise that those engaged in innovation confront four categories of problems or tasks. For each type, leaders need to organize a different type of team to address it successfully. Figure 4.1 arranges the four problems along a vertical continuum, from component-level problems at the bottom to architectural and contextual problems at the top.[2]

Figure 4.1 Relationship between Type of Project and Team

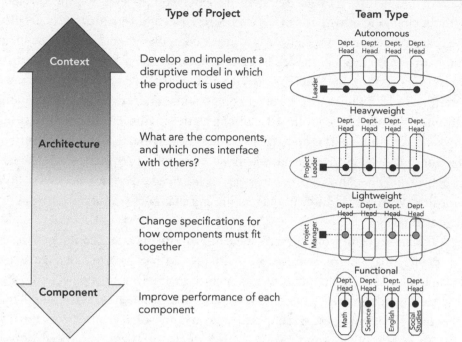

o = people; _ = direct reporting relationship; --- = indirect reporting relationship; oval = team

Functional Teams

The simplest type of problem is called a *functional* problem. These are problems that deal with improving just one part of a product or one step of a process. Because the work is self-contained—meaning it doesn't impact any other part of the organization—the work can be confined within each department.

To visualize a functional problem, imagine how Toyota changed its standard steering wheel for its standard 2014 Lexus GS 350 RWD sedan into a heated steering wheel for its premium Lexus GS 450h, a car that sells for roughly $12,000 more. Both cars are 110 inches long, 72 inches wide, and 57 inches tall. They are the same car, essentially. The only differences are in the upgrades that the GS 450h has at the component level, including the heated steering wheel.

To create that premium steering wheel, the Toyota engineering team responsible for designing steering wheels works only with other members within its silo. For this isolated problem, the team does not need to work with—or know much about — the members from other teams, like those who work on the front seats or headlamps. Toyota can swap in better components for the GS 450h without changing other parts of the car because its engineers previously detailed the required performance standards for each component so that it can be plug-compatible with any GS model. They also have specified how to manufacture each component to meet those performance standards, as well as how each must interface, or fit, with each of the other components. These detailed specifications minimize the need for coordination among all the engineers and manufacturing workers each time a part is updated. Everyone knows what to do to build the right sized and shaped GS component, whether it's standard, premium, or somewhere in between. This allows Toyota to swap in a heated steering wheel with little coordinative overhead and without making any changes to the architecture of the generic model.

A *functional* team works best to make improvements at the component level. We depict this type of team in the bottom right-hand corner of Figure 4.1. Toyota uses functional teams such as finance, marketing, manufacturing, and engineering to handle each of its business problems. Detailed specifications define what each functional group is supposed to do and how each group's work must fit together with another group's work. To the extent that Toyota can specify this in advance and there are no interdependencies, the groups can work independently and efficiently — with little coordinative overhead cost. Although many complain about working in silos when the work is interdependent with that of another group's, when they don't have this interdependence — a frequent occurrence within most organizations — a functional team is the best bet, as it avoids the bureaucratic bloat that ties many efforts down.

Lightweight Teams

The second type of task that innovators confront arises when a group decides to make improvements that affect how another group needs to do its job. When there is *predictable* interdependence between groups, managers should organize a *lightweight team* to handle the project. Toyota had to assemble a lightweight team in October 2013 when the company discovered that driver side airbags in some 2012 and 2013 Camry, Venza, and Avalon vehicles were inadvertently deploying without warning, a serious safety hazard. A functional team was insufficient to handle the immediate task because several Toyota departments needed to work together to coordinate a solution.

Representatives from a few departments came to the table. They played predictable roles, but their decisions were interdependent. The engineers investigated what caused the accidental deployments — surprisingly, spiders were the culprits! Spiders and their webs had clogged the air conditioner draining tubes, which caused water to spill over onto the airbag control module. In-house counsel was part of the temporary team and decided that even though only three airbag deployments and thirty-five warning light activations had been documented, a "better safe than sorry" recall of some 803,000 cars was warranted. This decision, in turn, required the involvement of the public relations department, which developed a communication plan for car purchasers and managed damage control with the media. It relayed the news that Toyota was recalling the vehicles to apply a sealant to keep out spiders and install a cover to eliminate the dripping — a simple solution that the engineering team had devised.[3]

Throughout this process, Toyota needed a coordinative or lightweight manager to oversee the problem and arrange for the various departments to innovate quickly to fix it. Lightweight managers shuttle back and forth among the groups working on a task to ensure that their work fits together correctly. We depict their role in Figure 4.1 as a dotted line connecting the manager with the lightweight team. The functional departments, however, retain primary responsibility for the work, as the solid vertical line in the diagram shows. The mindset of the team members is that the purpose of their membership on the team is to represent the abilities and interests of their departments as they work together across these departments.

Heavyweight Teams

So far we have discussed problems that involve incremental improvements or fixes to product components. But from time to time organizations are looking for a significant or breakthrough improvement — one that rethinks the architecture of the product itself. This can entail combining, eliminating, or adding new components or requiring that components assume different roles in the product's performance — in other words, the components and people responsible for them need to interact with one another in new ways that cannot be anticipated or specified in advance. Resolving these interdependencies often means people must trade off one department's interests in favor of another's to achieve an optimal level of system performance.

To address these challenges, organizations must create *heavyweight teams*.[4] This third type of team enables its members to transcend the boundaries of their functional organizations and interact in different ways. To be effective, members of heavyweight teams often must colocate, and a manager with significant clout must lead the team. Members bring their functional expertise with them as they join the heavyweight team, but their mindset must never be to represent the interests of their departments during the team's deliberations. Rather, they think of themselves as having collective responsibility to figure out a better way to knit things together to meet the overall project's goals.

When Toyota developed its Prius hybrid car, it could not use functional or lightweight teams because the hybrid entailed creating a completely different product architecture. New components had to be developed that interfaced with other new components in novel ways. To solve this problem, Toyota pulled key people from each department and put them together in a completely different location to serve as a heavyweight team. They brought their functional expertise to the team, but their role was not to represent the interests or needs of their respective departments. Together they created an elegant machine.[5] The internal combustion engine coordinates propulsion responsibility with an electric motor. The brakes don't just slow the car; they generate electricity. This in turn completely alters the role the battery plays.

Toyota kept its heavyweight team together for two more generations of the Prius to refine the architecture and ensure that it knew how the pieces of the system worked with one another. But once its engineers sufficiently understood this, they began codifying how to make each component and how each component must interface with all other affected components so that they were able to design next-generation Prius cars in functional teams, where they could minimize the coordinative overhead. Heavyweight teams should be temporary teams that accomplish an architectural redesign; they should not be permanent fixtures in an organization.

Autonomous Teams

The fourth type of team is an *autonomous team*. Autonomous teams are critical when the task at hand involves launching a disruptive model. This happens in the commercial sector when the mechanism for making money with a new innovation is incompatible with a company's existing profit formula. An autonomous team is a tool to create a new economic model that can profitably serve the new market.

Suppose Toyota believes that pure electric vehicles are a disruptive innovation that will one day transform how people drive. It already sells the hybrid Prius, but it wants to pioneer the pure disruption by commercializing a vehicle that runs on electricity alone rather than be disrupted by startup competitors. After a few calculations, however, Toyota's managers conclude that the pure electric cars make no business sense. Battery technology simply is not good enough yet to allow Toyota to build vehicles that its customers will buy. Making batteries good enough to work on mainstream highways would take massive upfront investment, and even then, Toyota would have to charge high prices and hope for green-energy subsidies from the government to squeeze out a profit. When Toyota's executives glance across the Pacific at Tesla, the American company that has made the most prominent foray into pure electric cars, they confirm their forecasts. Tesla's first product, the Roadster, hit the market in 2006 at a base price of $109,000, and despite the buzz, Tesla has continued to lose money despite past governmental aid and ongoing subsidies for consumers who purchase electric cars.[6]

This hypothetical is actually not far from the truth. In 2013 Toyota Chairman Takeshi Uchiyamada made this statement about electric vehicles: "The reason why Toyota doesn't introduce any major [pure electric vehicles] is because we do not believe there is a market to accept it." He predicted that at least two generational steps in battery technology are required before it is ready for prime time.[7]

No number of functional, lightweight, or heavyweight teams will make electric vehicles successful within Toyota's business model. Toyota would need to set up an autonomous team because the existing organization—from its designers and engineers to salespeople and dealership network—is structured to sell vehicles to customers who drive on mainstream highways and roads. Toyota cannot make a profit selling pure electrics in this context. But even as Toyota dismisses the opportunity, new entrants with different economic models are finding success selling pure electrics outside the mainstream market. Star EV, for example, sells electric vehicles for golfers, senior residential neighborhoods, airports, college campuses, warehouses, and security guards. The customers are delighted to ditch diesel and gasoline for a low-speed, rechargeable solution. Star EV is delighted to sell several thousand electric carts a year for $5,000 and up to a niche market. And

Toyota is delighted to keep focusing on selling more than nine million vehicles a year at $14,000 and up to its traditional market.

The reason an organization cannot successfully disrupt itself is that successful organizations can *only* naturally prioritize innovations that promise improved profit margins relative to their current economic model. The best way for an organization to go after a disruptive opportunity, therefore, is to create an autonomous organizational unit that has a different model, one that can find the new opportunity attractive.[8]

What does *autonomous* mean in this context? Geographical separation from the core business is not the critical dimension of autonomy. The key dimensions of autonomy relate to processes and priorities. The disruptive project needs to have the freedom to create new processes and to develop new priorities.[9] The people on the team must benefit from consistently prioritizing the disruptive opportunity over any temptation to compete against the industry leaders.

APPLYING THE TEAM FRAMEWORK TO SCHOOLS

The key to organizing the right group to lead a blended-learning project is first to match the problem to the type of team that can bring about the level of change you desire. At this point, you do not need to know exactly what model of blended learning you want to deploy or what the design of the program will be. But you do need to have a sense of the scope of the change that you want to realize. Classroom-level projects that do not require substantial or unpredictable changes to existing processes are the best fits for functional or lightweight teams. Architectural changes that require new types of interactions and coordination among different groups need a heavyweight team. Disruptive projects that do away with classrooms altogether and replace them with a new learning model are best suited to autonomous teams that can approach the solution from a new context and operate within a different set of priorities. Figure 4.2 shows how the team framework applies in the context of schools.

Functional Blended-Learning Teams

Sometimes an individual classroom teacher or an entire department of teachers wants to tackle a contained problem by moving their instructional practices forward and implementing blended learning within the walls of their own classrooms. In this circumstance, a functional team can work well because the way an individual class fits together with the rest of a school is well understood.

Figure 4.2 Relationship between Type of Project and Team at Schools

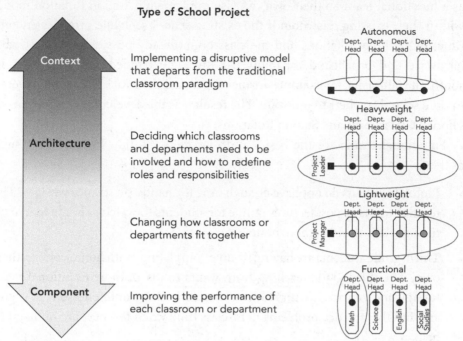

Type of School Project

Context — Implementing a disruptive model that departs from the traditional classroom paradigm

Architecture — Deciding which classrooms and departments need to be involved and how to redefine roles and responsibilities

Changing how classrooms or departments fit together

Component — Improving the performance of each classroom or department

Autonomous
Heavyweight
Lightweight
Functional

o = people; _ = direct reporting relationship; --- = indirect reporting relationship; oval = team

Functional teams are best suited to deliver sustaining innovations for problems whose solutions do not require coordination with other teaching groups or departments.

There are a variety of functional teams within a school—from an individual classroom teacher to the teachers in a middle or high school department or the teachers in a grade level in an elementary school. These functional teams make changes all the time without impacting the rest of the school. For example, if the science department introduces a new chemistry lab experiment, it does not need to coordinate the activity across departments. It simply makes the changes within the courses it controls.

Similarly, if an individual teacher wants to flip her classroom, she can. She simply changes how she runs her classroom. It has no impact on other classrooms, so her functional team of one can work, assuming she does not need assistance from other staff members to provide hardware for the students or help her record videos. Thousands upon thousands of teachers are making that decision on their own around the world today. In certain cases, individual teachers acting as a functional team on their own can also implement a Station Rotation model within their existing classroom if the existing school schedule provides enough time for multiple rotations and the classroom already possesses the necessary hardware and broadband capability. At Riverside Unified School District in southern California, for example, former superintendent Rick Miller empowered middle school teachers to innovate. The result was the development of dozens of Flipped Classrooms and Station Rotations.

Functional teams are the best way to create a solution for problems such as these:

- Biology students do not have enough time for hands-on science wet labs. The teacher wants to post lectures online for students to watch at home to free up time for labs during school hours.

- Third-grade students are having trouble completing math homework on their own. The third-grade teaching team wants to discontinue traditional math homework, replace it with students watching short online lessons at night, and flip the practice problems to in-class time when teachers are on hand to help.

- The district's IT department has installed Wi-Fi capability throughout the school, but the connection is unreliable. Teachers are complaining. The technicians need to figure out the best areas to place the routers.

- Middle school students are already rotating three times a week into a computer lab with their ELA teachers to practice spelling and reading comprehension skills, but the ELA teachers are struggling to use the data from the labs to match students to the right groups and assignments back in their classrooms.

Note that in the last example, students are already rotating between a computer lab and their classrooms, but the teachers want to improve the process. Instituting a Lab Rotation from scratch requires a lightweight or heavyweight team, depending on the level of changes in the school. But in this case, the basic rotation is already in place. The teachers merely need to tweak it, so a functional team can handle the project.

Usually functional teams find that a combination of team meetings, research into what others with the same problem did, and professional development are sufficient to find and implement a solution to their problem. In contrast, no amount of research and professional development are sufficient to address problems that require lightweight, heavyweight, or autonomous teams.

Lightweight Blended-Learning Teams

Other problems lend themselves well to a lightweight team. A typical school has a few lightweight teams. In a high school, the department heads often form lightweight teams to coordinate activities across the various subject areas. Similarly, if fourth-grade teachers decide to teach long division in a new way, a lightweight coordinative team could identify and agree on what subsequent changes this would require in the fifth-grade math curriculum. Lightweight teams can also help at the district level, such as to coordinate how changes in employee health plans impact the benefits, accounting, and human resources departments.

Lightweight teams suit situations in which more than one group must work together to solve a problem, but the interdependencies between the groups are predictable. Like functional teams, lightweight teams work best to bring about sustaining innovations. Milpitas School District in Northern California has been an early leader in employing blended-learning solutions. Its superintendent, Cary Matsuoka, has used a variety of tactics to get there. One of its schools, Burnett Elementary, has employed a bottom-up approach, as it allows its teachers who want to innovate—a coalition of the willing—to take the lead in developing their own blended-learning models and work in tandem with district personnel on acquiring the necessary hardware and furniture to support it. Alison Elizondo, a fourth-grade teacher, now employs a Station Rotation model that she developed with support from the district to help students learn to teach themselves, set goals, work with others, and use feedback to track their own progress.

 WATCH CLIP 16: Teachers at Burnett Elementary school work in lightweight teams with district personnel to provision their blended classrooms

www.wiley.com/go/blended16

Lightweight teams are the best solution for problems such as these:

- Teachers want their students to be able to use the learning lab three times a week, so the school needs to schedule time in coordination with all other teachers to be sure the room is available.

- Middle-school teachers want to use online learning for a portion of each instructional period but need support from district technology staff to set up the computers and internet access in classrooms.

- First-grade teachers want fifth-grade students to serve as reading buddies while other students are doing online reading practice or meeting in small groups with the teacher. The basic rotation is already in place, but the reading buddy program is a new element.

In each of these circumstances, a lightweight manager can shuttle back and forth among the departments to ensure that everyone's work fits together. Team members should represent the interests of their departments or classrooms throughout the process.

Heavyweight Blended-Learning Teams

Some problems go beyond how classrooms or departments work together. They require changing the architecture of the school or district itself. Giving teachers full autonomy to develop models and choose software content within their classrooms can be important to solve certain problems, but that approach has its limits, given that teachers cannot unilaterally change certain school architectures—such as the use of time and bell schedules—or district processes. In these cases, the best group to lead the change is a heavyweight team. Members of heavyweight teams should colocate, and a manager with significant clout should lead. The most important rule for team members is to leave behind departmental interests and instead work collectively to meet the project's goal.

A school can form a heavyweight team by choosing experts from different parts of the school community—mostly teachers and administrators, but also counselors, other staff members, and parents. Districts can also create heavyweight teams; these take several forms at that level, but charter and pilot schools are among the most common. These schools give educators the freedom to step outside the departmental structure of the traditional district school to create new architectures for learning. Although heavyweight teams are well suited for designing new processes and breakthrough changes for schools, autonomous teams are better at leading a disruption that no longer uses traditional classrooms. Heavyweight teams are ideally suited for designing an innovative configuration of classrooms, departments, and other components within the school and district.

Implicit in all of these team descriptions is the fact that ultimately success comes from not only forming the right type of team but also having the right members on that team. With changes at the functional or lightweight team level, classroom teachers who are ready and eager to innovate and solve problems can take the lead in many cases, especially if their principal or superintendent empowers them. At the level of the heavyweight team, the need for a person with significant decision-making authority often means that people in formal leadership roles need to be more involved. For example, if a school needs students to have more time to learn than the traditional schedule allows or to learn in a differently configured space with other teachers from other departments, most individual teachers don't have the decision-making authority to make those changes. Picking the right mix of team members who are already excited to innovate—but also involving skeptics to hear their views or keep them involved so they don't derail a project in a heavyweight team—can be an important, but tricky, balancing act.

Milpitas has employed heavyweight teams in addition to lightweight teams to drive changes in some of its schools. A few years ago, for example, Cary Matsuoka asked his teachers and principals one question: If you could design the ideal school, what would it look like?[10] With a set of design parameters and ideas in place from the district leadership, different teams of teachers and administrators embarked on a three-month design process and then pitched their new models to Matsuoka, his cabinet, and the teachers' union. The critical challenge was to personalize learning for different student needs, given that over half of the districts' students are immigrants. Proposals at two schools, Randall Elementary and Weller Elementary, to transform the schools into blended-learning environments that leveraged the Lab Rotation model were chosen, and the schools embarked on significant redesign.

Heavyweight teams specifically work well to address problems such as these:

- The principal wants to rethink the bell schedule, teacher roles, and curriculum to implement a blended-learning solution to improve reading and math scores across the school.

- The district superintendent wants to close the achievement gap by switching from a seat-time system to a competency-based system across all her schools.

- The principal at a high school wants all his students to get more small-group instruction by rotating students between online and face-to-face groups for core instruction, which will require fundamental changes in the school schedule.

At the beginning of this chapter we discussed a suburban district that wanted to deepen the impact of its technology deployment. We observed that the district relied on functional teams to implement the blended-learning program when it should have organized a heavyweight team. The functional teams—namely, individual teams of teachers across the schools—dutifully attended professional development sessions and tried to weave the new systems and tools into their existing programs. Although change certainly occurred within the classrooms, there were limits to how broad the change could be. A heavyweight team could have stepped away from daily operations; designed sweeping changes to scheduling, teacher roles, and curriculum based on a collective effort to architect the best solution; and then implemented the technology in a much more comprehensive and strategic way.

Autonomous Blended-Learning Teams

In contrast to functional, lightweight, and heavyweight projects, some initiatives are intended to replace the traditional classroom with an entirely new education model. Whereas functional, lightweight, and heavyweight teams are generally well suited to address rallying cries that are core opportunities, nonconsumption opportunities require a different team structure. Leaders can best bring about disruptive change by creating an autonomous team, which has the freedom to rebuild the budget, staffing plan, facilities design, and curriculum from the ground up. Such autonomy is crucial because successful disruption is a two-part game—the new technology is the first part, but a new context is equally important, if not more so. Without a new context, the technology ends up layered on top of the existing model, and when the dust settles, little is different. This explains why the factory-style classroom persists in roughly its same form, and with roughly its same results, despite America's massive investment in education technology over the years.

One way to understand this two-part game is to think about how the legislative process works.[11] A congresswoman might see a pressing social need and draft the perfect piece of legislation. But then the budget committee chair introduces amendments to keep it within budget; the Chamber of Commerce demands changes in order to give its support, so that the bill does not interfere with the interests of businesses across the country; a powerful senator from Connecticut insists on a few more changes to sweeten the bill for his constituents; and in the end, the final bill that the president signs into law looks nothing like the congresswoman's initial idea. This happens not because of any maliciousness on the part of any of these actors per se, but because each is representing and protecting legitimate interests as well. As a result, for any one of them to sign off on the bill, each needs to be sure that the bill does not do any great harm to those interests.

Similarly, a new technology may have the potential to transform a factory-based classroom into a fully student-centered model. But the teacher who chooses the technology does not have resources to buy new furniture, so she has to keep her existing classroom setup. No one else is interested in adjusting the bell schedule, so the teacher cannot deploy the technology on a flexible schedule according to individual student needs. The principal plans to evaluate teachers based in part on their ability to deliver whole-class instruction, so the teacher has to be sure to preserve that aspect of the traditional classroom. She adjusts the model once again. In the end, the final implementation looks very similar to the original classroom model, with the technology added on top. No matter how much of a breakthrough a particular technology is, when it arrives in the context of the existing system, the existing system starts to shape the technology to conform to its dimensions.

In contrast, if the teacher works with the principal and joins with other teachers to form a "school within a school," separate from the traditional context, her idea stands a much better chance. The principal or senior leader should work with the team to identify clear goals and outcomes and then give the team complete autonomy — to the extent possible by law — over budgets, staffing choices, facility design, and curriculum. The virtue of autonomous teams is that they provide a natural mechanism to break free from the tenacious grasp of these established priorities and start anew in a fresh context.

It takes a senior administrator with significant authority over these elements of a school model to have the power to shepherd a disruptive project through the system and protect it from stakeholders who would morph it back into the traditional shape. Some principals are lucky enough to have that level of jurisdiction, such that they can set up and protect the autonomy of a school-within-a-school. But this is rare. In most cases, the district and school board must be involved to authorize and set aside resources for the disruptive project, as well as to free the team from traditional input-based regulations.[12] In some cases states must grant waivers as well. States can also foster school transformation by setting up their own autonomous teams, and those that want to lead the way with innovation should make ready use of the power of this organizational structure. Leaders can use autonomous teams to solve problems such as these hypothetical scenarios:

- Several high schools in rural Oklahoma are having problems offering enough advanced courses to allow students to satisfy the prerequisites of top colleges. The principals want to band together to create a cyber academy that makes online courses available to supplement face-to-face courses.

- Parents at a well-ranked high school want their students to be able to accelerate through some subjects to make time for them to develop deeper expertise in others. This is not the school's current priority, so the parents wonder if they can set up an adjunct learning studio next to the high school, where students could drop in throughout the day for special blended programs.

- A district has a problem with high school dropouts, particularly as a result of teenage pregnancies. The superintendent wants to set up a new learning center to recover these students and help them graduate.

Each of these examples involves making changes that go a level deeper than components, or even architecture. They require changing the very priorities of the teachers, administrators, and other personnel in the school system. Every day each of these people faces dozens of decisions about how to allocate resources and effort. School principals must decide how much time to devote to student discipline, whether to adjust the budget, and when to walk the hallways. Teachers must decide which standards to emphasize, when to devote special attention to a specific student, and how much to worry about end-of-year tests. Each participant in the system sets priorities again and again to solve certain problems until these priorities become engrained as culture.

Reluctance to use autonomous teams is largely to blame for how hard it is to find schools that have converted traditional classrooms into flexible, student-centered learning studios in which the students genuinely control the pace of their learning. "Spotting kids learning at their own pace is like catching a glimpse of Bigfoot," quipped Alex Hernandez, a partner at the Charter School Growth Fund, a nonprofit that funds high-performing charter school operators to expand their impact. "We all know about Bigfoot, but beyond a few grainy photos, few can claim they have actually seen it in the wild." The culture of the traditional classroom is so deeply accustomed to students moving in standardized batches at a set pace that setting a new priority for flexibility and self-pacing is extraordinarily difficult within that context. But an autonomous team, with the freedom to adjust staffing, budgets, facilities, and curriculum, has the necessary headroom to set new priorities and reinvent the culture—made up of all of the existing processes and priorities—from the ground up.

USING MULTIPLE TYPES OF TEAMS

Whenever a school, district, or charter management organization is solving for a variety of problems and trying to undertake a system-wide transformation, it will likely need to use several different teams for different purposes at different times. The New York City Department of Education, for example, uses multiple teams to move toward personalized learning for its students through its iZone initiative, which works with schools, the education technology marketplace, policymakers, and the Department of Education itself to spur innovation. The iZone team has found that in order to drive the kind of innovation it needs in its schools, it must work at three levels. First, it uses heavyweight teams that include practitioners—teachers, principals, and central office staff—to design and test new learning models and help the practitioners approach the work with new assumptions. Second, it works with policymakers and central office staff to gain regulatory relief and move away from old, self-imposed processes that inhibit innovation. When teams at the district or state level are changing processes—how existing functional teams interact with each other and how they do their jobs—these teams should be lightweight. When the task is to rethink what regulatory departments and staffing should exist in the ideal as well as how these parts interact, however, then a heavyweight team is necessary at first.

Finally, the iZone has determined that it must have teams that work closely with education vendors and schools to aggregate demand so that vendors help solve the right problems and the district is a receptive place in which to work. Because the project manager in this case plays a coordinating role, the necessary team is a lightweight one that involves people from the schools, the department, and the vendors themselves.[13]

THE COST OF GETTING IT WRONG

Great opportunities can be missed and thousands, or even millions, of dollars wasted when leaders do not organize strategically before attempting to blend. One of the most common mistakes is asking classroom teachers to use technology to personalize learning and then expecting them to create a truly transformative learning model on their own. Functional teams do not have the power to abandon the traditional classroom entirely or to implement a disruptive model independently, even with the best professional development and technology budgets.

The other side of the coin is that some schools create heavyweight or autonomous teams to handle problems that functional or lightweight teams could handle more efficiently and less bureaucratically. Many teachers have found that they can flip their classrooms or create stations within their classrooms on their own, with only a slight nod of approval from the administration and a resourceful spirit about cobbling together the technology. In fact, we have heard several accounts of teachers who learn about blended learning at a conference or training and then go home and rearrange their classrooms that very weekend to start experimenting with a Flipped Classroom or Station Rotation. Of course, we recommend a more thorough planning process before making any switch, and we note that in many cases Station Rotations can cause a significant enough architectural shift that they require heavyweight teams. But the point remains that classroom teachers can and should act entrepreneurially and decisively on their own when they want to bring about classroom-level improvements. Quality professional development and transition funds would help their cause, but a heavyweight team would only slow them down.

The other principle to reinforce is that heavyweight and autonomous teams must behave in a certain way to be effective. For heavyweight teams, the requirements are to colocate, appoint a person with significant clout and the power to make decisions as the team leader, and pledge to represent their collective interests and set aside the narrower interests of their classrooms and departments. For autonomous teams, success is predicated on securing authority over staffing, budgets, facilities, and curriculum for the students in their charge. Furthermore, a senior leader at the very top needs to protect and defend the fledgling disruptive project from those who want resources to go toward only sustaining innovations. Plenty of people in the existing system will fight for fancier traditional classrooms and more resources for the factory model, rather than diverting funding and time to nonconsumption problems. The best senior leaders look into the future, see the benefits that disruptive innovations can bring to their system, and take a firm stance in protecting the autonomous project. As we discuss at the end of Chapter Three, senior leaders should communicate that failure to act disruptively poses a substantial threat to the organization's success. Then, after forming an autonomous team to lead the project, the senior leader should drop the focus on the threat and instead communicate that the project presents a vast upside opportunity for students, teachers, and the community as a whole. By choreographing this dance wisely, senior leaders play an indispensable role in allowing the organization, and students in particular, to benefit from disruptive opportunities.

To Sum Up

- After defining their rallying cries, leaders should organize the right teams to lead the project. Functional, lightweight, and heavy-weight teams are best suited to address rallying cries that are core opportunities, whereas nonconsumption opportunities require an autonomous team.
- Functional teams are best suited to improving one component of a product or one step of a process. Toyota uses functional teams to swap in different headlamps, steering wheels, and trim for different versions of the same basic car model. Schools should use functional teams, made up of teachers or staff within the same department, to make changes that are not interdependent with other parts of the school.

(continued)

(continued)

- Lightweight teams work well when a group decides to make improvements that affect how another group needs to do its job and when the relationship between the groups is predictable. Toyota used a lightweight team to coordinate a response to the issue of spiders and spider webs clogging the air conditioning draining tubes in certain car models. Schools should use lightweight teams to coordinate projects that implicate more than one set of teachers, but in predictable ways.

- Heavyweight teams are the best fit for those tasks requiring that both components and the people responsible for them interact with one another in new ways that cannot be anticipated or specified in advance—in other words, the problem requires a new system architecture. Toyota used a heavyweight team to design the Prius, a hybrid that necessitated a completely different architecture from its gasoline-powered predecessors. Schools should use heavyweight teams to implement sustaining innovations that require a fundamental redesign of how classrooms and departments interact.

- Autonomous teams are essential for disruptive innovations. They allow innovators to step outside of the existing context—including staffing, budget, facilities, and curriculum—to pioneer a new model based on a benefit such as personalization, access, or cost control. If Toyota someday decides to take part in the disruption of gasoline-powered vehicles by electric vehicles, it will need to establish an autonomous team that is attracted to the initially modest profit opportunity of selling electric carts. Schools should use autonomous teams when they want to do away with the factory-based classroom completely and replace it with a disruptive blended-learning model.

- Leaders do not need to know what model of blended learning they want to deploy or what the design of the program will be at this point. But they do need to have a sense of the scope of the change that they want to realize. Before moving forward with the next steps toward blended learning, take the time to set up the right type of team.

NOTES

1. Julia Freeland, "Blending toward Competency: Early Patterns of Blended Learning and Competency-Based Education in New Hampshire," Clayton

Christensen Institute, May 2014 (http://www.christenseninstitute.org/wp-content/uploads/2014/05/Blending-toward-competency.pdf). This white paper examines blended learning in thirteen New Hampshire schools moving toward competency-based education. It concludes that, "Based on this small, early-stage sampling, blended-learning models that tend to be disruptive relative to the traditional classroom appear especially well suited to support competency-based education at scale.... On the other hand, the schools that were still tethered to time-based practices used sustaining blended-learning models, namely the Flipped Classroom and Station Rotation."

2. This section is adapted from Chapter Nine of *Disrupting Class*. The model of team structure around which that chapter is structured was developed by Kim Clark and Steven Wheelwright of the Harvard Business School. See Steven C. Wheelwright and Kim B. Clark, *Revolutionizing Product Development* (New York: The Free Press, 1992).

3. Nathan Ingraham, "Spiders Force Toyota to Recall 800,000 Vehicles," *The Verge,* http://www.theverge.com/2013/10/18/4852840/spiders-force-toyota-to-recall-800000-vehicles (accessed October 21, 2013).

4. Much of this section on heavyweight teams specifically is adapted from Chapter Nine of *Disrupting Class*.

5. In contrast, most of Toyota's competitors designed their hybrid cars in lightweight teams. Their cars simply did not perform as well as the Prius—a fact that has been reflected in Toyota's dominant share of the hybrid car market.

6. In 2009 Tesla received a $465 million loan guarantee from President Obama's administration, supplemented in 2012 by a $10 million grant from the California Energy Commission. "The Other Government Motors," *Wall Street Journal*, updated May 23, 2013, http://online.wsj.com/news/articles/SB10001424127887324659404578499460139237952 (accessed November 8, 2013). Tesla repaid the loan early, but it has still posted a net loss each year, a circumstance that Toyota seeks to avoid.

7. Eric Loveday, "Toyota Sees No Market for Pure Electric Vehicles," *Inside EVs,* October 2, 2013, http://insideevs.com/toyota-sees-no-market-for-pure-electric-vehicles/ (accessed November 8, 2013).

8. *Innovator's Solution,* pp. 198–199.

9. Ibid.

10. Christina Quattrocchi, "What Makes Milpitas a Model for Innovation," EdSurge, January 7, 2014, https://www.edsurge.com/n/2014-01-07-what-makes-milpitas-a-model-for-innovation.

11. This story is adapted from Chapter Three of *Disrupting Class.*

12. Principals' control over school leadership responsibilities varies across the nation. According to "The MetLife Survey of the American Teacher," "Principals are least likely to report that they have a great deal of control in making decisions about finances (22%). Fewer than half of principals report having a great deal of control in making decisions about removing teachers (43%) or about curriculum and instruction (42%). In contrast, most principals say they have a great deal of control in making decisions about teachers' schedules (79%) and hiring teachers (74%)." "The MetLife Survey of the American Teacher: Challenges for School Leadership," MetLife, Inc., February 2013, p. 28.

13. See iZone, "About the Office of Innovation," http://izonenyc.org/about-izone/ (accessed May 30, 2014), as well as Innovate NYC Schools, "About Innovate," http://www.innovatenycschools.org/about-innovate/ (accessed May 30, 2014). The insight for the importance of New York City's multi-tiered approach stemmed from a conversation with Steven Hodas of Innovate NYC Schools during a meeting at the U.S. Department of Education on May 28, 2014.

Part 3

Designing

Understanding | Mobilizing | Designing | Implementing

Chapter 5

Motivate the Students

With a rallying cry in mind and the right team assembled, you are ready to start designing your blended-learning solution. Ultimately that solution will have many dimensions, including a strategy for staffing, devices, content, facilities, model, and culture. But the starting point for design, before any of these considerations, is to crawl inside the head of students and look at school through their eyes. The key premise of this chapter, and one of the most important findings for designing a blended model, is that when schools get the design right from the students' perspective, so they feel that school aligns well with the things that matter to them, students show up to school motivated and eager to learn. It's not unusual to hear from parents at student-centered schools that their children complain on Saturdays because they can't wait until Monday for more school.

On the other hand, when teams design school without regard to the students' perspective, they face resistance at every turn from the very people they are trying to serve. Some students will be compliant enough to go along with it or fortunate enough to have a personality that happens to work in the given design, but too many will eventually sour on the classroom experience, and school becomes a battle. In the unfortunate words of one middle school student, "School made me hate school."

The first task for blended-learning teams therefore is to understand the student perspective and to design with student motivation as a guiding star.

THE IMPORTANCE OF STUDENT WILLINGNESS TO LEARN

At a back-to-school event we attended, twenty children gathered in a circle around their new teacher, Mr. Allen, on a colorful ABC rug. After welcoming the students back to school, Mr. Allen held up a pitcher full to the brim with water and explained that the water represented all of the amazing knowledge in that classroom for the children to soak up during the year ahead. Everything the children might ever want to explore was stuffed inside that water.

Then he held up a clear bowl. "This is your brain," he explained. "See how it's empty and cup shaped? It's perfect for holding that knowledge. But some students come to school like this." He turned the bowl upside down and poured water from the pitcher onto the underside of the bowl, so the water ran down the sides and splattered to the ground. The children squealed, amazed that the teacher had poured so much water right onto the rug. "Some students choose not to try to learn, and it's sad for them, because look at that waste of knowledge."

Next Mr. Allen pulled the bowl away from the pitcher and dumped several cups of water directly onto the rug. "Other students decide not to come to school at all," he said. "They don't get enough sleep, their families don't really care about school, and they're often late to class. How sad for them. Look at all that waste of knowledge."

Finally, the teacher turned the bowl right side up and said, "I can see that this room is full of students with brains like this." He poured the remaining water into the bowl until it was completely full. "I can see that you are going to fill your brains with all of the adventures that await you in this classroom. Be like this bowl, ready to learn."

Like Mr. Allen, most teachers share an eagerness for their pupils to seize the day and the ample learning opportunities presented to them. America spent $673 billion on PreK–12 public education in fiscal year 2014.[1] U.S. teachers each devote over one thousand hours per year to teaching, which represents more hours per year than in almost any other country in the world.[2] Libraries are stacked with books; backpacks are so full that students roll them with luggage handles; and now, with the Internet, the amount of knowledge available seems limitless. If only students could be like those right-side-up bowls, willing to capture the outpouring.

Sadly, however, most teachers say that their biggest struggle with students is that they lack the motivation to learn. In a 2013 survey of five thousand teachers, student motivation ranked as the top challenge for teachers, followed by student attitude toward learning, student distractions during class, and student behavior during class time.[3] If America is working so hard to dish up learning, why are so many students not fully partaking in what's being served?

THE JOBS-TO-BE-DONE THEORY

Schools are not alone in struggling to design an offering that their end users will willingly show up to devour. More than 75 percent of new products introduced each year fail, and that's true even if they are backed by big companies, popular brand names, and aggressive advertising. One classic example, which MSN Money named on its top-ten list of biggest product flops of all time,[4] is the McDonald's Arch Deluxe, a premium sandwich topped with an unnaturally round piece of peppered bacon, which McDonald's introduced in 1996 for adults with a more refined palate—the latte drinkers of the world. McDonald's spent $100 million in advertising, but the product failed miserably.

Companies struggle so desperately to predict whether a customer in a given demographic category will buy a new product because from the customer's perspective the market is not structured by customer or product category.[5] Customers just find themselves needing to get things done. They have "jobs" that arise regularly that demand resolution, so they look around for a product or service that they can "hire" to help them out. This is how customers experience life. The Arch Deluxe simply didn't provide a compelling fix for a job that enough people were trying to do.

On the other hand, some companies launch successful products and services again and again. They have a knack for understanding the circumstances in which customers find themselves and for looking at the world through the eyes of those customers. This lets them see the job that customers are confronting and the results they need to achieve for which their products might be hired as a solution. The job, and not the customer demographic or even a customer-needs analysis, is the best framing of the question. Most home-run new-product introductions are the result of marketers understanding—either implicitly or explicitly—the job to be done and then finding a way to help people do that job more effectively, effortlessly, swiftly, and affordably. Another name for this type of product is a *killer app*—a solution that nails the job so beautifully that customers can scarcely remember how they survived before it arrived.

Companies and organizations often fall into the trap of thinking that just because a product or service is beneficial to a customer, the customer will embrace it. This is especially true of organizations with a social mission, such as those with an education, wellness, or environmental-protection objective. So-called social enterprises are notorious for identifying a solution that is irrefutably salutary and worthwhile but is unlikely to work unless it helps users more affordably, conveniently, and effectively do what they already had been trying to get done. The graveyard of failed products is populated by things that people *should* have wanted—if only they could have been convinced those things were good for them.

Hiring Milkshakes

In *Disrupting Class* we illustrate the jobs-to-be-done theory by telling the story of a fast-food restaurant chain's effort to improve its milkshake sales. The example captures the spirit of jobs-based design in a classic way and bears repeating.

Some time ago, a fast-food restaurant chain resolved to improve sales of its milkshakes.[6] Its marketers first defined the market segment by product—milkshakes—and then identified the customer demographic who historically bought the most milkshakes. Next the marketers invited people who fit this profile to evaluate what sorts of changes would improve the shakes—should they be thicker, cheaper, chunkier? The panelists gave clear feedback, but the consequent improvements to the product had no impact on sales.

A new researcher took a different approach. He spent a long day in one of the restaurants to try to see the situation from the customers' point of view. He was surprised to find that nearly half of all milkshakes were purchased in the early morning. These customers almost always were alone, they did not buy anything else, and they promptly got in their cars and drove off with their milkshakes.

The researcher returned the next morning and confronted these customers as they left the restaurant, milkshake in hand, and essentially asked (in language that they would understand), "Excuse me, but could you please tell me what job you were trying to do when you came here to hire that milkshake?" As they struggled to answer, he helped them by asking, "Think about a recent time when you were in the same situation, needing to get the same job done, but you didn't come here to hire a milkshake. What did you hire?" Most of them, it turned out, bought their milkshakes to do essentially the same job: they faced a long, boring commute and needed something to make the commute more interesting. They weren't yet hungry, but knew that they'd be hungry by 10 A.M.; they wanted to consume something now that would stave off hunger until noon. And they faced constraints: they were in a hurry, they were wearing work clothes, and they had (at most) one free hand.

In response to the researcher's query about what other products they hired to do this job, the customers realized that sometimes they bought bagels to do the job. But these were dry and tasteless. Spreading cream cheese on the bagels while driving caused serious problems. Sometimes these commuters bought a banana. But it didn't last long enough to solve the boring-commute problem, and they were starving by 10 A.M. Doughnuts were too sticky and made the steering wheel gooey. The milkshake, it turned out, did the job better than any of these competitors. It took people twenty minutes to suck the thick milkshake through the thin straw, which gave them something to do with that free hand while they drove. They had no idea what the milkshake's ingredients were, but that didn't matter to them because becoming healthy wasn't the job they were hiring the milkshake to do. All they knew was that at 10 A.M. on days when they had hired a milkshake, they didn't feel hungry—and the shake fit cleanly in their cup holder.

The researcher observed that at other times of the day parents often bought milkshakes, in addition to a complete meal, for their children. What job were the parents trying to do? They were exhausted from repeatedly having to say no to their kids. They hired milkshakes as an innocuous way to placate their children and feel like loving parents. The researchers observed that the milkshakes didn't do this job well, though. They saw parents waiting impatiently after they had finished their own meal while their children struggled to suck the thick milkshake up through the thin straw. Customers in the same demographic were hiring milkshakes for two very different jobs. But when marketers had asked a busy father who needs a time-consuming milkshake in the morning—and something very different later in the day—what attributes of the milkshake they should improve on, and when his response was averaged with those of others in the same demographic segment, this had led to a one-size-fits-none product that didn't do well either of the jobs it was being hired to do.

Once marketers understood the jobs that the customers were trying to do, however, it became clear how to improve the milkshake to do the different jobs even better, and which improvements were irrelevant. How could they better tackle the boring morning commute job? Make the shake even thicker so that it would last longer. Swirl in tiny chunks of fruit so that the drivers would occasionally suck a chunk into their mouth, which would add a dimension of unpredictability and anticipation to their monotonous morning routine. Just as important, they could move the dispensing machine in front of the counter and sell customers a prepaid swipe card so that they could dash in, gas up, and go. Addressing the other job to be done would require a very different product and experience.

Hiring (or Avoiding) the Gym

Designing the right milkshake experience helps fast-food chains entice more people to purchase milkshakes, but this example may feel far afield from the question of how to design education experiences that students embrace. An example from the health care sector, which is similar to the education sector because it likewise grapples with the question of how to help people do things that are good for them, helps bring the jobs-to-be-done theory closer to home.

Just as teachers struggle to help students be willing and eager to learn, many companies struggle to motivate their employees to take care of their physical health—an important goal for companies that want to minimize the cost of employee medical coverage. Several of America's largest companies offer subsidized fitness club memberships to encourage employees to lose weight and remain fit. But they find that only a fraction of their employees participate, and almost all of those people are already in good physical condition. The problem is that *maintaining health* is a job that only a minority of people prioritize in their lives. For the rest, becoming healthy becomes a priority job only after they start to feel the consequences of illness. Companies can try mightily to convince employees to engage in wellness behaviors, but if those messages do not align with jobs the employees are already trying to do, all those membership dues go to waste.[7]

But if the companies could understand their employees' jobs and create an offering that did those as well as theirs, they would get both done. For example, the computer maker Dell discovered that many of its employees prioritize the job of "improve my financial health" above "maintain my physical health." In 2014 it offered its team members a $975 discount off their medical coverage if they showed improvement toward a fitness goal. Many employees gladly became fitter in exchange for the $975. The "Well at Dell" program accomplished Dell's job by catering to the job-to-be-done of its employees.[8]

STUDENTS' JOBS TO BE DONE

Similar to people who deprioritize the job of "maintain my physical health," many students languish in school or do not come to class at all because education isn't a job that they are trying to do. Education is something they might choose to *hire* to do that job—but it isn't the job. Teachers can work extraordinarily hard to improve the features of their products, in the hope that more engaging lessons, media, and student-response clickers will improve student motivation. But their efforts are in vain if they are aimed at providing an even better way for students to do something that they were never trying to do in the first place. Of course, schools can try punishments and rewards to coerce students to learn. Ultimately, however, if this is the best school can offer, many students will hire other solutions to solve the problems that arise in their lives, and school will descend to a lower and lower priority.

This is not to say that a school should not instill in students certain core knowledge, skills, and dispositions; rather, that in order to accomplish these objectives, the school must create an experience that is intrinsically motivating for students. School can be a place where students find joy in learning. The key is to crawl into the learners' skin and see their circumstances—including their anxieties, immediate problems, and innate motivations—from their point of view. The jobs-to-be-done theory is a tool to help you do that.

We have observed that there are two core jobs that are the highest priority for most students. First, they want to feel successful. They want to feel that they are making progress and accomplishing something, rather than experiencing nothing but repeated failure or running up against walls.[9] Second, they want to have fun with friends. That means they want positive, rewarding social experiences with others, including with peers, teachers, coaches, advisors, and other potential friends.

Just as the milkshake competes with bananas, doughnuts, and bagels for the morning commute job, schools compete with gang membership as something that students can hire to experience success and have fun with friends; other choices are dropping out of school to take a job or hang out with friends, playing video games, playing pickup basketball, and any number of other nonacademic options. Too often, schools are sorry competitors for these alternatives. Factory-type classrooms are structurally incapable of allowing teachers enough time to give all students daily, personal feedback on their progress. Students must wait for intermittent feedback on homework and exams, and in many cases teachers simply do not have time to provide much more than a single grade or marking on these efforts. When students do get their grades, most fall short of feeling that motivating affirmation from success; by design, most teachers award the privilege of feeling successful to only the best students and send the rest home with something less than an A.

Factory-style classrooms also struggle to help students have fun with friends. Sixty percent of participants in a Harris Poll said that either they have experienced bullying in school or someone they know has experienced it. Furthermore, among parents with children in the K–12 grades, over a third believe that bullying is a problem at their child's school.[10] Although not all students experience negative relationships to this extreme, the question arises: are traditional classrooms optimized to help students form positive relationships? Teachers are responsible for instructing large batches of diverse students, and they have limited time to connect with each student one-on-one. Whole-group lecture offers little opportunity for students to form relationships with each other or with the teacher during that time. Schools themselves are stretched to provide a full suite of academic, extracurricular, and social services. The elimination of bullying and the assurance of a safe, positive environment can fall through the cracks.

Students who do not hire school to do their job but instead focus their attention on things besides education are not unmotivated. They are plenty motivated—to feel success and have fun with friends. The problem is that a surprising number of students just don't or can't feel successful each day and find rewarding relationships at school. Instead, school makes them feel like failures—academically, socially, or both.

THE ARCHITECTURE OF A JOB

There are three levels in the architecture of a job. Figure 5.1 depicts this architecture. To design education as the solution that students want to hire depends on educators getting each of these levels right.

At the foundational level is the job itself—the fundamental result that the customer needs to achieve. For many morning commuters who end up hiring milkshakes, the job is to mitigate the boredom of the long drive and stave off morning hunger.[11] The second level in the architecture is composed of all the experiences in purchasing and using the product that its vendor must provide, so that they add up to "nailing" the job perfectly. Once innovators understand what these experiences must be, they can implement the third level in the architecture of a job: they can integrate properly by knitting together the right assets—human resources, technologies, ergonomic features, packaging, training, support and service capabilities, distribution and retail systems, and branding and advertising strategies—that are required to provide each of the experiences necessary to do the job perfectly.

Suppose the fast-food restaurant that wanted to improve early-morning milkshake sales applies the theory in Figure 5.1 to design the perfect customer experience, step by step. What design decisions would it make? First, starting at the bottom of the diagram and working up, it would observe the morning

Figure 5.1 Three Levels in the Architecture of a Job

What and how must we integrate to provide these experiences?

What are the experiences that we need to provide to get the job done perfectly?

What's the job to be done?

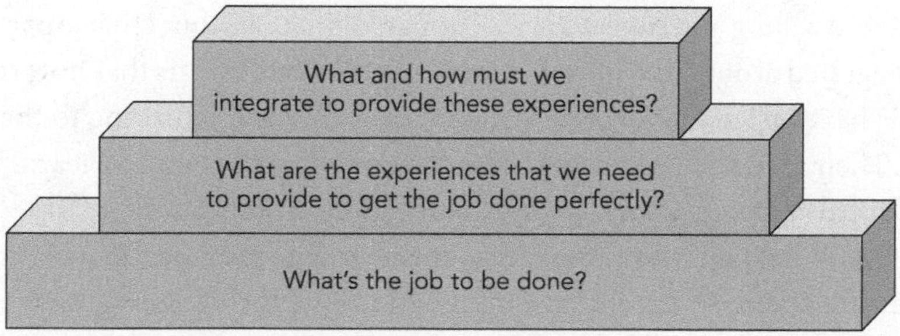

Source: Adapted from Clayton M. Christensen, "Module Note: Integrating Around the Job to Be Done," Harvard Business School, 2010.

commuters and identify the basic job that is motivating their detour off the road for a milkshake. The restaurant chain would then brainstorm all of the experiences that it could provide to fulfill perfectly the morning commute job. What experiences do customers with this job need to have as they are learning about this milkshake brand for the first time? What about when they are making the purchase each day? And then when they get in their cars to consume it, what should that experience be like? Should the milkshake be more viscous or more fluid? Healthy, unhealthy, or doesn't matter? In a paper or plastic cup?

Finally, as the top level of the diagram depicts, the restaurant chain would review its existing operations and ask how they should integrate everything together. If they need to make the product more viscous so that it lasts through the entire morning commute, what new ingredients do they need to procure? Or to make the milkshake chunkier, how should they change the recipe? Should they move the dispensing machine in front of the counter so that customers can serve themselves without ever having to wait in a line? How should the restaurant modify other systems—from advertising and container design to employee training and distribution—to optimize them for delivering the right experiences to customers with this job?

If the chain wanted to improve milkshake sales among other customers with different jobs to be done, then it would need to repeat the same three-step analysis for the new set of circumstances. Ultimately, and perhaps counter-intuitively, understanding the job—more than understanding the customer—is what matters.[12]

FULFILLING THE JOB FOR STUDENTS

The jobs-to-be-done perspective is helpful for designing a blended model that students are willing and eager to hire. The parents at one school that is particularly well-integrated around the jobs that matter to students told us that now that their students have tasted that experience, they can't imagine returning to the factory model. Their students are ready—even hungry—to show up and learn. That's a powerful advantage, even a *killer app*, in the game of education.

Let's walk through the three levels in the architecture of the jobs that most students are trying to do and see the implications for designing better blends.

With respect to the ground level, we state earlier in this chapter that the two jobs that appear to be the highest priority for most students are to feel successful and make progress, and to have fun with friends. Education itself is not the job; rather, it's one option that students can hire to get their jobs done.

The next level up of the job architecture involves imagining all the experiences that education needs to offer students to provide an irresistible solution for getting these jobs done. Summit Public Schools, a charter school network based in Redwood City, California, stands out as among the most groundbreaking innovators with respect to providing experiences that help students make progress every day and have fun with friends. We use it as an illustration of the types of experiences that leaders might want to consider as they imagine all of the ways that schools can help students want to hire education.

Several years ago, a group of parents in Silicon Valley came together to reimagine the middle and high school experience, with the goal of radically improving student readiness for college and for life after school. They hired Diane Tavenner, a former assistant principal at Mountain View High School, to launch Summit Public Schools and serve as its CEO. Diane opened Summit's flagship school in 2003, and has since added five additional schools, which serve roughly 1,600 students in grades 6 through 12.

By 2011 Summit had already achieved national acclaim. *Newsweek* listed it as one of the top ten most transformational high schools in America, and its schools consistently outperformed their peers on California's Academic Performance Index (API).[13] But that fall, the network's leaders decided to make a change. They were concerned about data that showed that although nearly all of Summit's students had gone on to college, some students were struggling when they arrived there.[14] The leaders began thinking about ways to design a set of experiences that better prepared students with the content knowledge, cognitive skills, habits of success, and real-world practice necessary to thrive in college and beyond. At first they experimented with a Station Rotation model for math at two of their schools, but over time they evolved to deliver a much more personalized, Flex model for all subjects across all the Summit schools. Their efforts are already paying off, they report, even as they continue to experiment, learn, and iterate accordingly.

WATCH CLIP 17: Summit Public Schools structures the school day to deliver personalized learning through the Flex model.

www.wiley.com/go/blended17

Summit's SMART goal is to personalize learning so that 100 percent of its students are prepared to succeed in college and life. To get there, it developed experiences that help students want to hire education so that they show up ready to learn. For the purposes of this chapter, we describe eight meta-experiences that Summit identified as critical from the students' perspective.

1. Student agency. Summit believes that for students to feel successful and make progress every day, one essential element is empowering them to set individual learning goals for their own personal learning plans and then providing them with enough time and the right processes each day to make progress toward those individualized goals. Faculty believe students need to experience making personal decisions about the direction of their learning and choosing from multiple options to learn the required concepts. Summit even extends this to incorporating student feedback into improving its school design and asking students to rate the menu of lessons its teachers develop.

2. Individual mastery. Summit's faculty think that students should make progress as quickly or slowly as they are able to demonstrate their preparedness to move on, and that each student's pace should be individual, not collective. As Tavenner says, when you realize how irrational the current system of schooling is—in which students advance based on time regardless of whether they have mastered material, which has significant repercussions for their odds of success on future work—and then you give students a rational, competency-based schooling system—one that just makes sense because it is set up for them to be successful—they want more of it. Inherent in this concept is that students work on skills that are "just above" their own current capabilities: not too difficult and not too easy, with occasional opportunities to stretch or challenge themselves.[15]

3. Access to actionable data and rapid feedback. Following from the emphasis on student agency and individual mastery, Summit decided that giving students rapid feedback and data about their performance would be a critical experience for them to accomplish their job of feeling successful. Without data, students would not know how they were doing and what they needed to do to be successful. But armed with data and rapid feedback that was actionable—meaning students could use it to figure out where they needed to do more work and improve their performance—students would be able to achieve success.[16] Having data also helps students have positive experiences with their friends—from fellow peers to teachers—because they can collaborate productively on how to make progress.

4. Transparency in learning goals. To help students understand what success means, Summit thinks it is also important to provide students with a clear view of what they are trying to achieve, not just in the course of a given unit but over their entire academic career at Summit. This means that students should have not only a clear picture of what competencies they will be expected to master but also a sense of the time frame in which they must master those competencies to stay on track to realize their broader goals for success in life.

5. Sustained periods of quiet, solitary reading time. Although having opportunities for students to engage in productive group work is vital—so students can master teamwork skills, but also to help students have fun with friends—Summit's philosophy is that all too often schools overlook the importance of providing students with quiet time when they can immerse themselves in a book. Students often do not have this type of an experience at home, and without this opportunity they may struggle to build the reading capacity they need to be successful in so many other parts of their schooling. Training students to set apart time for extended focus on a book is an important experience that Summit believes is necessary for students to fulfill their success job.[17]

6. Meaningful work experiences. Summit's theory is that students are more likely to hire school when their experiences there help them connect the acquisition of knowledge with the ability to be successful in life. School is better when it feels relevant. As Tavenner says, students are smart. They will opt out of something that they know is not what schools say it is if it does not appear to help get them where they want to go. In many cases, this means that schools have to help students understand the range of career opportunities and life pathways that are possible so that they can develop a broader notion of what they might want to do when they grow up—beyond what the adults in their immediate lives have done—and to see how learning would be critical to achieving those goals. Incorporated in this experience is not only connecting what students do as part of their schooling to what and why it will make them successful, but also giving students the opportunity to work—and have fun—with friends, teachers, and others in the community.

7. Mentoring experiences. Mentoring is a big deal at Summit. School leaders knew that mentors would be vital to help students make progress toward rigorous but attainable goals and that students would benefit from that social relationship if the mentors were good. Summit views mentorship as a critical part of helping students learn to build social capital—or networks of people—that students can use to achieve success throughout their lives.

8. Positive group experiences. Summit also believes that students must have positive group experiences in which they work with others to tackle hard projects and discuss issues that are of importance to them. Fostering these experiences helps students have fun with their friends and builds their capacity to relate to and get along with others.

Other Circumstances. We have not listed the full set of experiences that Summit decided was important to help students make daily progress and have fun with others, nor has Summit likely thought of everything. One important question to ask when brainstorming the student experiences that are best for your community is whether there are circumstances that beg for remediation before any other learning experiences, however well-designed, can make much impact. For example, certain communities face a persistent problem of students being too tired to learn effectively. Dr. John Ratey, a neuropsychiatric expert at Harvard Medical School, said that one of the biggest problems among American adolescents is sleep deprivation. His research shows that teenagers need more sleep than adults and on average are chronically sleep deprived.[18]

Ratey also found that many communities do not provide children and youth with enough physical exercise. Although in some communities students undoubtedly get plenty, this is not the case for all. Ratey preaches that one of the best ways to help students experience success in school is to ensure that they get adequate exercise. He calls for portable playground equipment (such as balls, tricycles, and scooters), which he says encourage more physical activity than fixed playground structures, and for thirty minutes of vigorous physical activity at the start of each school day in communities where lack of exercise is a problem.[19] Of course, just because a school provides these remediating experiences does not mean that academic progress will result, but the *lack* of these must-haves can create up-front barriers to success.

Furthermore, researchers have found that adverse, stressful experiences during childhood are hugely detrimental to a child's ability to learn. These experiences include physical and sexual abuse, physical and emotional neglect, and various kinds of household dysfunction, such as having family members who were incarcerated, mentally ill, or addicted. Dr. Nadine Burke Harris surveyed more than seven hundred patients at her San Francisco clinic and found that among those who had not experienced any of these severe traumas in their youth, only 3 percent had been identified as having learning or behavioral problems. Among those who had experienced four or more of these stressful incidents as children, the figure was 51 percent.[20]

This research paints a bleak picture of the situation that some students face. Of course, schools cannot solve this societal problem on their own, but at the least, school leaders can be aware of the high correlation between adverse childhood experiences and difficulty in feeling successful and making progress at school. For many students, extra counseling, mentoring, and social services are among the most important experiences that schools must consider as a starting point for helping those students get their jobs done.[21]

Other populations of students have other circumstances to consider—from special physical or mental-health needs to atypical extracurricular or work-related realities. All these merit consideration when designing the right experiences for a given population of learners. Therefore the search for "best practices" is ill-advised. It is better to instead analyze a set of real circumstances and then design student experiences that are the best match for each context.

Researchers can help with this effort by studying which experiences are the most effective in a range of circumstances. For example, some teachers report that in circumstances where behavior problems and attention deficit disorders are rampant, the shift to giving students more choice and control makes a big difference. They say that offering options—like allowing students to use standing desks, opt for a beanbag chair, move around more, eat a snack when hungry, and choose among learning modalities—can be more powerful than Ritalin. Others have told us that the percentage of special needs and English language learners drops dramatically over time when students are learning at the right level—not too easy or hard—and when learning is personalized. We hope researchers will study these sorts of correlations to provide evidence-based recommendations for experiences that work best in specific circumstances.

WHAT TO INTEGRATE, AND HOW

The final step in fulfilling a job, as depicted at the top of Figure 5.1, involves understanding what resources an organization must have and how to integrate those resources and processes to deliver the experiences identified in the previous step of the figure. In the case of Summit's effort to provide students with the eight experiences we highlight, school leaders continue to think about how to integrate Summit's resources—from its facilities and teachers to its technology and budgets, how to adjust scheduling, what processes or routines to establish or change, and how to engage its community. Its answer continues to evolve, but some pieces are emerging as staples for integrating a cohesive, deliberate program.[22]

To create the experiences of student agency and individual mastery, Summit believed there was no available software that provided the right functionality. So it partnered with several organizations—the Girard Education Foundation, an education philanthropy based in San Diego; Illuminate Education, a student data platform company; and the Alvo Institute, a company that helps schools design blended-learning environments—to create new software called Activate Instruction. This free online tool gives students access to a variety of learning resources curated by teachers and organized by competency in what it calls "playlists." Students working on Activate have multiple options—from online videos to articles and games—for how they learn any given competency through the playlists.[23]

This in turn allows Summit to offer students eight hours a week in school and eight hours a week at home of what it calls Personalized Learning Time. During this time, students cycle through the process that Figure 5.2 illustrates. They set learning goals for the week; develop a plan to achieve the goals using Activate's playlists; and work through the plan. When they feel ready, they can take assessments, which are available on demand, to show evidence that they have

Figure 5.2   The Learning Cycle at Summit Public Schools

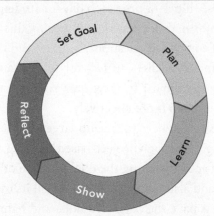

Source: Image courtesy of Summit Public Schools from November 2013 PowerPoint.

mastered the concepts or skills. That means that if students already believe they understand a concept, they can take an assessment at the outset and skip ahead. If they fail, then they work through their individual playlist until they are capable of showing evidence of mastery.

After taking assessments, students receive pass/fail feedback, as well as a detailed explanation of their performance. This short-cycle feedback loop allows students not only to make progress—and feel ownership of their progress—in steady, frequent increments, but also to have access to actionable data. With these data in hand, each Friday students sit down with their mentors to reflect on their weekly progress, how they feel about their learning experience, what worked well, and what to improve.

Because students can progress as fast as they master material, Summit had to create, up front, a coherent scope, suggested sequence, and associated playlists of resources for the entire set of competencies a student should master—meaning all the way through high school. That means for teachers, there is no lesson planning the night before. The ancillary benefit of this is that Summit posts this scope and sequence in its software so that students can see what's ahead. Summit even has a graphical line in its student-facing data system that moves with the calendar to help students see where they should be in their learning if they want to complete high school on time and that allows them to make adjustments accordingly.

To give students sustained periods of quiet, solitary reading time, the school created Summit Reads, a block of time each day for students to free read. Summit uses an e-reading platform, called Curriculet, during this period, to deliver texts that contain a layer of embedded questions, quizzes, and rich media annotations. Curriculet allows Summit teachers to test for understanding in real time and provides them with a dashboard to view quiz results, time on task, and other metrics that help them coach more effectively.

Summit uses these experiences to free up large blocks of time for students to tackle "deeper learning"[24] through project-based learning, which Summit believes is uniquely capable of accomplishing the dual purpose of helping students fulfill their jobs to be done and also helping Summit fulfill its own job of ensuring that 100 percent of students have the cognitive skills and habits of success necessary to succeed in college and life. Exhibit 5.1 shows a typical daily schedule for a Summit student and how project-based learning figures prominently into the day. Exhibit 5.2, at the end of this chapter, displays sample schedules from other blended schools.

Exhibit 5.1 A Day in the Life of a Summit Public Schools Student

7:30	Begin to arrive; work on personalized learning plan
8:25	Schools start with project time (math and science)
10:20	Break
10:35	Personalized Learning Time
11:35	PE or sustained reading time (using Curriculet)
12:35	Lunch and recess outside
1:20	Project time (English and history)
3:15	School ends; can stay and work on personalized learning plan

Note: On Fridays, the student spends most of the day on a personalized learning plan and has a one-on-one check-in with her mentor.

In addition, Summit provides its students with eight weeks a year of "Expeditions," in which students learn largely off-campus in the real world. Students explore their passions in everything from elective courses to real internships to learn about career options. Expeditions give students the chance to build strong relationships with their Expedition teachers and people in outside community organizations. Summit also has an internal mentorship program, which consists of weekly ten-minute, student-led, one-on-one meetings with an assigned teacher who becomes a student's academic coach, college counselor, family liaison, and advocate. Students lead one to three meetings a year with their mentor and family. Each teacher mentors roughly fifteen students per year.

Finally, both the expeditions and project-based learning provide students with ample time for positive group experiences. Summit supplements this with forty-five minutes per week of community time, in which students meet together in small groups to engage in discussions about issues important to them.

BLENDED LEARNING'S ROLE IN FULFILLING STUDENT JOBS

Schools like Summit are taking advantage of two breakthroughs to make it easier for them to integrate the right academic and social experiences from a student jobs-to-be-done perspective. First, online content is improving such that it is gradually becoming capable of serving as the backbone for student learning in some courses and subjects for some students. As schools are able to deliver content via online platforms, teachers are left with more time and energy to devote to creating the most positive, interactive learning experiences possible for students on their campuses. Summit teachers are able to invest more time in one-on-one mentoring because they are no longer focused on their next lecture. Instead, they can turn their attention to developing students' habits of success by creating deep personal relationships with students. Second, in some cases online content is accelerating the mastery of basic skills and compressing the amount of time spent on them. This opens up blocks of time for activities like project time and Socratic discussions, which not only help *schools* accomplish their job of developing articulate, critical thinkers, but also, conveniently, help *students* fulfill their job of having fun with friends. Similar to Summit, Acton Academy, which we introduce in Chapter Two, compresses core learning to a two-and-a-half-hour personalized-learning period each day. This gives the school time to offer three two-hour project blocks each week, a Socratic seminar each day, game play on Fridays, ample art and PE, and numerous other highly social experiences.[25] Schools should be on the lookout for ways to make learning more efficient to open time for students to develop what they consider to be fun relationships with their peers and teachers.

One way of thinking of this is that as digital learning becomes ubiquitous, students will have — although it may seem counter-intuitive — far more time for hands-on, project-based learning experiences. Many cities are already seeing an increase in makerspaces (also known as "hacklabs" and "hackerspaces"), community-oriented creative spaces. We suspect that as schools blend more online experiences into their programs, they will find not only that they have more time for students to have these experiences, but also that the hands-on practice sessions and face-to-face social experiences that are uniquely available through projects and expeditions are part of what has been missing for students all along. Fortunately, project-based and expeditionary-learning experiences not only provide a counterbalance to children's screen time — an idea that appeals to many adults — but are also uniquely suited to helping students do the jobs that they are prioritizing.[26]

THE DANGER OF ASKING STUDENTS TO CHANGE JOBS

After identifying their rallying cries and organizing to innovate, blended-learning teams embark on the challenging and exciting task of designing the learning model. This chapter makes the strong recommendation that teams anchor their efforts in the jobs that students are already trying to do in their lives. Again, for most students these jobs are to make progress each day and to have fun with friends. Teams should then brainstorm all of the experiences that add up to getting these jobs done perfectly. Finally, teams should consider which resources they need and how to integrate the resources to deliver the desired experiences. In the next few chapters, we dive deeper into the third level of the architecture of a job: bringing together teachers, other staff, the physical and virtual environment, the model, and the culture into a seamless, integrated solution.

As the late educator Jack Frymier often said, "If the kids want to learn, we couldn't stop 'em. If they don't, we can't make 'em." The good news is that society's jobs to be done and students' jobs to be done overlap some. Society wants students to make academic progress each day and to engage in constructive social relationships. When these ideals are central to school design, students are most likely to engage.

To Sum Up

- School can be a place where students find joy in learning. When a school gets the design right from the students' perspective, such that it aligns perfectly with the things that matter to them, they show up to class motivated and eager to learn. The key is to design with empathy. The jobs-to-be-done theory is a tool to help design from that vantage point.
- The first level in the architecture of a job is simply identifying the job to be done. Generally speaking, the two jobs that are the highest priority for most students are to feel successful and make progress, and to have fun with friends. Education itself is not the job; rather, it's one option that students can hire to get their jobs done.
- The second level is identifying all of the experiences that schools need to provide to get the jobs done perfectly. For Summit Public Schools, these include delivering student agency, individual mastery, access to actionable data and rapid feedback, transparency in learning goals, sustained periods of solitary reading time, meaningful work experiences, mentoring experiences, and positive group experiences.
- Some of the experiences that help students get the job done are universal, but others depend on the circumstances of individual student populations—for example, some communities need to design experiences that remediate for sleep and exercise deprivation or for traumatic home lives. Other circumstances require different experiences.
- The third level in the architecture of a job is identifying what to integrate and how to deliver the experiences necessary to get the job done. Summit Public Schools integrated personalized learning time, the learning cycle, project-based learning, expeditions, and other processes and routines to deliver its full set of experiences for students.
- Blended learning makes it easier for educators to deliver the array of academic and social experiences that can make school the best place for students to get their jobs done.

Exhibit 5.2 Sample Daily Schedules

1. KIPP Comienza Community Prep, Huntington Park, California[27]
Grades K–4
  Station Rotation

7:30	Breakfast and family-literacy activities
7:45	School-wide morning meeting
8:05	Math block with station rotations
9:25	Recess
9:40	Writers' workshop
10:20	ELA stations with phonics, guided reading, and word work
11:30	Art, Spanish instruction, or science
12:30	Lunch and play
1:15	Values circle: Check in on behavior and choices
1:30	Readers workshop: Independent reading based on reading level
2:00	Reading comprehension block with the whole class
2:45	Spiral review, student choice, standards review, or extension
3:20	Ethnic studies class: Identity, social sciences, and history
4:00	End of day

2. Gilroy Prep, a Navigator School, Gilroy, California
Grades K–4
  Lab Rotation

8:00	Whole school "boot up" with songs
8:10	Math class begins with tech-enriched, whole-group instruction
9:10	Adaptive software on Chromebooks with pull-outs for interventions
9:40	Recess
9:55	ELA with pull-outs for phonics and reading
11:00	Successmaker math in the computer lab
11:30	Science or PE
12:15	Lunch
1:00	Accelerated Reader on the iPad
1:30	Successmaker math in the computer lab
2:00	Writers' workshop, reading comprehension, spiral review
3:15	End of day
3:15	Enrichment for older kids if needed

3. Acton Academy, Austin, Texas

Grades 1– 12 (sample schedule for grades 6– 8 only)

   Flex

	Activity	Behavior norm
8:00	Free time	Free time
8:30	Huddle	Collaborative
8:55	Core Skills (reading, writing, math, and Civilization)	Silent time (individual work)
10:00	Break	Free time
10:15	Core Skills, continued	Collaborative (individual work, but with peer support)
11:40	Lunch	Free time
12:15	Project Time	Collaborative
2:45	Clean Up	Collaborative
3:00	Huddle	Collaborative
3:15	End of day	

Note: PE is Mondays and Thursdays for an hour before lunch. Students can earn an hour of game time, which occurs on Fridays before afternoon Clean Up.

NOTES

1. "United States Federal, State and Local Government Spending," usgovernmentspending.com, http://www.usgovernmentspending.com/us_education_spending_20.html (accessed December 13, 2013).

2. "Education at a Glance 2013," OECD, p. 251, http://www.oecd.org/edu/eag2013%20(eng) — FINAL%2020%20June%202013.pdf

3. HotChalk Education Index 2013 Mid-Year Report, http://www.education inamerica.com/research/hotchalk-edu-index/infographic/ (accessed December 13, 2013).

4. Kim Peterson, "10 of the worst product flops ever," MSN Money, March 28, 3013, http://money.ca.msn.com/savings-debt/gallery/10-of-the-worst-product-flops-ever?page=11 (accessed December 20, 2013).

5. This section and the next two sections of Chapter Five are based largely on *Disrupting Class,* Chapter Seven.

6. The product and company in this example have been disguised.

7. This section is adapted from the insightful work of Clayton M. Christensen, Jerome H. Grossman, and Jason Hwang, *The Innovator's Prescription: A Disruptive Solution for Health Care* (New York: McGraw-Hill, 2009), pp. 157–178.

8. Many people assume that the best way to determine the job to be done is to assess a person's needs. The Well at Dell example shows why this is wrong. Everyone has the *need* to maintain physical health. Not everyone, however, is trying to do that job. The key is to observe what people are *motivated* to do, not what they *need* to do.

9. There are several points of evidence supporting this observation. First, when we use the phrase "want to feel successful," we do not mean the kind of surface-level idea of success that constitutes praising a child no matter how she performed on a given activity, under the mistaken idea that building "self-esteem" in this vein is a good idea. Instead, we mean true success, when the student in fact accomplishes and achieves something real and makes progress. A discussion of the perils of the former can be found in George Will's discussion of Po Bronson and Ashley Merryman's book, *NurtureShock: New Thinking About Children.* See George F. Will, "How to Ruin a Child: Too Much Esteem, Too Little Sleep," *Washington Post,* March 4, 2010, http://www.washingtonpost.com/wp-dyn/content/article/2010/03/03/AR2010030303075.html. Further evidence that feeling successful is a primary job of students—and of all people—emerges from the field of cognitive science. As Daniel T. Willingham writes in Chapter One of his book *Why Don't Students Like School? A Cognitive Scientist Answers Questions about How the Mind Works and What It Means for the Classroom* (San Francisco: Jossey-Bass, 2009):

    > Solving problems brings pleasure. When I say "problem solving" in this book, I mean any cognitive work that succeeds; it might be understanding a difficult passage of prose, planning a garden, or sizing up an investment opportunity. There is a sense of satisfaction, of fulfillment, in successful thinking. In the last ten years neuroscientists have discovered that there is

overlap between the brain areas and chemicals that are important in learning and those that are important in the brain's
natural reward system …. Many neuroscientists suspect that
the two systems are related. Rats in a maze learn better when
rewarded with cheese. When you solve a problem, your brain
may reward itself with a small dose of dopamine, a naturally
occurring chemical that is important to the brain's pleasure system. Neuroscientists know that dopamine is important in both
systems—learning and pleasure—but haven't yet worked out
the explicit tie between them. Even though the neurochemistry
is not completely understood, it seems undeniable that people
take pleasure in solving problems …. It's notable too that the
pleasure is in the solving of the problem. Working on a problem
with no sense that you're making progress is not pleasurable.

In addition, in a book by Susan A. Ambrose, Michele DiPetro, Michael W.
Bridges, Marsha C. Lovett, and Marie K. Norman, *How Learning Works:
Seven Research-Based Principles for Smart Teaching* (San Francisco: Jossey-
Bass, 2010), the authors cite several other studies that support this hypothesis. In particular, the authors dedicate a chapter to the research on motivation,
in which they summarize that "When students find positive value in a learning goal or activity, expect to successfully achieve a desired learning outcome,
and perceive support from their environment, they are likely to be strongly
motivated to learn." In particular, they write, "there are two important concepts that are central to understanding motivation: (1) the subjective value of
a goal and (2) the expectancies, or expectations for successful attainment of
that goal. Although many theories have been offered to explain motivation,
most position these two concepts at the core of their framework (Atkinson,
1957, 1964; Wigfield & Eccles, 1992, 2000)." The ability to experience success, in other words, is one of the central underpinnings of motivation. As
the authors write, "Although one must value a desired outcome in order to
be motivated to pursue it, value alone is insufficient to motivate behavior.
People are also motivated to pursue goals and outcomes that they believe
they can successfully achieve."

Richard E. Mayer and Ruth C. Clark, in their book *eLearning and the
Science of Instruction: Proven Guidelines for Consumers and Designers of
Multimedia Learning Second Edition* (San Francisco: Wiley, 2008), also

discuss how learners experience enjoyment as they successfully solve problems. As Barbara Gaddy Carrio, Richard A. DeLorenzo, Wendy J. Battino, and Rick M. Schreiber note in *Delivering on the Promise: The Education Revolution* (Bloomington, IN: Solution Tree Press, 2009), "A fundamental principle of the RISC Approach to Schooling is that student motivation and engagement have a great deal to do with student success."

What is distinct about understanding motivation from the jobs-to-be-done perspective is that we learn that all students are motivated to feel success; but for many, school is not something they can hire to experience success. Therefore students often turn to other avenues, but that does not mean these students are unmotivated.

10. Harris Interactive, "6 in 10 Americans Say They or Someone They Know Have Been Bullied," Harris Poll, February 19, 2014, http://www.harris interactive.com/NewsRoom/HarrisPolls/tabid/447/ctl/ReadCustom%20 Default/mid/1508/ArticleId/1383/Default.aspx (accessed April 13, 2014).

11. Jobs don't have solely a functional dimension; customers also have social and emotional jobs.

12. The national educational toy store franchise Learning Express Toys is another example of an organization that views its market structure—intentionally or unintentionally—in terms of jobs to be done. As a result, it is expanding at an average of one new toy store per month. Its more than 130 franchise stores are small in terms of square feet, but each store is usually hopping with customers. Learning Express has discovered a sizeable market of people with a particular job related to toys: "I need a nice gift for a child's birthday party that starts this afternoon!" The company designs every detail of the customer experience in ways that add up to nailing that job perfectly. The stores are often located in outdoor retail spaces (as opposed to indoor shopping malls) with ample parking so that customers can get in and out quickly. They arrange their selection of toys by gender and age to help customers zero in on the right range of options immediately. Inventory is limited compared to a larger toy store such as Toys R Us, but Learning Express scrutinizes each toy in stock for its quality and play value. This relieves customers from having to do much sorting or comparison, plus expert staff in bright red aprons roam the store to offer assistance.

In the back corner of each store is a play area and train table to entertain young shoppers while their parents make their purchases. At the checkout stand, Learning Express offers birthday cards that are arranged by child's age, free gift-wrapping, and free personalization. In short, Learning Express offers such a convenient, effective way for people to choose the perfect toy, for every child, for every occasion when time is tight, that its business is booming. Shoppers can stop in on the way to a party or the post office and do their entire job in one quick errand. Learning Express understands the job its customers need to do and has integrated its activities to enable customers to do the job as well as possible.

13. "High School Rankings 2011: *Newsweek* Ranks America's Most Transformative," *Newsweek,* June 21, 2011, http://www.newsweek.com/high-school-rankings-2011-newsweek-ranks-americas-most-transformative-67911 (accessed December 26, 2013). Many people also know Summit Public Schools from its starring role in the documentary *Waiting for Superman.*

14. Matt Wilka and Jeff Cohen, "It's Not Just About the Model: Blended Learning, Innovation, and Year 2 at Summit Public Schools," FSG, http://www.fsg.org/Portals/0/Uploads/Documents/PDF/Blended_Learning_Innovation.pdf. Incidentally, the percentage of Summit Public School's former students who were succeeding in college—55 percent—was far higher than the national average, but Diane and the school's teachers felt strongly that their mission was to educate all students to be successful in life. If any students were failing in college because they were not prepared adequately in any way, then they believed they were not meeting that mission.

15. There is considerable evidence that, as cognitive scientist Daniel Willingham writes, "Working on problems that are of the right level of difficult is rewarding, but working on problems that are too easy or too difficult is unpleasant." A key to helping students experience success is borrowing a concept from the world of gaming and allowing students to learn at the point that will maximize their chances of success while still being sufficiently challenging or interesting that they will experience that triumph as a real moment of progress so that they will want to keep learning. Daniel Willingham, *Why Don't Students Like School: A Cognitive Scientist Answers*

Questions about How the Mind Works and What It Means for Your Class-room, (San Francisco: Jossey-Bass, 2009), Ch. 1.

This idea relates to the notion of the Zone of Proximal Development, which was developed by Lev Vygotsky, a Soviet psychologist. See the Wikipedia entry, "Zone of proximal development," for a high-level summary of the concept at http://en.wikipedia.org/wiki/Zone_of_proximal_development#cite_note-4 (accessed April 7, 2010). An often-cited definition of this term is "the distance between the actual developmental level as determined by independent problem solving and the level of potential development as determined through problem solving under adult guidance, or in collaboration with more capable peers," as written in his own work (see L. S. Vygotsky, *Mind in Society: Development of Higher Psychological Processes* [Cambridge: Harvard, 1978], p. 86).

In addition, the gaming industry teaches us that people are most motivated when success is almost within reach, but still on the horizon. William "Bing" Gordon, a top executive in the video game industry, said that "one principal of gamification is you only get motivated when you're 90 percent of the way to success." Kevin Werbach, "Gamification" course, Coursera, https://class.coursera.org/gamification-003/lecture (accessed April 13, 2014), timecode: 07:37.

16. Data and feedback are not always good for learning. When a student receives feedback but cannot do anything useful with that feedback, it has a negative influence on student learning. Conversely, when the student can do something with the data, then it has a positive impact on learning. According to *Delivering on the Promise: The Education Revolution* (Kindle Locations), pp. 1624–1630:

> Relative to student feedback, findings from research might best be summed up by saying that feedback in and of itself is not necessarily useful. In fact, the long-used practice of simply telling students which answers are right and which are wrong (a practice with which most readers likely have considerable firsthand experience) has a negative influence on student learning (see Bangert-Drowns, Kulik, Kulik, & Morgan [1991], cited in Marzano, 2006). Conversely, ensuring that students are clear about the criteria that will be used to judge

their responses, providing students with the correct answers, giving them explanations about why their responses were correct or incorrect, and asking students to continue responding to an assessment item until they correctly answer are all practices that research shows can result in statistically significant gains in student achievement (Marzano, 2006).

17. More researchers are worrying that the practice of scanning and skimming when people read online is having a negative impact on the ability of people to read longer texts and engage in deeper reading. See Michael S. Rosenwald, "Serious Reading Takes a Hit from Online Scanning and Skimming, Researchers Say," *Washington Post*, April 6, 2014 (http://www .washingtonpost.com/local/serious-reading-takes-a-hit-from-online-scanning-and-skimming-researchers-say/2014/04/06/088028d2-b5d2–11e3-b899–20667de76985_story.html). We also recommend this thoughtful response to this article: Dan Willingham, "Don't Blame the Internet: We Can Still Think and Read Critically, We Just Don't Want To," RealClearEducation, April 16, 2014 (http://www.realcleareducation.com/articles/2014/04/16/dont_blame_the_web_we_can_still_think_and_read_critically_we_just_dont_want_to_942.html).

18. John Ratey keynote presentation, "Learning & the Brain Conference," Boston, MA, November 16, 2013.

19. John Ratey, *Spark: The Revolutionary New Science of Exercise and the Brain* (New York: Little, Brown and Company, 2008).

20. Paul Tough, *How Children Succeed* (New York: Houghton Mifflin Harcourt, 2012), pp. 9–19.

21. Farsighted leaders might also consider using high school to teach parents how to be parents before they become parents. In the not-too-distant past, courses like home economics, auto repair, and wood- and metalworking were offered in most high schools to prepare young people for at least some of the mechanics of adulthood. Parents who are trapped in a multigenerational cycle of educational underachievement and poverty would certainly benefit from learning how to break the cycle with their own children. Clayton M. Christensen, Michael B. Horn, & Curtis W. Johnson, *Disrupting*

Class: How Disruptive Innovation Will Change the Way the World Learns (New York: McGraw-Hill, 2011), p. 155.

In addition, Russell Simmons and the David Lynch Foundation work to help schools implement a small time period of transcendental meditation each day to help students deal with extreme stress and improve their readiness to learn. See Russell Simmons, *Success Through Stillness: Meditation Made Simple* (New York: Gotham, 2014) and the David Lynch Foundation, http://www.davidlynchfoundation.org/

22.   Our friend Alex Hernandez, a partner at the Charter School Growth Fund, makes an important point when thinking about how to design schools, which echoes this framework.

> We advise our school designers not to start with the school schedule when they advise schools. The reason is, blended learning is this big, open canvas and what you do when you start with a schedule is you basically drop a thousand constraints [on that canvas]. You're giving away stuff that you're not even prepared [to], or have thought about giving away. And so where we do ask folks to start is, we say, "Start with the learning environment. And I don't care if it's thirty kids or it's ninety kids. And let's not think too much about the space at this point. Think about the experiences that you want students to have academically, socially. And, yeah, let's not do too many, but let's just think through, like, if we wanted to do three or four of these different experiences during a certain block of time." So you start putting boundaries around these experiences. How do you create these experiences for students? And that's the beginning of School Design.
> And then once you've kind of mapped that out, we do a lot of drawing, we do a lot of visualization—you can start saying, "Okay, how do kids cycle through this environment?" And sometimes by just saying, "Hey, we're going to cycle kids through this," all of a sudden your design starts breaking. So then you start modifying. You want to make sure that every kid's getting the experiences that you intend them to get and not just because you have time to do one-to-one for ten kids

and the other ninety kids get left out in your school model. And, that's the beginning of iteration, and so, the key is don't give away your constraints too early. Because it's not really that useful to know what you can't do; what's really useful is figuring out what you can do.

See Brian Greenberg, Rob Schwartz, and Michael Horn, "Blended Learning: Personalizing Education for Students," Coursera, Week 2, Video 2: Key Elements of the Student Experience, https://class.coursera.org/blended learning-001

23. "Summit Public Schools," Clayton Christensen Institute's Blended Learning Universe, http://www.christenseninstitute.org/summit-public-schools/ (accessed December 29, 2013).

24. The Hewlett Foundation defines deeper learning as using knowledge and skills in a way that prepares students for real life. Students master core academic content—reading, writing, math, and science—while learning how to think critically, collaborate, communicate effectively, direct their own learning, and believe in themselves (or gain what is known as an "academic mindset"). See http://www.hewlett.org/programs/education-program/deeper-learning (accessed on January 27, 2014).

25. Alex Hernandez, "Which Way for K12 Blended Learning? (Part 1: Boarding the Mayflower)," Blend My Learning, February 12, 2013, http://www.blend mylearning.com/2013/02/12/which-way-for-k12-blended-learning-part-1/ (accessed December 29, 2013).

26. Some have worried about how to ensure the quality of project-based learning. VLACS Aspire, winner of a 2013 Next Generation Learning Challenge (NGLC) grant, aims to tackle that problem. Through a model called "experiential blended learning," VLACS Aspire offers students extended learning opportunities (ELOs) for credit. These opportunities involve outside-of-school projects, such as internships that are based on students' interests. For both online coursework and real-life work completed through ELOs, the students' online teacher administers performance assessments to measure progress. Over time, the emergence of a strong ecosystem to support performance assessments at VLACS Aspire and other schools is likely

to make quality control associated with project-based and experiential learning easier and more reliable. See Julia Freeland, "Blending toward Competency: Early Patterns of Blended Learning and Competency-Based Education in New Hampshire," Clayton Christensen Institute, May 2014, http://www.christenseninstitute.org/wp-content/uploads/2014/05/Blending-toward-competency.pdf

27. KIPP Comienza Community Prep and Gilroy Prep schedules are available at this online course: Silicon Schools Fund and Clayton Christensen Institute, "Blended Learning: Creating the Ideal Student Experience in a Blended Learning Classroom," hosted by Khan Academy, https://www.khanacademy.org/partner-content/ssf-cci/ccss-ideal-student-experience/sscc-learning-environments/a/example-blended-learning-school-schedules (accessed May 31, 2014).

Chapter 6

Elevate Teaching

A recurring theme in this book is that blended learning entails more than layering technology on top of traditional classrooms; it involves a deeper redesign of the instructional model. Ideally, the design effort should begin with a singular devotion to fulfilling the students' jobs to be done and then consider how to integrate the other parts of the school—from the teachers to the facilities, curriculum, and culture—to deliver the right experiences.

The responsibility to integrate teachers successfully into the design is no small matter. Intuition and a good deal of evidence show the lasting influence that good teachers have on student outcomes.[1] Students cannot afford a failed experiment with teacher integration. Furthermore, over three million adults in the United States alone have devoted their careers to the teaching profession, and society depends on continuing to recruit and retain capable talent in the future. Getting this right for teachers is important.

One of the most widely read blogs ever on the Christensen Institute website is "Will Computers Replace Teachers?"[2] The topic hit a nerve. Everyone sees that online software is taking on an instructional role, and the inevitable question follows: just how far will this phenomenon go? In Chapter Two we predict that once online learning becomes good enough, schools will be able to rely on it to deliver high-quality learning adapted to each student. That will free schools to focus more on other critical jobs, but it also presents the risk that as schools delegate content and instruction to an online platform, on-site faculty will feel replaced, "check out," and neither offer much support to students nor shift their roles to focus on the development of higher-order thinking skills and dispositions. This is a risk, because teachers are critical to the success of blended learning. In the good blended-learning programs we have observed, although the teacher role shifts in profound ways—teachers may no longer be lesson planning and leading an entire class on the same activity—they are still engaged and working with students even more actively in a variety of ways. In the bad blended-learning programs that we have observed, the teacher feels replaced and often sits in the back of the room, disgruntled and disengaged from the students, who in turn tend not to learn nearly as much as they might with an engaged, enthusiastic teacher.

The responsibility to design well for teachers is significant. It may be the single most important determinant of whether the rise of blended learning will net out as a win. In this chapter, we first consider ways to integrate the teacher role advantageously from the student perspective. Second, we think through the opportunities from the teacher perspective. How can we ensure that the design helps teachers fulfill their own jobs and priorities?

DESIGNING THE TEACHER ROLE FROM THE STUDENT PERSPECTIVE

Because students' circumstances and learning needs are as diverse as students themselves, there is no single definition for the ideal teacher. But two observations about the world of today's learners provide clues about how to integrate teachers into students' lives in ways that will help students learn and get their jobs done.

Move Beyond Lockstep Instruction

The first observation is that, as we've discussed, relying on a factory model of instruction does not fit with what it means to become career-ready in today's world. The classic image of a teacher at the chalkboard, overhead projector, or electronic white board delivering — or even facilitating — whole-class instruction is inappropriate as the norm. The future awaiting today's youth demands something new from schools. Factory-style classrooms that reward students for "just showing up and staying awake" no longer cut it.[3]

Even the United States military, an organization long characterized by rigid, authoritarian discipline, is reconsidering its traditional top-down approach to instruction.[4] According to General Martin Dempsey, chairman of the Joint Chiefs of Staff (America's top military officer), the United States military used to look to recruit people who were "physically fit, educated, and disciplined." In today's world, however, they mostly want someone "who can communicate, who is inquisitive, and who has an instinct to collaborate."[5]

Given the need for soldiers who can analyze intelligence data in real time, think entrepreneurially, and own the mission, the military has found that integrating military instructors as drill sergeants no longer works as well. General Dempsey said that military leaders are transitioning away from being the "sage on the stage," where in essence "you sat there and [the drill sergeant] yelled at you and you took notes and you got out of boot camp," to being "guides on the side."[6] He believes a leader needs "to be more an orchestrator and inspirer than a traditional hard-charging, follow-me-up-the-hill commander."[7]

The shift in the military's approach points to a path forward for schools. Top-down, teacher-centered, monolithic instruction is an uninspiring choice for generating the entrepreneurial, inquisitive problem solvers that today's employers are paying top dollar to recruit.[8] Even as many teachers across the United States have attempted to shed aspects of the lecture format over the last several decades, the factory-model classroom design limits the ability to move toward a rigorous, student-centered approach that both equips students with knowledge and skills and allows them to develop critical dispositions and creativity. As schools consider how to integrate teachers into their blended-learning designs, they have an exciting opportunity to think beyond a role that has time- and lecture-based elements geared for producing the factory workers of yesterday.

A story from the evolution of Summit Public Schools illustrates the importance of seizing the opportunity. In the pilot year for Summit's Flex model of blended learning, some teachers at first insisted that students should always be introduced to new material through a teacher's lecture. Other staff members were less sure. So

Summit ran an experiment. Teachers offered lectures to introduce new material, but, in keeping with the Flex model design, students had the option of whether to attend. At first, all the students attended the lectures because they were in the habit of doing so. But over time, the numbers started to dwindle. Meanwhile, as the data came back, they showed that the lectures were not producing great results for those who did attend. In response, teachers worked hard to improve their lectures, but week after week, the results for students attending the lecture were unexceptional and attendance continued to decline.

One week, seemingly out of nowhere, the results flipped. Students who had attended the lectures produced remarkable results. The teachers who had originally proclaimed the importance of the lecture appeared triumphant. But when the Summit team members looked closer at the data, they realized something else had changed. There were only a small number of students attending the "lecture," which had in essence been transformed into small-group instruction or tutoring. Teachers were no longer lecturing, but were instead answering questions and facilitating discussions. Not only that, but both students and teachers enjoyed this type of engagement and found it to be productive. Shedding assumptions of what teaching has to look like as schools redesign learning environments is critical to unlock the potential of blended learning.

Fill the Mentoring Gap

A second observation concerns integrating teachers to help students fulfill their jobs. Because of some fundamental changes in society, more and more students need teachers to serve as mentors not only to help them build positive relationships and have fun with friends, but also to help them succeed in life. With online learning delivering some part of a course's content and instruction, blended-learning programs create more time for teachers to fill this important role.

The word "mentor" comes from Greek mythology, in which it appears as the name of the son of Alcimus. Mentor took charge of Odysseus's son Telemachus when Odysseus left for the Trojan War. Later, when Athena visited Telemachus, she disguised herself as Mentor to encourage Telemachus to stand up for worthy causes. In other words, the original character named Mentor had a caregiver assignment; a second character, Athena, who assumed the identity of Mentor, provided encouragement and practical plans for dealing with personal dilemmas. As it relates to the role of teachers, the term has something in common with both senses of the word.

Former *New York Times* writer Paul Tough has done some of the best investigative journalism about the difference that a good mentor can make even for seemingly irrecoverable youth. He published a story about Keitha Jones, a seventeen-year-old who grew up in Roseland on Chicago's South Side, a once-prosperous area that has since declined into one of the worst-off neighborhoods in the city by just about any measure. Keitha's mother was a crack addict; her father, who lived a few blocks away, had fathered at least nineteen children in the neighborhood; police frequently ransacked her crowded, chaotic house by turning over tables and emptying shelves to look for guns and drugs; and beginning when Keitha was young, an older relative who stayed in the house from time to time sexually molested her repeatedly.[9]

High school was where Keitha let her anger out. Her classmates regarded her as one of the most violent kids at a violent school. Eventually, the principal requested that the local office of the Youth Advocates Program, or YAP, assign her a mentor. YAP is a nonprofit organization that uses intensive mentoring and "wraparound advocacy" to try to keep at-risk youth with their families rather than in foster care. YAP assigned Keitha to a part-time advocate named Lanita Reed, a thirty-one-year-old Roseland resident who owned Gifted Hanz, a beauty salon that brightened up the otherwise blighted block of 103rd Street.[10]

Reed began by teaching Keitha to shampoo and braid clients' hair and then taught Keitha to care for her physical appearance, including getting her nails done and her hair styled. After that the inner makeover began. The two discussed boys, absentee fathers, drugs, anger, and prayer. Reed was also instrumental in seeing that the sexual predator was incarcerated and ensuring that the state did not place Keitha or her sisters in foster care.[11]

Ultimately, Reed helped Keitha change her outlook on life at the advanced age of seventeen, when many people think a child is beyond hope. Keitha graduated from high school and enrolled in Truman College, where she planned to pursue a cosmetology degree. Paul Tough concluded his story with the observation that time and again, mentors have proven capable of "rewiring a personality" and achieving a rapid and unexpected transformation against even the starkest odds.[12]

An increasing number of students need this kind of wraparound advocacy and intensive mentoring. As one example, a worrisome trend that speaks to the importance of having mentors is that fewer children come from stable two-parent homes today than they did a generation ago. Sixty-four percent of children from birth to seventeen lived with two married parents in 2012, down from 77 percent in 1980. Only 59 percent of Hispanic children and 33 percent of African American children lived with two married parents in 2012.[13]

The decline in stable two-parent homes hurts children on average. Paul R. Amato, professor of sociology and demography at Pennsylvania State University, conducted a meta-study about the effects of divorce on children. He found that children with divorced parents are worse off on average than those with continually married parents on measures of academic success (school grades, test scores), conduct (behavior problems, aggression), psychological well-being (depression, stress), self-esteem, and peer relations (number of close friends). Of course, children growing up with continuously partnered parents may also evidence maladjustment if they are exposed to stressful circumstances, such as poverty, serious conflict between the parents, violence, neglect, and substance abuse. Correspondingly, some children of divorced parents have circumstances that allow them to cope well.[14] But on average, Amato found that children with divorced parents are worse off than those with continually married parents.

Given societal trends, schools are asked more and more to be the ambulance at the bottom of a cliff.[15] Steve Gates, YAP Chicago director, made the connection between family breakdown and schools when he said that "there is a very direct correlation between family issues and what the kids present in school. The lapses in parenting, the dysfunction—it all spills over to the kids, and then they take that to school and the streets and everywhere else."[16]

Schools cannot substitute for a stable, nurturing home. They can, however, help when children need a mentor. Many schools already do. In some cases, it's the only hope for a child to be successful. And even children from functional homes stand to benefit from outside mentors.

Big Picture Learning schools integrate teachers as mentors by assigning each student to a small learning community of fifteen students called an "advisory." An advisor works closely with the group of students and forms a personal relationship with each advisee. Each student works individually with her advisor to identify her interests and personalize her learning. The students have internships as well, which allows them to work individually with an outside mentor and learn in a real-world setting. In addition, the school reaches out to parents and families to help shape the student's personalized learning plan. Taken together, these sources of adult influence form a stronghold of mentoring and relationship that backs up each student.

 WATCH CLIP 18: Big Picture Learning deploys teachers as mentors and prioritizes internships as key elements of its student experience.

www.wiley.com/go/blended18

Schools across the country are integrating teachers as mentors in a variety of ways. For example, some schools assign students to have the same teacher for multiple years so that each student has a stable and continuous relationship in her life. Blended learning can help; because software can deliver lessons tailored to each student in a classroom of mixed ages and levels, it can free up schools to keep groups of students together with one teacher over many years, even as the students' academic abilities progress.

Over time, we suspect that additional schools will turn to online learning to deliver content and instruction and then adjust their recruiting, training, and teacher evaluation processes to cultivate a team that includes many with a mentoring responsibility and fewer who lesson plan and lecture to an entire class in lockstep fashion. Summit Public Schools, for example, has chosen to integrate mentorship into its design by training teachers to forget about their next lecture and focus instead on developing deep, personal relationships with students—as academic coaches, college counselors, family liaisons, and advocates. Mentors each have stewardship over ten to fifteen students and meet with them at least weekly. Summit includes mentoring as one of seven dimensions that it measures to rate teacher effectiveness. Teachers progress on a continuum ranging from basic to expert, based on principal evaluation, peer evaluation, and self-evaluation, and Summit offers personalized professional development to support them.[17]

DESIGNING THE TEACHER ROLE FROM THE TEACHER PERSPECTIVE

We know the role of teachers is crucial from the student perspective. But to gain teachers' buy-in, a redesigned school must benefit teachers as well. Teachers have personal jobs to do in their lives, and the magic happens when schools design experiences that fulfill the jobs of both students and teachers. A case study from the hair color industry provides an analogy for why designing with teachers in mind is critically important.

The ColorMatch Conundrum

Max Ladjevardi and his wife, Bibi Kasrai, never intended to start a hair color business. But one day, while shopping at a True Value hardware store for paint for some door frames in their home, they had an inspiration. Needing to match the paint color exactly, Max handed the True Value clerk a chip of the existing paint to help him find the best match. The couple watched as the clerk used a color sensor to formulate an exact color match. They wondered: "What if a similar technology could be used in hair salons to ensure that clients end up with exactly the right color there as well?"[18]

The market seemed ready for this idea. The vast majority of American women, and many men as well, used hair color. Max and Bibi knew of many individuals who were disappointed, or even horrified, by the result of a botched coloring attempt. The couple decided to engineer a simple handheld device, roughly the size of a small blow dryer, that could analyze hair color with near-perfect accuracy and recommend the best color formulation. They planned to manufacture it for $200 to $300 per unit and sell it under the name ColorMatch.

From the perspective of individuals seeking the right hair color, the technology was a hit. ColorMatch promised to take the guesswork out of hair coloring and ensure the right match every time. The problem, however, was that Max and Bibi could not convince hair salons to buy ColorMatch devices. In time the reason became clear. In their hearts, hair-color professionals saw their jobs differently from their clients. Whereas clients hired the salon to help them achieve just the right cut and color, hair-color professionals showed up at the salon every day for a different reason. They wanted a vocation in which they could express themselves as artists; cosmetology seemed to offer that. Professional colorists took pride in mixing up the perfect custom formula for each of their clients. Although they cared that their clients felt happy with the outcome, they framed the issue differently. From their perspective, they hired hair products and color treatments that allowed them to fulfill their jobs as artists. Small wonder ColorMatch was never a commercial success, given this framing. Rather than help colorists do the jobs they felt called to do, ColorMatch did the opposite. It actually offended the artistic sensibility and implied that technology could replace the delicate craft of color formulation altogether.

The lesson from ColorMatch is that for an innovation that requires the adoption and use of multiple stakeholders to succeed, it must fulfill all of the jobs of all of the stakeholders or else it will not work for any of the stakeholders.[19] That's partly why schools are complicated environments for innovation. Trying to overlay the jobs of multiple stakeholders—from students and teachers to administrators, school boards, parents, and policymakers—is like trying to win on a six-layer chessboard. (And some would say that is a conservative estimate of the number of layers!) The good news, however, is that several opportunities to improve teachers' job satisfaction also benefit students. To spot the opportunities, we need to borrow a theory that American psychologist Frederick Herzberg developed to clarify the art of employee motivation.

Motivator-Hygiene Theory

Frederick Herzberg wrote one of the most popular *Harvard Business Review* articles ever: "One More Time, How Do You Motivate Employees?" The article, which has sold more than 1.2 million reprints since its publication in 1968, debunks the idea that job satisfaction is one big continuum, with very happy on one end and absolutely miserable on the other. The surprising finding is that employees can love and hate their jobs at the same time.[20]

This is possible because two sets of factors affect how people feel about their work. The first set, called *hygiene* factors, affects whether employees are dissatisfied with their jobs. The second set, called *motivators,* determine the extent to which employees outright love their jobs. It's important to note that in Herzberg's categorization scheme, the opposite of job dissatisfaction is not job satisfaction, but just the absence of dissatisfaction. Similarly, the opposite of loving your job is not hating it, but the absence of loving it.

Here are the motivators, in order of their impact on satisfaction (from highest to lowest):

- Achievement
- Recognition
- Work itself
- Responsibility
- Advancement
- Growth

And here are the hygiene factors, in order of their impact on job dissatisfaction (from highest to lowest impact):

- Company policy and administration
- Supervision
- Relationship with supervisor
- Work conditions
- Salary
- Relationship with peers
- Personal life
- Relationship with subordinates
- Status
- Security

So what does this mean? Allowing employees to find places to achieve, gain recognition, exercise responsibility, and have a career path has a greater tendency to motivate employees than do salary levels, corner offices, or vacation time. But conversely, these other factors can make people quite dissatisfied with their jobs. To put it another way, to make teachers perform better in their jobs, the schools should work on improving the motivators; financial incentives and the like will not do much.[21] But to keep teachers from leaving because of dissatisfaction, schools need to ensure adequate hygiene factors.

Integrating Teacher Motivators into Blended Designs

The traditional teaching job lacks many of the essential motivators. Teachers often work in isolation from other adults, which means there is little or no opportunity for recognition for their efforts. Just as in nursing, there is no real career track. Opportunities for increased responsibility and career advancement are slim. Aside from becoming the head of a department, the only other way for most teachers to move up in this line of work is, in fact, to stop teaching so they can be "promoted" into an administrative job.[22] And aside from occasional workshops or required training programs, teachers have limited opportunities for growth in the job after the first few years.[23]

But blended learning creates an opportunity to blow apart that construct; if the blended program is designed well, the role of teachers can amplify motivators in ways that are difficult in the traditional, analog classroom.[24] As you move forward with blended learning, here are five ways you can restructure the role of teachers to maximize their motivators:

Extending the reach of great teachers[25]

Digital technology opens up the possibility for great teachers to reach more students. Sal Khan is the most prominent example. His lessons reach roughly ten million people per month. Similarly, in South Korea, many teachers at Megastudy reach thousands of students a year and make millions. One teacher reaches 150,000 students online per year and earns $4 million a year.[26] Although Herzberg might say that the financial reward is a hygiene factor, because in this case money is aligned with—and therefore a proxy for—achievement and recognition, it shows that great teachers can achieve more and garner increased recognition and growth as a result of broader reach. Even in quieter ways, as schools construct blended-learning environments within the community, they can allow teachers to feel the sense of achievement, recognition, responsibility, and advancement that comes from posting a Flipped Classroom lecture for others to use, managing an online community of practice, serving as lead guide in a large Flex studio with far more students than in a typical class, or leading a professional development webinar about a topic of expertise.

Assigning individual teachers specialized responsibilities

The growing number of formal and informal learning options is causing an unbundling of the teacher role. Whereas in the factory model teachers are responsible for everything that happens in the classroom, in blended models students often experience multiple learning modalities originating from multiple sources. This creates opportunities for teachers to specialize, particularly in schools where teachers teach in teams (more on this shortly). Teachers can choose among options such as becoming:

- Content experts who focus on developing and posting curriculum
- Small-group leaders who provide direct instruction as part of a Station or Lab Rotation
- Project designers to supplement online learning with hands-on application
- Mentors who provide wisdom, social capital, and guidance
- Evaluators to whom other educators can give the responsibility of grading assignments and, in some cases, designing assessments
- Data experts

And the list goes on. According to Herzberg, specialization unlocks the motivators of responsibility, growth, and advancement. With the implementation of blended learning, even teachers who continue to be solely responsible for their students' progress begin to specialize in a way, as they are often no longer responsible for lesson planning and for delivering a lesson to an entire class of students; now they can specialize in working one-on-one with students and in small groups, mentorship, facilitating discussions and projects, and so forth.

Allowing teachers to teach in teams

As we've seen with Summit Public Schools, Teach to One, and more, many blended-learning programs are tearing down the walls between classrooms and creating learning studios with multiple teachers working in a variety of roles with many more students. Although many say that those who become teachers do so expressly to work in a solitary environment where they can close the classroom door and be the star, with all eyes on them during their lecture performance, we see something different.[27] Just as Herzberg's research suggests, many teachers savor the feeling of recognition for their achievements with students that comes from their fellow teachers. The existing teaching environment all too often isolates them from opportunities to experience those feelings on a frequent basis. Working in a team environment not only creates those opportunities but also unlocks a variety of opportunities for advancement, such as to create master teachers within a team and other roles, as discussed earlier.

Awarding teachers micro-credentials for the mastery of skills

The logic behind moving to a competency-based system with multiple pathways for students also makes sense for teachers.[28] An online platform could allow teachers to show what they know and share that through a badge or other micro-credential. Herzberg found that when workers are given new and more difficult tasks, they experience the motivators of growth and learning. Digital technology makes it possible to administer such a system at scale. Although the idea is still underdeveloped, many are working on creating just such a system, including Summit Public Schools, which is now using the Activate system that it helped develop for students for the ongoing professional development of its teachers.

Granting authority to blended-learning teams

The very process of designing and implementing blended learning that this book outlines can give teachers wide leeway to innovate. Herzberg found that when organizations remove some controls while retaining accountability, the motivators of responsibility and achievement skyrocket. The Digital Age is beckoning schools to innovate, and that fact in itself gives leaders the impetus to create broad growth opportunities for teachers.

DOING RIGHT FOR STUDENTS AND TEACHERS

At their July 2013 convention, delegates to the National Education Association, the largest labor union in the United States, approved a policy statement that supports digital learning.[29] We think they got it right with this decision, not only in terms of the opportunities that online and blended learning introduce for students to make progress every day and have fun with friends, but also in terms of benefitting teachers. From a teacher's point of view, the rise of blended learning means broad new opportunities to access intrinsic motivators related to professional achievement, recognition, responsibility, growth, and others.

Why not start now to give teachers an immediate career opportunity by recruiting them to join a blended-learning team, such as those that Chapter Four describes? Despite the complexity of trying to meet the needs of students and teachers simultaneously, blended learning presents several opportunities to innovate in ways that get the jobs done for both groups.

To Sum Up

- Teacher quality significantly impacts student outcomes. Students cannot afford a failed experiment with teacher integration. Getting the design right for teachers may be the single most important determinant of whether the rise of blended learning will net out as a win overall.
- Students in today's world stand to benefit from teachers shifting away from top-down, monolithic instruction and toward filling gaps that open in students' lives for trusted guides and mentors.
- According to the motivator-hygiene theory, teachers are likely to feel job dissatisfaction as a result of poor hygiene factors, such as upsetting school policies, annoying supervisors, or inadequate salary. At the same time, they are likely to feel job satisfaction as a result of motivators, such as the opportunity for achievement, recognition, and intrinsically rewarding work.
- If designed well, blended-learning programs can amplify motivators in ways that are impossible in the traditional, analog classroom.

NOTES

1. A Harvard study about the lifetime impact of high "value-added" teachers, measured by the increase in average test-score gains among students over the course of the year, found that students assigned to a high value-added teacher (top 5 percent) are more likely to go to college and earn higher incomes, and are less likely to have children as teenagers. On average, having such a high value-added teacher for one year raises a child's cumulative lifetime income by $80,000. The study used school district and tax records for more than one million children. It found that "on average, a one standard deviation improvement in teacher value-added in a single grade raises earnings by 1.3 percent at age 28. Replacing those teachers whose value-added is in the bottom 5 percent with an average teacher would

increase the present value of students' lifetime income by approximately $250,000 per classroom." Raj Chetty, John N. Friedman, and Jonah E. Rockoff, "The Long-Term Impacts of Teachers: Teacher Value-Added and Student Outcomes in Adulthood," National Bureau of Economic Research, September 2013, http://obs.rc.fas.harvard.edu/chetty/w19424.pdf.

In addition, The MetLife Survey of the American Teacher has long pointed to the impact of teachers as well. See for example, "The MetLife Survey of the American Teacher: Teachers, Parents and the Economy," MetLife, Inc., March 2012.

2.   The author is Thomas Arnett, a research fellow for the Christensen Institute's education practice.

3.   Paul Tough, *How Children Succeed: Grit, Curiosity, and the Hidden Power of Character* (New York: Houghton Mifflin Harcourt Publishing Company, 2012), p. 161.

4.   Heather Staker wishes to thank her mother, Kathy Clayton, for introducing her to this insight about the military via her book *Teaching to Build Faith and Faithfulness: Ten Principles for Teachers and Parents* (Salt Lake City, Utah: Deseret Book, 2012), p. 112.

5.   Thomas Friedman and Michael Mandelbaum, *That Used to Be Us: How America Fell Behind in the World It Invented and How We Can Come Back* (New York: Farrrar, Straus, and Giroux, 2001), p. 91.

6.   Gregory Ferenstein, "Thomas Friedman to United States: Innovate or Else," *Fast Company*, September 6, 2011, http://www.fastcompany.com/1778214/thomas-friedman-united-states-innovate-or-else (accessed March 7, 2014).

7.   Friedman and Mandelbaum, *That Used to Be Us*, p. 92.

8.   "The number of jobs involving more complex interactions among skilled and educated workers who make decisions is growing at a phenomenal rate. Salaries reflect the value that companies place on these jobs, which pay 55 and 75 percent more, respectively, than those of employees who undertake routine transactions and transformations." Johnson, Manyika, and Yee, p. 26 (introduction, n. 17).

9.   Paul Tough, *How Children Succeed*, pp. 2, 43–45.

10. Ibid., pp. 22, 45.

11. Ibid., pp. 45–46.

12. Ibid., pp. 47, 153.

13. "America's Children: Key National Indicators of Well-Being, 2013," ChildStats.gov, http://www.childstats.gov/americaschildren/famsoc1.asp (accessed March 8, 2014).

14. Paul R. Amato, "The Impact of Family Formation Change on the Cognitive, Social, and Emotional Well-Being of the Next Generation," *Future of Children*, Vol. 15, No. 2, Fall 2005, p. 77, http://futureofchildren.org/futureof children/publications/docs/15_02_05.pdf

15. According to "The MetLife Survey of the American Teacher," "A majority (64%) of teachers reports that in the last year, the number of students and families needing health and social support services has increased, while 35% of teachers also report that the number of students coming to school hungry has increased. At the same time, many teachers have seen reductions or eliminations of health or social services (28% overall, including 34% of high school teachers) and after-school programs (29% overall, including 32% of high school teachers)." "The MetLife Survey of the American Teacher," March 2012, p. 8.

16. Paul Tough, *How Children Succeed*, pp. 42–43.

17. The other dimensions are Assessment, Content, Curriculum, Instruction, Knowing Learners and Learning (special education, English Language Learners, etc.), and Leadership. The Summit continuum places teachers on one of four levels: basic, proficient, highly proficient, and expert. Each of the four steps typically takes two years to master. Tom Vander Ark, "How Frames, Plans, Platforms & PD Support Great Teaching," Getting Smart, August 24, 2013, http://gettingsmart.com/2013/08/how-frames-plans-platforms-pd-support-great-teaching/ (accessed March 8, 2014).

18. This story first appeared in this case study: Clayton M. Christensen and Matthew Beecher, "The ColorMatch Hair Color System," Harvard Business School, N9–607–030, January 29, 2007.

19. The authors of *Disrupting Class* elaborate on this idea as follows:

> Many companies have offered products or services that they could see would improve student learning—if only teachers would just use them correctly! Many an education technology company has struggled with this—and few have lived to tell about the struggles. Wireless Generation had such a product with its mobile educational assessment solutions, but unlike most education technology companies, its product became a success. What was the difference? Just as in the story about digital photos, most education technology companies are not offering a product that helps a teacher do more efficiently what they are already trying to do and prioritizing, and instead have the result of layering "just one more thing" on top of a teacher's already busy work day.
>
> By contrast, Wireless Generation's handheld device … helps its target teachers do more easily something that they were already doing—and it allows them to do it with greater ease so it improves and simplifies their lives rather than further complicates them. [p. 180]

20. These next sections draw heavily from the referenced article: Frederick Herzberg, "One More Time: How Do You Motivate Employees?" *Harvard Business Review*, 1968, http://www.facilitif.eu/user_files/file/herzburg_article.pdf

21. For further evidence on the inability of financial incentives to motivate most teachers, given today's disagreements on the goal of schooling and what actions will lead to what results for students, see the analysis in *Disrupting Class* derived from the Tools of Cooperation theory. Clayton M. Christensen, Michael B. Horn, and Curtis W. Johnson, *Disrupting Class: How Disruptive Innovation Will Change the Way the World Learns, Expanded Edition* (New York: McGraw-Hill, 2010), p. 234.

22. "The MetLife Survey of the American Teacher: Challenges for School Leadership," MetLife, Inc., February 2013.

Traditionally, career progress for leadership in education has meant that effective teachers leave the classroom for school-based or district-level roles developing teaching and learning, or to become principals. Some teachers are committed to classroom teaching but also aspire to grow and contribute professionally in ways that the classroom alone cannot provide. Innovative teachers are defining "hybrid teaching roles" that keep them part-time in the classroom combined with other roles of service and leadership in education—"teacherpreneurs" in the phrase coined by one group of teacher leaders, in their vision of the future of their profession. These opportunities are envisioned as new pathways for leadership and as ways to strengthen the profession, job satisfaction, and retention of effective teachers. [p. 41]

23. According to "The MetLife Survey of the American Teacher," teacher satisfaction is at its lowest level in twenty-five years. Less-satisfied teachers are more likely to report being in schools where budgets, opportunities for professional development, and time for collaboration all declined. "The MetLife Survey of the American Teacher," February 2013, p. 6.

   In the survey the prior year, teachers with lower job satisfaction were more likely to report that their job was not secure, that they were not treated as a professional by the community, that they had seen average class size increase, and that the number of students coming from difficult backgrounds or needing help—for example, the students lacked health, social services, and food or were being bullied—had increased. "The MetLife Survey of the American Teacher," March 2012, p. 7.

   Unfortunately, the MetLife Survey reports its results based only on a satisfaction versus dissatisfaction continuum and does not appear to use Herzberg's findings to assess teachers' love of their job on one continuum and their job dissatisfaction on a separate continuum.

24. For a more thorough discussion of the benefits blended learning can bring to the teaching profession, we recommend John Bailey, Bryan Hassel, Emily Ayscue Hassel, Carri Schneider, and Tom Vander Ark, "Improving Conditions & Careers: How Blended Learning Can Improve the Teaching Profession," Digital Learning Now! Smart Series, May 2013.

In addition, the paper also makes the case that blended learning will allow for an improvement not only in career opportunities but also in pay for teachers. There is some evidence that this could be true from schools such as Rocketship Education, which pays teachers' salaries 10 to 30 percent above the local salary schedule. Whether this hygiene factor is realized at scale will depend on how schools shape their blended-learning environments in the years ahead as well as on a slew of policy, regulatory, and bargaining agreement decisions.

25. See the work of Public Impact's "Opportunity Culture," which is an effort to extend the reach of excellent teachers and their teams. "Opportunity Culture," Public Impact, http://opportunityculture.org/ (accessed June 1, 2014).

26. Amanda Ripley, "The $4 Million Teacher," *Wall Street Journal*, August 3, 2013, http://online.wsj.com/news/articles/SB100014241278873246359045786839780253571520.

27. In *Disrupting Class*, we also remind people that in the shift from the one-room schoolhouse to the classroom-based factory-model of schooling, "A profession whose work primarily was in tutoring students one on one was hijacked into one where some of the teacher's most important skills became keeping order and commanding attention" (p. 111).

28. For more on this important topic, we recommend Karen Cator, Carri Schneider, and Tom Vander Ark, "Preparing Teachers For Deeper Learning: Competency-Based Teacher Preparation and Development," Digital Promise and Getting Smart, April 2014.

29. See "NEA Policy Statement on Digital Learning," http://www.nea.org/home/55434.htm (accessed March 8, 2014).

Chapter 7

Design the Virtual and Physical Setup

Some readers may be surprised that we waited until Chapter Seven to talk about technology and devices in a book about blended learning. But placing this topic this late in the book was purposeful. The problems, goals, teams, and student and teacher experiences are much more important to tackle first. Too often schools lead with the technology rather than with these considerations. With that foundation in place, we now turn to the technology questions.

In 1981 the Osborne Executive came to market and became the first commercially successful portable computer. It was roughly the size of a sewing machine and was advertised as the only computer that would fit underneath an airline seat. It was revolutionary. Fast forward to today, though, and the comparison between the Osborne Executive and the Apple iPhone is laughable. The Executive weighed roughly one hundred times as much, had nearly five hundred times as much volume, and was ten times more expensive in today's dollars and somewhere on the order of one-hundredth as fast as the iPhone—with a lot less functionality.[1]

The rate of technological change in the past several decades has been breathtaking. This presents a challenge when discussing how to integrate specific software, devices, Wi-Fi, and furniture to support a successful student experience. Attempting to provide the latest is an exercise in futility, as the chosen equipment will soon be outdated, often before it is even installed.

The discussion is important, however, because successful blended learning depends on making the right bets on integrating technology into schools. Given this paradox, our goal with this chapter is to zoom out and introduce a set of concepts that clarify how and why technology is changing and then zoom in and invite you to draw your own conclusions about the implications for any given moment in which you find yourself. The engineering concepts of *interdependence* and *modularity* are the centerpiece for this chapter because they point to answers for a range of questions about technology and infrastructure, including these:

- For software, should we buy online content from one provider per subject, or do we need to offer students options from multiple providers, or should our teachers develop online content themselves? What are the tradeoffs among these different approaches?

- For devices, what are the key considerations and options?

- For building design, if we have the opportunity to break ground on a new campus, should we stick with the traditional school architecture or build something different?

- In general, where are technology and infrastructure in schools headed, and what are the implications for today?

Let's step back to consider these questions from a conceptual perspective, with the hope that that lens will sharpen the focus as you look at the best options for your circumstances.

PRODUCT ARCHITECTURE AND INTERFACES

In the engineering world, a product's *architecture* refers to all of its constituent components and subsystems and how they fit together.[2] For example, the architecture of a table lamp includes such components as an electrical cord, the body of the lamp, a socket for the light bulb, and the lampshade on the top. The point where two components of a product fit together is called an *interface*. For a table lamp, the point where the light bulb twists into the socket is an example of an interface.

Interdependent Architecture

When a product is first developed, the interfaces between the parts are messy, in the sense that they are *interdependent*. The design and fabrication of part A affects the way that parts B and C must be designed and built, and vice versa. They also tend to be unpredictable. How parts A, B, and C affect each other is not always certain. The company making the product usually needs to control every aspect of design and production or else risk encountering manufacturing surprises and performance issues. New high-tech military aircraft like Lockheed Martin's F-22 fighter jet are an example of this type of product. The F-22 required the best engineers in the world working together in concert to manage the unknowns that arose inevitably in the process of creating a new high-performance machine. The final product is the best-performing fighter jet in the world. But maintenance is a bear. If an F-22 breaks down, don't count on a local aviation mechanic to fabricate new parts any time soon. The instruction handbook simply does not exist yet to allow for anyone other than Lockheed Martin to make and assemble components easily.

Lockheed Martin has to control the design and manufacture of every critical component of the system to ensure that all the pieces fit properly together. Integrating like this allows companies to optimize the functionality and reliability of the product. Because they control each step of the process, they can squeeze as much performance out of the new product as possible. The drawback, however, is that customization in an interdependent architecture is prohibitively expensive. There is as yet no instruction handbook with clear standards and specifications to allow a variety of vendors to make compatible parts.[3]

Modular Architecture

Over time, the interfaces among components of a product become cleaner and generally understood. Anyone who wants to make a light bulb can easily find specifications for the size and shape that a light bulb must be to fit into a lamp socket. The product now has a *modular* rather than an interdependent architecture. The components in a modular architecture fit together in such well-understood and well-defined ways that it does not matter who makes each component, as long as it meets the predetermined standards or specifications. Modular components are plug-compatible, which makes it easy to swap different modules in and out to configure a customized result. Printers, cameras, and

Table 7.1 Key Differences between Interdependence and Modularity

Interdependent architecture	Modular architecture
• Optimizes functionality and reliability	• Optimizes flexibility and customization
• Requires companies to integrate	• Allows companies to outsource
• Industry standards and specifications are not possible	• Industry standards and specifications are crucial
• Synonymous with proprietary architecture	• Synonymous with open architecture

thumb drives that plug into any device with a USB port; electric appliances that plug into any wall socket; even shoe stores that offer a range of colors, brands, and styles for any particular shoe size—all are examples of modularity.

Industries become modular when an interdependent product's functionality and reliability improve enough to overshoot customers' requirements. This forces manufacturers to compete differently. Customers stop looking for better raw performance and start asking for products that are flexible and easy to customize to tailor to their individual needs.

Table 7.1 summarizes the essential differences between interdependent and modular architectures.[4]

THE SHIFT IN PERSONAL COMPUTER ARCHITECTURE

In the early 1980s Apple Computer sold the best personal computers in the business. It did this by integrating to develop and build every part of the machines from top to bottom—including product design, assembly, the operating system, and the application software. From this so-called "vertically integrated" position, Apple developed a proprietary, highly interdependent architecture that crushed its more modular competitors in terms of performance.[5] Apple machines shot quickly to the top as the easiest-to-use, least-likely-to-crash desktops around. The far left side of Figure 7.1 depicts the dimensions across which Apple vertically integrated to control all the components and interfaces within its sophisticated, high-performing machine.

But then in the mid-1980s the market shifted. Desktop computers became good enough in terms of basic functionality and reliability, and customers started

Figure 7.1 The Shift from Integration to Modularity in the Personal Computer Industry

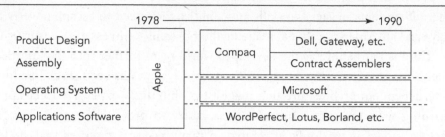

to demand something else: the flexibility to install non-Apple software, such as WordPerfect and Lotus. These products were plug-compatible with Microsoft's DOS operating system, thanks to a well-defined interface, and customers took notice. As customers became less willing to pay for further improvements in performance and reliability, the companies that offered modular solutions (such as those on the far right side of Figure 7.1) gained the advantage. At this point Apple could have decided to modularize its design and sell its operating system for other computer assemblers to use to thwart the rise of Microsoft's Windows. But Apple did not, and Microsoft, Dell, and other suppliers took the lead.

Clayton Christensen says that the phenomenon in Figure 7.1 "looks like the industry got pushed through a bologna slicer."[6] When functionality and reliability become more than adequate, the industry shifts from left to right, and a population of specialized companies whose rules of interaction are defined by a modular architecture and industry standards comes out in front on the other end.

Industries tend to swing like a pendulum between interdependent and modular architectures. In the 1990s, the pendulum swung back toward favoring some interdependence. Customers began demanding the ability to transfer graphics and spreadsheet tables between different types of files. This created a performance gap, which swung the industry back to an appetite for interdependent architecture. Microsoft responded by integrating its software suite (and later its web browser) into the Windows operating system. This quickly put nonintegrated companies, such as WordPerfect and Lotus, out of business. As we'll see, Apple's and Microsoft's interdependent architectures have implications for school technology decisions today.[7]

THE SHIFT TOWARD MODULARITY IN EDUCATION

In recent decades, society has called on schools to do a better job of ensuring that *all* students master the skills and abilities they need to escape poverty and have an "all-American shot at realizing their dreams"—in essence, ensuring that no child is left behind as the developed world races further into the knowledge economy. Until recently, however, the school system has been stuck in a highly interdependent architecture that makes it prohibitively expensive to customize learning with the surgical precision necessary to prevent any stragglers. The factory model is vertically integrated in many ways: it requires that students complete one grade in its entirety before moving on to the next grade; they must progress through subjects in linear order, so as not to interfere with teachers' scope and sequencing; and their attendance and participation must comply with a complex web of local, state, and federal regulations, which, although designed to ensure reliability and performance, result in the exclusion of flexibility and customization.[8]

Demand among parents, students, and society at large, however, is starting to shift. Recall that in the mid-1980s, customers began wanting the ability to choose among software providers, such as WordPerfect and Lotus, rather than rely on Apple software as their single option. A similar thing is beginning to occur in K–12 education. Right around the time schools began serving two to three meals a day, providing dental care and child care, and expanding to offer more pre-K and extended-day seat time, the system hit a tipping point where it overshot some students' and parents' needs in terms of functionality. Not all students are overserved, of course. Those with the most complicated needs and highest functionality requirements—often students in low-income communities—need even more programs that are vertically integrated and comprehensive. But a tier of students is emerging for whom the fully integrated, interdependent model is more than adequate in terms of offering comprehensive functionality, and now the greater need is for choice, flexibility, and the opportunity to customize.

The school system is responding in part by beginning to offer better modular interfaces between courses so that students can choose from a variety of course providers. Roughly 58 percent of high schools in California had students taking A La Carte online courses in the 2013–14 school year, up from roughly 48 percent in 2012–13.[9] From Minnesota to Florida and from Wisconsin to Utah, state-level "Course Access" programs that provide students with expanded course offerings from diverse, accountable providers are gaining popularity.[10] This rising interest in facilitating modular courses points to a growing demand among many communities for customized course selection instead of for further functionality along the lines of the factory model.[11]

The shift to a Course Access mindset is only one way that the system is transitioning from an interdependent to a modular architecture. Similar evolutions are under way in at least three other aspects of schooling:

- Course content itself is becoming modular.
- Computing devices in schools are taking on modular architectures.
- Physical facilities are morphing into a more modular design.

The shift from integration to modularity takes place on a continuum—it's not a matter of purely one or the other. Furthermore, there's no one right place to be on the continuum: interdependent architectures have their advantages and disadvantages, but so do those that are modular. For these reasons, blended-learning teams have to reach their own conclusions about the tradeoffs they are willing to make and how modular they want their course content, devices, and facility arrangements to be, given their circumstances. Breaking down the alternatives allows us to gain a clearer picture of the range of options for setting up the virtual and physical environment.

INTEGRATED VERSUS MODULAR ONLINE CONTENT

Developing a strategy to find the right online content for a blended program is not easy. Schools are scattered across the integration/modularity continuum in this regard. On one end of the continuum, many believe that they need the performance that integration offers; in response, they build their own online content or at the least license fully integrated solutions from a single provider. On the other end, seeing that no one offering can well serve each student's distinct needs, some schools are developing an appetite for the customization that a modular approach offers; this motivates them to look for a multi-provider option. Figure 7.2 depicts this continuum and four common strategies for securing online content.

Moving from left to right on this continuum, let's consider the four strategies in turn.

Figure 7.2 The Integration/Modularity Continuum for Online Content

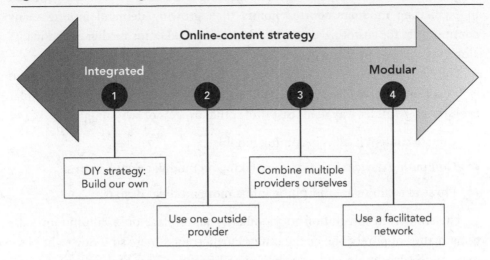

Strategy #1: DIY—Build Our Own

One of the first questions most blended leaders consider is whether to build or buy. Should schools build their own online courses and content or use off-the-shelf content that a third party has developed? This question arises regardless of the amount of content schools need—whether full courses with online teachers of record for A La Carte programs, full courses for Flex programs, or supplemental digital content to plug into one of the stations in a Rotation model. Regardless of model, leaders must grapple with the alternatives of DIY (do it yourself) or outsourcing.

Many blended programs survey the range of possibilities for third-party content and decide to build their own. The reasons we hear are usually something like "The only affordable third-party content is not rigorous enough" or "Vendor content doesn't align to our high standards and tests." In short, the school leaders and teachers believe the functionality and performance of the outside content is not good enough—or if it is, it's too expensive.[12] As a result, they must vertically integrate to develop the content themselves. Quakertown made this choice when it decided to build the Infinity Cyber Academy using courses its own teachers developed. Flipped Classroom teachers make this choice each time they decide to record their own mini lesson to post online rather than search the Internet for something readymade.

The main advantages of the DIY strategy are the opportunities to control quality, design the content according to local standards and testing requirements, avoid the high dollar cost of premium third-party alternatives, and preserve the traditional role of face-to-face teachers as the source of content and instruction. In addition, some educators enjoy developing the skill set of building an online course, lesson, video, or software program, and they seek out that opportunity rather than wanting to delegate it.[13]

The main reason other programs decide against the DIY strategy is that they realize that developing content in-house is not as low cost as they at first thought and that they do not have the time or money to develop the in-house expertise required to produce content that is high quality. Without ready access to capital markets, schools, districts, and nonprofits of any stripe struggle to scrape together enough resources to develop online content that is much richer than digital textbooks or online lectures.[14] They see the growing libraries of third-party courses and modules and decide to leave the software development to software developers, rather than try to build that competency themselves.[15]

Strategy #2: Use One Outside Provider

When we surveyed forty blended-learning programs in 2011—just as blended learning was becoming part of the national conversation—we found that 60 percent were following strategy #2 on the continuum: Use one outside provider per course or subject. They were not integrated to the point of developing content themselves, nor were they modular to the point of trying to piece together segments of content from a variety of providers. They were in between on the continuum. In some cases the programs were using a full-course provider (such as K12, Inc., Apex Learning, or Florida Virtual School). In other cases they took a slightly more modular approach and complemented their face-to-face classes with a supplemental provider (such as DreamBox Learning, ST Math, or Scholastic). But in both cases they relied on only a single outside provider for the online content for any given course or subject, rather than try to mix and match modules from a variety of sources to create a patchwork solution.[16] As of the writing of this book, many blended programs continue to rely on one provider. Carpe Diem uses Edgenuity, Flex Public Schools use K12, Inc., and Wichita Public Schools uses Apex Learning; others use Compass Learning, Rosetta Stone, or Pearson.

Although using a single online provider doesn't give these schools the customization they may prefer within a course, its simplicity and reliability are worth the tradeoff. These operators never worry about having to coordinate data across multiple online providers—even as those who chose a supplemental provider must work with independent data from both their offline and online instruction. Furthermore, the software providers point out that at least their content is more customizable than an old-school textbook. The best courses build multiple pathways right into the software to adjust for a student's progress. Large online providers are better able to stomach the fixed costs required to develop these sophisticated courses, and as a result, some are becoming remarkably adaptive, engaging, and aligned to the latest cognitive-science research.

Integrated software has its drawbacks. One is that the technology tends to be expensive if it's any good, particularly if it is going to offer customization. Customization has a price tag. A software representative from a highly regarded provider that offers built-in customization for students told us that it generally takes nine months and contributions from over thirty employees to develop a year-long online course, "soup to nuts." Another provider, Florida Virtual School, has said in the past that it costs roughly $300,000 to develop a course.[17] Providers who stand any chance of covering their costs have to compete against each other for big contracts from large school districts. That forces them to design directly to the lowest common denominator across the factory system; otherwise districts—which are beholden to state and federal accountability—simply cannot adopt their products. It also forces them to confine the software within the traditionally defined subject disciplines. The bottom line is that fixed costs force online content providers to play into and preserve the rigidities of the education system's interdependent architecture that online learning is purported to overcome.

Strategy #3: Combine Multiple Providers

Some schools decide that they do not want to develop their own content, but they need a more flexible solution than relying on a single provider for an entire course or subject. They want modularity within the course to allow for a variety of pathways for each student. As early as 2011, when we surveyed the forty blended-learning programs, a few organizations—Alliance College Ready Public Schools, KIPP Empower, Rocketship, and what was then called School of One—had decided they needed modular course content and were striving to patch together a variety of mostly proprietary programs into a unified platform, ideally one in which students had to sign on only once to access all the providers ("single sign on") and teachers could monitor progress across the variety of providers on a single dashboard. The intention behind this strategy was to maximize customization for each student. Depending on what worked best, a student could learn to calculate area by using the animated sheep game in DreamBox Learning, then switch to ST Math to tackle fractions with Gigi the Penguin,[18] and then, tired of animated characters, resort to ALEKS for straight-up long division.

Some of the complaints we hear from schools that take this approach are:

"The technology is five years behind where it needs to be."

"The software content providers are proprietary. It's impossible to get the data out of them. And when we do, the data don't connect easily to the standards and the data from other providers."

"Where are the algorithms that create the individualized student playlists for us? This is too much work."

Judging from the content of their complaints, these educators appear to be pushing the industry toward modularity rather than waiting for it to shift on its own; therefore they are dealing with the corresponding headaches of a still-immature technology. Many persist, however, because they sense that a more modular world for online content will multiply the power of schools to realize the full promise of personalized learning for their students.

Strategy #4: Use a Facilitated Network

A new wave of disruptive innovation is emerging, with the potential to swing the industry toward the far right end of the integration/modularity continuum. Software platforms are emerging that facilitate the development, sharing, and curating of user-generated content in modular bites. A prime example of this is the Khan Academy platform, which hosts over one hundred thousand exercise problems and a growing library of thousands of microlectures via video tutorials stored on YouTube.[19] The fascinating thing about this platform is that it did not start out as a product to serve schools and districts. It began in 2004 when its founder, Sal Khan, started tutoring his cousin Nadia in mathematics using

Yahoo's Doodle notepad. Wanting an easier way to distribute the tutorials to other friends and relatives, Khan began posting the tutorials on YouTube. In time, millions of people tuned in to watch. Khan responded by developing a full platform that facilitates not only micro lectures but also pre-tests, practice exercises, and a "Knowledge Map" to track progress. The platform is open and nonproprietary; it has an open API, which means that other software can easily interface and be compatible with it. In other words, Khan does not make or even curate all the content on the platform. Volunteers are building on it by adding new topics—such as biology, art history, and computer science—and by translating it into other languages.[20]

Like Khan Academy, this new wave of disruption looks more like tutorial tools than integrated courseware. Rather than being pushed into classrooms through a centralized procurement process, tools like Khan Academy are being *pulled* into use through self-diagnosis—by teachers, parents, and students. Other so-called "facilitated networks" like this are emerging that allow parents, teachers, and students to offer microinstruction to other parents, teachers, and students.

The arrival of facilitated networks brings two main benefits. The first is hypercustomization. One day, modular platforms will amass hundreds of millions of micro tutorials, on-demand assessments, and other learning objects that users will be able to browse and select to assemble customized courses based on the needs of each learner. Western Governors University (WGU) already does this in part at the higher education level. Students log in to the WGU platform, which runs on Salesforce software, to access a massive library of learning resources, meticulously curated and organized by degree plan and learning objective. From this library they choose whichever items appeal to them—as few or as many as they need. Then, when they're ready, they complete an assignment or assessment to prove mastery of the objective, and they move on.

The second benefit of facilitated networks is affordability. In contrast to proprietary, integrated software, content that's available through facilitated networks is, on average, much less expensive to make and often free to use. Think Yahoo's Doodle notepad: tools like that allow users to create simple modules, and over time, the tools improve to facilitate the production of increasingly more sophisticated content. The availability of these tools knocks down barriers to entry, and that floods the market with a supply of content. This drives down costs, and voilà!—modular content becomes plentiful, sophisticated, and extremely inexpensive.

Together, the benefits of flexibility and affordability look like they are pushing the traditional, integrated instructional model through a bologna slicer. Figure 7.3 illustrates how this is playing out for a hypothetical sixth grade English/Language Arts course; a similar pattern is under way for other disciplines.

The most likely scenario is that over time, the emergence of facilitated networks—like Khan Academy—on which lots of users write content that uses the standards of the platform, as opposed to forcing a retrofitting between proprietary software programs like DreamBox Learning and ST Math, will solve the modularity problem for blended programs. Already, as of this writing, several platforms are emerging that allow—or soon will allow—users to write and add content, including Agilix's Buzz, Activate Instruction, Knewton, and Declara.[21] The specifications that make the interfaces between content providers work will emerge in de facto fashion, as blended programs vote with their feet—or clicks—and settle on a few of the best of third-party platforms such as these.[22]

Figure 7.3 The Shift from Integration to Modularity in a Hypothetical Sixth Grade English/Language Arts Course

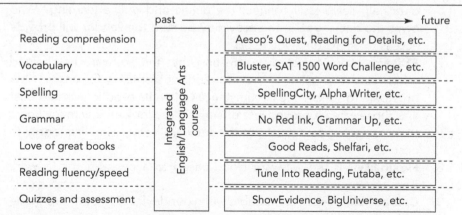

Note: This figure is for illustrative purposes only and is not comprehensive.

Twelve Other Considerations When Choosing Software[23]

Apart from the question of whether to build, buy, or look for a combined solution for software, a number of other issues are worth considering:

1. **Existing inventory**—What do you already have? Schools and districts often already have subscriptions to software and web-based services that are sitting unused.

2. **Full-time or supplemental**—How many hours of content do you need—enough for the entire course or only a few hours to supplement other sources of instruction?

3. **Price**—What can you afford? Often there is a tradeoff between flat, sequential content that is free or nearly free versus adaptive, engaging content that provides premium services.

4. **Student experience**—Can students see where they are, what they have accomplished, and what they need to do next? Can they see their metrics and get real-time feedback? Can they choose among different pathways? Is it engaging and intrinsically motivating for the entire time?

5. **Adaptability or assignability**—Do you want software that slows down, speeds up, and optimizes the path based on the performance of each student? Or do you need software that puts teachers in control to select which modules to assign? Or something that allows for a little of both?

6. **Data**—Does the software provide actionable data for teachers? Do data help seamlessly connect the online and offline learning? Who owns the data—you or the provider? Be sure the vendor will provide access to all the data you need.

7. **Efficacy**—Look for studies attesting that the software has helped other students achieve the learning outcomes you desire. Ask providers to specify the circumstances when its product worked best and those when it proved less effective. Also look at how many hours the average student must use the software before significant growth occurs.

8. **Flexibility**—Is the software cloud-based to allow students to work from anywhere?

9. **Compatibility**—Is it compatible with your devices? Is it interoperable with other software you plan to use, such as the learning management system?

10. **Alignment**—Is it aligned to Common Core or other applicable standards?
11. **Provisioning**—How easy is it for you to provision new users with usernames and passwords by connecting directly from your student information system to the software?
12. **Single sign on**—Can students enter their username and password one time and be logged in to all their software, or do they have to learn multiple sign-on processes?

In sum, understand your model and make sure to match the software to the design. You may want to revisit these questions after making the final choices about your blended model, which we walk you through in Chapter Eight.

Also, the Blended Learning Universe (BLU) provides searchable information about the software that the organizations in its collection are using. Appendix 7.1 provides a snapshot of the online content that these organizations use according to data in the BLU as of May 2014.

INTEGRATED VERSUS MODULAR OPERATING SYSTEMS

The selection of instructional content benefits from weighing integration versus modularity, but what about devices? This is a new way of thinking about the device question. Most commonly, device selection at schools begins with a debate about the right form factor—with desktops, laptops, netbooks, and tablets as the top four contenders. Schools usually opt for laptops and netbooks, although beginning in late 2012, sales of Apple's iPads tablets dominated the K–12 market.[24] School leaders who select laptops and netbooks say that although tablets are great for consuming content, they are lousy for creating it. Tablet purchasers, on the other hand, claim that despite the limited functionality of a tablet, its portability and touchscreen interface make it a compelling tool, especially for very young children—and it's not hard to add a physical keyboard.

The question of form factor is important, but in the end the modularity issue may trump the debate. Until recently, schools have mostly purchased either Apple devices, which use Apple's OS X operating system, or so-called PCs that run the Windows operating system. Both of these operating systems are proprietary and integrated, although Apple's is more so. Apple devices feature an interdependent interface not only between OS X and certain Apple software, but also between the devices themselves and the operating system.[25] Hackers have made progress in figuring out how to run OS X on non-Apple devices, but not without a struggle. Simply put, Apple software is designed only for Apple hardware.

For many, this proprietary architecture is the essence of Apple's allure. Apple engineers have the luxury of pushing the technological frontiers of what's possible as they design their machines, without having to kowtow to externally imposed industry standards. OS X is widely regarded for its reliable functionality—no crashes, no intrusion of annoying pop-up dialogue boxes, very few viruses.

Other schools opt for Windows-based devices. Windows is more modular than OS X, in that it uses a modular interface to allow for plug-compatibility with third-party hardware. Dell, HP, Lenovo, Asus—multiple device manufacturers use the Windows operating system. Although Windows is modular at the hardware interface, the story is different for the interface between Windows and software. Microsoft designs Windows to integrate seamlessly with its own software—the Microsoft Office suite and the Explorer browser. It's less open about making the software interface easy for others to use, so companies that want to compete against Microsoft with office productivity and browser software struggle to develop tools that run on Windows as dependably as the Microsoft products do.

For decades, scarcely anyone noticed or cared that Windows has an interdependent architecture at the software level. But this is changing. Computing is becoming more internet-centric; the work people want to get done on computers involves connecting with apps and content that live "in the cloud," meaning on a network of remote servers that the Internet hosts, rather than on a personal computer's hard drive. So if most of the software people want is cloud-based and online, why pay Microsoft or Apple for proprietary, integrated software that's tied in with their operating systems? The shift toward internet-centric computing is creating demand for dis-integration between operating systems and software.

Enter a third option that is starting to take schools by storm. Google first announced the sale of Chromebooks—personal computers running the Chrome operating system—in June 2011. By 2013, Chromebooks had come out of nowhere to grab a fifth of U.S. K–12 purchases of mobile computers.[26] The Chrome operating system is a Linux-based system designed by Google to work primarily with web applications. It's built on the open-source project called Chromium OS, which enlists volunteer developers around the world to test, debug, and improve on the operating system's source code. This helps Chromebooks get better over time, without the massive fixed costs that Microsoft and Apple incur when they try to improve Windows and OS X, respectively. In addition, Chromebooks do not have installed software on their local hard drives, except for the browser, a media player, and a file manager. Don't expect to see word processing or spreadsheet software stored on the device. Instead, Chromebooks rely exclusively on the Internet to connect users to the web apps they need to get their work done, whether that's sending email, creating documents, or taking an online course.

The upsides of these architecture choices are manifold: for one, Chromebooks are inexpensive. They sell for under $300 per unit. Their limited functionality means that they boot up lightning-fast—ten seconds max. Relative to Windows-based devices, they are much less likely to get a virus because Linux is set up to ensure a virus-free environment. They are also easy to keep up to date; Google pushes auto updates to the Chrome OS, without requiring any work on the user end.

The question of interdependence versus modularity suggests that devices like Chromebooks will give closed-architecture devices tough competition in the years ahead. Internet-centric computing, focused on web apps and cloud storage, will force a gradual evolution in product architecture—away from interdependent, proprietary architectures that had the advantage in the not-good-enough era toward modular designs in an era of performance surplus.[26] That's not to say that Chromebooks are right for everyone. They require wireless[27] connectivity—the rough estimate is at least 100 Mbps of broadband for every thousand students.[28] They also only support software that is web-compatible, so they are not a good fit for students who want to use downloaded software. The expectation, however, is that in time an increasing number of blended programs will gravitate toward the type of open architecture that Chromebooks introduce.

INTEGRATED VERSUS MODULAR PHYSICAL SPACE

The energy that is dis-integrating and modularizing the virtual environment is flowing outward to affect the physical environment as well. In an aesthetic sense, one could argue that the traditional architecture of factory-type schools has coalesced around a proprietary design that—although reliable and orderly—has little to offer in terms of openness or flexibility. Linda Darling-Hammond of Stanford University characterizes the traditional architecture as follows:

> The office is the first thing one sees, the quietest and best-outfitted part of the school, a forbidding place with its long high counter separating the office staff from others who enter. The next sight is a glass-enclosed trophy case and a bulletin board of announcements about meetings, sports events, and rules to be followed. Long clear corridors of egg-crate classrooms are broken by banks of lockers and an occasional tidy bulletin board. Classrooms look alike, teachers' desks at the front of each room commanding rows of smaller desks for students.[29]

Victoria Bergsagel, the founder and director of Architects of Achievement, made this comment about traditional buildings: "If Rip Van Winkle were to wake up today, he'd probably still recognize our schools. We went from the Industrial Age to the Information Age, and we're kind of going into the Innovation Age, but if you look at our schools, they still look like the factory model with cells and bells, especially in the upper grades."[30]

For many, particularly those who are seeking to bring sustaining improvements to the traditional model through Station Rotations, Lab Rotations, and Flipped Classrooms, the basic layout of egg-crate classrooms may be perfectly adequate. Many blended programs, however, are choosing to rearrange their furniture and physical space to align with the principles of student agency, flexibility, and choice that are at the core of their new models. Table 7.2 summarizes some of the ways that schools—some that are blended and others that are not—are rethinking physical space.

Of course, money is the main barrier that prevents schools from making changes to align their physical space to the principles and goals of their blended initiatives. Often the best you can do is hack your current space with simple workarounds and then wait until funding becomes available for larger changes. The real example of a missed opportunity, however, is when leaders get the chance to build a new building or renovate an old, and they choose to perpetuate the integrated factory-type blueprint. Who wants to be the school district that builds the last twentieth-century building?

Table 7.2 Examples of the Shift in School Design to Open Architecture

Program	Description
Summit Public Schools	In two of its schools, Summit removed walls to create seven-thousand-square-foot open-architecture learning facilities that each accommodate two hundred students in individual workstations and four workshop rooms for breakout sessions.[31] Summit now prefers furniture with wheels so that it's easy to rearrange. It has mounted IKEA 4x4 cubbies on wheels and affixed whiteboards on the back to make the furniture modules adaptable in different circumstances.[32]
Marysville Getchell High School	On this campus outside of Seattle, the four buildings each have load-bearing walls around their outermost edges so that the interior walls may be knocked down or moved without compromising the stability of the structure. They have interior windows from the classrooms to the hallway to increase the amount of natural light. They use fold-up tables and chairs to keep the space flexible.[33]
Hellerup School	Located in a suburb of Copenhagen, Denmark, this school's four-story building has almost no walls, save for an administrative office upstairs. Its open design and absence of classrooms allow students from all grades to intermingle. The open library in the center of the building doubles as seating during assemblies.[34]
Columbus Signature Academy	The architects of this school in Columbus, Ohio decided not to use the word "classroom" anymore. Instead, they call all the spaces "studios." The footprint of each studio is double-sized and houses a double group of students in a two-teacher cohort. The interior of the building has either no walls or glass walls separating studios from corridors and breakout spaces.[35]
The Met	The Met, a Big Picture Learning School, has more than sixty sites across the United States. Learning environments have demountable walls and ample storage space for student projects. The spaces are designed to provide a variety of options for students: quiet space, meeting space, common space, and advisory space.[36]

(continued)

Table 7.2 (continued)

Program	Description
New Learning Academy	Located in the county of Kent, England, this school features, at the heart of its design, a learning plaza large enough to house 120 students. The school uses the flexibility of the plaza for five activity modes: (1) Campfire—allows for class work; (2) Watering Hole—allows for small-group work; (3) Cave—allows for self-study; (4) Studio—allows for projects; and (5) Multiple intelligences—allows for a mix of modes.[37]
Ridge Middle School	In Mentor, Ohio, math teacher Tommy Dwyer removed desks to create a more open space. He covered the walls with Plexiglas boards on which students can do their work, which had the added effect of removing any sense of the front of the classroom. Students sit in groups around tables. Their chairs are on wheels so they can scoot themselves to the wall to use the Plexiglas boards as scrap paper.[38]

ALIGNING YOUR STRATEGY TO YOUR CIRCUMSTANCES

We take the position that the shift to modular architecture at schools is by and large a great thing for the future of learning. As the specifications for modular interfaces coalesce—as industry standards and platforms develop that facilitate sharing—users will be able to mix and match components from best-of-breed suppliers to respond adroitly to the specific needs of individual students. Devices will tap into the innate modularity of the Internet at a fraction of the cost of devices with yesterday's proprietary operating systems. Physical architecture will adjust to align with the energy, openness, and choice that the virtual architecture enables.

In the early stages of blended learning, however, modularity is not always technologically possible. It's tempting to want to make the leap to a modular world immediately, but leaders must take inventory of individual circumstances to identify the right timing. Getting this timing right is a critical part of integrating the school's infrastructure to support the jobs that students and teachers are trying to do.

To Sum Up

- Interdependent architectures optimize functionality and reliability, but they require integration to do all the work of building and assembling the product in-house. Modular architectures optimize flexibility and customization. They use standard interfaces that make it possible for independent organizations to build and assemble components interchangeably.
- The factory model of schooling is vertically integrated to provide everything in one package. For many students, the fully integrated model is more than adequate in terms of offering comprehensive functionality, and now the greater need is for choice, customization, and modularity.
- Schools are using four strategies—ranging from integrated to modular—for securing online content for their blended programs: building their own, using one outside provider per course or subject, combining multiple providers themselves, or using a facilitated network. Each strategy has advantages and disadvantages.
- Schools must consider the level of modularity of the operating systems they choose. Apple devices are the most integrated, PC devices with the Windows operating system are less so, and Google Chromebooks are growing in popularity thanks to their extreme modularity. Open-architecture devices are poised to unseat proprietary devices in the years ahead.
- In an aesthetic sense, the egg-crate architecture of factory-type schools represents a proprietary design that limits customization and flexibility. Many blended programs are rearranging their furniture and physical space in a more open, modular way to align with the principles of student agency, flexibility, and choice that are at the core of their new learning models.

APPENDIX 7.1: SNAPSHOT OF ONLINE CONTENT IN USE AMONG K–12 BLENDED PROGRAMS

These data represent online content that was listed in connection with 120 programs in the Blended Learning Universe as of May 2014. The programs are of widely varying size; in some cases they are large districts, in others they are single schools. The data are not weighted to reflect this size difference.

Content Provider	Number of Programs
Khan Academy	25
Compass Learning	25
Achieve3000	18
ST Math (MIND Research Institute)	16
Self-developed	15
DreamBox Learning	13
Apex Learning	12
Edgenuity	10
Aventa Learning	9
ALEKS	8
K12, Inc.	8
Edmentum	7
i-Ready	6
Accelerated Reader	5
OER	5
Think Through Math	5
CK-12	4
Mangahigh	4
Raz-Kids	4
Rosetta Stone	4
Connections Academy	3
Florida Virtual School	3
History Alive!	3
Newsela	3
Reading Plus	3
TenMarks	3
Virtual Nerd	3

Content Provider	Number of Programs
Headsprout	2
HippoCampus	2
IXL Math	2
Lexia Reading Core5	2
myON	2
NoRedInk	2
NovaNET Courseware	2
Reading A-Z	2
Reflex	2
Renaissance Learning	2
Revolution K12	2
Scout (from the University of California)	2
SpellingCity	2
Virtual High School	2
Wowzers	2
AcademicMerit	1
AlephBeta Academy	1
American Institute for History Education	1
Big Universe	1
Blended Schools Consortium	1
blendedschools.net Languages Institute	1
BrainPOP	1
Brightstorm	1
BYU Independent Study	1
Cyber High	1
Destination Reading	1
Earobics Reach	1
EdisonLearning	1
Edmodo	1
Educurious	1
eDynamic Learning	1
enVisionMATH	1
eSpark Learning	1

(continued)

Content Provider	Number of Programs
Curriculet	1
IDEAL-NM	1
Imagine Learning	1
Istation Reading	1
Membean	1
Middlebury Interactive Languages	1
MIT OpenCourseWare	1
mylanguage360	1
National University Virtual High School	1
Odysseyware	1
READ 180	1
Reasoning Mind	1
Revolution Prep	1
ScienceFusion	1
Sevenstar Academy	1
StudySync	1
SuccessMaker	1
Teaching Textbooks	1
The Keystone School	1
Ticket to Read (Voyager Sopris Learning)	1
Utah Electronic High School	1
Vermont Virtual Learning Cooperative	1
Vmath (Voyager Sopris Learning)	1
WriteToLearn	1

NOTES

1. The observation about speed is based on the finding that the Osborne Executive has about 1/100th the clock frequency of a 2007 Apple iPhone with a 412-MHz ARM11 CPU. See J. VanDomelen, "More Cores in Store," Mentor

Graphics, http://blogs.mentor.com/jvandomelen/blog/2010/07/02/more-cores-in-store/ (accessed April 15, 2014).

The processor in the Osborne Executive, the Intel 8088, had a maximum CPU clock rate of between 5 and 10 MHz. "Intel 8088," http://www.princeton.edu/~achaney/tmve/wiki100k/docs/Intel_8088.html (accessed July 23, 2014).

2. This section and the next are adapted from Chapter Five of Christensen and Raynor, *The Innovator's Solution*, pp. 125–148 (ch. 3, n. 17).

3. The example of the F-22 is from Ben Wanamaker, "When Will Plug and Play Medical Devices and Data Be a Reality?" Clayton Christensen Institute, August 15, 2013, http://www.christenseninstitute.org/when-will-plug-and-play-medical-devices-and-data-finally-be-here/ (accessed June 2, 2014).

4. According to Christensen and Raynor, "pure modularity and interdependence are at the ends of a spectrum: Most products fall somewhere between these extremes." *The Innovator's Solution*, p. 128.

5. As Walter Isaacson's biography on Steve Jobs details, Jobs was a fanatic about the importance of an integrated product regardless of the circumstance. For example, "Jobs's objections to the cloning program were not just economic … He had an inbred aversion to it. One of his core principles was that hardware and software should be tightly integrated. He loved to control all aspects of his life, and the only way to do that with computers was to take responsibility for the user experience from end to end." Walter Isaacson, *Steve Jobs* (New York: Simon & Schuster, 2011), Kindle Locations 5886–5889.

   Jobs was of course right that having an integrated product is the way to create the best possible product with the most pure functionality and beauty in simplicity and design. What Jobs did not accept was that there are certain circumstances when customers no longer value the best product in terms of raw functionality and desire the customizability that comes with a modular architecture.

6. Christensen and Raynor, *The Innovator's Solution*, p. 133.

7. Ibid., pp. 135–136.

8. Clayton M. Christensen, Michael B. Horn, and Curtis W. Johnson, *Disrupting Class* (New York: McGraw-Hill, 2011), pp. 33, 38.

9. Brian Bridges, "California eLearning Census: Increasing Depth and Breadth," California Learning Resource Network, April 2014, http://www.clrn.org/census/eLearning%20Census_Report_2014.pdf; Brian Bridges, "California eLearning Census: Between the Tipping Point and Critical Mass," California Learning Resource Network, May 2013, http://www.clrn.org/census/eLearning_Census_Report_2013.pdf

10. Examples of states that have authorized by law a Course Access program include Florida, Louisiana, Michigan, Minnesota, Texas, Utah, and Wisconsin. To learn more, we recommend reading John Bailey, Nathan Martin, Art Coleman, Terri Taylor, Reg Leichty, and Scott Palmer, "Leading in an Era of Change: Making the Most of State Course Access Programs," Digital Learning Now and EducationCounsel, LLC, July 2019, http://digitallearningnow.com/site/uploads/2014/07/DLN-CourseAccess-FINAL_14July2014b.pdf

11. The concepts of interdependence and modularity help explain why the Course Access movement is poised to gain steam in the years ahead. More parents and students want to be able to choose from a portfolio of options, rather than continue to support a fully integrated system that cannot accommodate customization.

    The system can respond to this demand by adjusting education policy at all levels to do a better job of satisfying the three requirements of a modular world: *specificity* regarding which attributes of an online course (or any modular course) are crucial for the course to be plug-compatible with a student's overall learning plan; *verifiability*, so that both suppliers and customers can measure those attributes and verify that the specifications have been met; and *predictability*, to help students and schools anticipate that enrollment in a particular course will lead to the desired results. The observation about the three requirements of a modular world is from Christensen and Raynor, *The Innovator's Solution*, pp. 137–138.

12. We note that many schools, however, underestimate the costs of building and maintaining their own content in terms of the amount of staff time it takes.

13. The Blended Learning Implementation Guide 2.0 provides helpful tips for teachers who want to produce their own online content. The Guide is a joint project of Digital Learning Now!, Getting Smart, and The Learning Accelerator. John Bailey, Nathan Martin, Carri Schneider, Tom Vander Ark, Lisa Duty, Scott Ellis, Daniel Owens, Beth Rabbit, and Alex Terman, "Blended Learning Implementation Guide: Version 2.0," DLN Smart Series, September 2013 (http://learningaccelerator.org/media/5965a4f8/DLNSS .BL2PDF.9.24.13.pdf), p. 34.

14. Michael B. Horn, "Beyond Good and Evil: Understanding the Role of For-Profits in Education through the Theories of Disruptive Innovation," in Frederick M. Hess and Michael B. Horn (eds.), *Private Enterprise and Public Education* (New York: Teachers College Press, 2013).

15. Schools that want to develop their own online content should be creative about looking for ways to produce high-quality content despite a limited budget. The School for Integrated Academics and Technologies (SIATech), a charter management organization that provides workforce training for high school dropouts, outsources to software developers in India to help lower the cost of developing its online courses. Staker, *The Rise of K–12 Blended Learning*, p. 136 (see ch. 1, n. 6).

16. We found that the market of companies and organizations providing content to the forty organizations was highly fragmented. K12, Inc., had the biggest presence, with five implementations of its Aventa Learning products, three implementations of its K12, Inc.-branded courses, and one implementation of the A+ program by American Education Corporation, which K12, Inc. had acquired. Apex Learning and NROC were the next largest, with seven and four implementations respectively. Some of the organizations told us that they use more than one content provider. At the time, School of One told us that it uses over fifty content providers for its math program. Staker, *The Rise of K–12 Blended Learning*, p. 161.

17. This $300,000 figure is based on an estimate from the 2008–09 school year. Katherine Mackey and Michael B. Horn, "Florida Virtual School: Building the First Statewide, Internet-Based Public High School," Clayton Christensen Institute, http://www.christenseninstitute.org/wp-content/uploads/2013/04/Florida-Virtual-School.pdf, pp. 9–10.

18. MIND Research Institute, the creator of ST Math (the ST stands for Spatial-Temporal), makes ongoing investments in mathematics and neuroscience research to study the mechanisms associated with working memory, conceptual thinking, and learning. Its rigorous questioning of the circumstances that optimize learning are paying off, as ST Math is a leader in promoting student growth in math performance among elementary students.

19. Full disclosure: the Clayton Christensen Institute partnered with the Silicon Schools Fund to add partner content on the Khan Academy platform on how to create high-quality blended-learning experiences. See https://www.khanacademy.org/partner-content/ssf-cci.

20. *Disrupting Class* discusses and foretells this evolution in Chapter Five, particularly pp. 133–141.

21. Vendors of learning management systems (LMSs) for higher education are starting to open their platforms to third-party apps and resemble facilitated networks as well. They are becoming a "marketplace for add-ons," rather than proprietary, single-provider platforms. The shift can be seen in the five largest LMS vendors: Blackboard, Desire2Learn, Instructure, Moodle, and Sakai. Carl Straumsheim, "The Post-LMS LMS," Inside Higher Ed, July 18, 2014, http://www.insidehighered.com/news/2014/07/18/analysts-see-changes-ahead-lms-market-after-summer-light-news#sthash.Cwx82q QH.nqj5hAYi.dpbs

22. This change may not be too far off. One sign that changes are afoot—that the functionality and reliability of integrated online courses have become more than adequate—is that salespeople at big online-content companies start complaining that their customers are treating their product "like a *commodity*!" We've already heard this very comment from a few online-course providers, which is telling. This is evidence that integrated solutions—particularly those that serve schools with strategy #2 on the continuum—are overshooting the needs of their customers in terms of performance and that schools are starting to shift to prefer a more modular strategy. *The Innovator's Solution* explains how the commoditization of proprietary solutions signals that customers are ready for the benefits of modularity (Christensen and Raynor, p. 130) (ch. 3, n. 17).

23. Many of these ideas are from Brian Greenberg, Rob Schwartz, and Michael Horn, "Blended Learning: Personalizing Education for Students," Coursera, Week 5, Video 3: Criteria to Pick Software, https://class.coursera .org/blendedlearning-001. See also "Ten Ways to Save Money on EdTech," The Blended Learning Implementation Guide 2.0, p. 33.

24. "Individual Computing Devices at 10% Penetration in K–12 Education by 2017," Futuresource Consulting, December 5, 2013, http://www.future source-consulting.com/2013–12-computers-in-education-research.html (accessed March 22, 2014).

25. The Apple app store is interdependent with OS X, but its APIs create a modular interface that allows for a wide range of third-party software to run on Apple devices. Apple must approve the software, however, before it is made available on the store.

26. "Google's Chromebook Accounted for 1 in Every 4 Devices Shipped into US Education Market in Q4," Futuresource Consulting, January 2014, http://www.futuresource-consulting.com/2014–01-Google-Chrome book.html (accessed June 3, 2014).

27. Christensen and Raynor, *The Innovator's Solution*, p. 131.

28. Christine Fox, John Waters, Geoff Fletcher, and Douglas Levin, "The Broadband Imperative: Recommendations to Address K–12 Education Infrastructure Needs," State Educational Technology Directors Association (SETDA), September 2012, p. 2.

29. Linda Darling-Hammond, *A Right to Learn: A Blueprint for Creating Schools That Work* (San Francisco: Jossey-Bass, 1997), p. 149.

30. Katie Ash, "Digital Learning Priorities Influence School Building Design," *Education Week*, March 11, 2013, http://www.edweek.org/ew/articles/2013/ 03/14/25newlook.h32.html (accessed April 14, 2014).

31. Diane Tavenner, "Embarking on Year Two: Moving Beyond Blended Learning," Blend My Learning, November 27, 2012, http://www.blend mylearning.com/2012/11/27/embarking-on-year-two-moving-beyond- blended-learning/ (accessed April 15, 2014).

32. Brian Greenberg, Rob Schwartz, and Michael Horn, "Blended Learning: Personalizing Education for Students," Coursera, Week 5, Video 8: Facilities and Space pt. 2, https://class.coursera.org/blendedlearning-001

33. Ash, "Digital Learning Priorities."

34. Erin Millar, "No Classrooms and Lots of Technology: A Danish School's Approach," *Globe and Mail*, June 20, 2013, http://www.theglobeandmail.com/report-on-business/economy/canada-competes/no-classrooms-and-lots-of-technology-a-danish-schools-approach/article12688441/ (accessed April 14, 2014).

35. Bob Pearlman, "Designing New Learning Environments to Support 21st Century Skills," in *21st Century Skills: Rethinking How Students Learn*, edited by James Bellanca and Ron Brandt (Bloomington, Indiana: Solution Tree Press, 2010), pp. 129–132.

36. Ibid., pp. 136–138.

37. Ibid., pp. 142–144.

38. Jason Lea, "Mentor Public Schools Experiment with Blended Learning Classroom," MentorPatch, May 7, 2013, http://mentor.patch.com/groups/schools/p/mentor-public-schools-experiment-with-blended-learninda7b16f78e (accessed April 14, 2014).

Chapter 8

Choose the Model

You know the problems you want to solve, and you've organized your teams. You have mapped out the experiences you want to provide to students, the opportunities you want teachers to have in their jobs, and the technology and physical spaces you would like your schools to have. Now it's time to figure out how to operationalize this vision. That most likely means picking from among the blended-learning models we introduced in Chapter One and then customizing them to fulfill your vision.

In 2013, Todd Sutler, Brooke Peters, and Michelle Healey embarked on a road trip across the United States, Finland, and Italy to research preferred practices for their charter school in Brooklyn. Under the banner of the "Odyssey Initiative," the team toured the facilities, talked to the students, and surveyed the teachers at more than seventy innovative schools.[1] The CityBridge Foundation and NewSchools Venture Fund sponsored a similar journey that same year, as they sent twelve teachers across the country to tour blended-learning programs before implementing blended classrooms in their home schools in Washington, D.C.

A multi-stop tour is certainly not realistic or necessary for everyone, but shopping for the best model to fit your circumstances is a good idea nonetheless.[2] Five years ago we could not have recommended this approach, for the simple reason that the basic models of blended learning were still amorphous and few could testify to their effectiveness. The best advice at the time was to start with a blank sheet of paper, call on one's latent creative powers, and piece together a blended-learning model from scratch based on student jobs, teacher resources and opportunities, available technology, and other stakeholder preferences.

But today, enough schools and programs have implemented each of the models that everyone else can benefit from their work, rather than reinvent the wheel. In a word, the next step for successful blended learning is *replicate*. Beg, borrow, and steal from the examples of successful blended-learning models already in place. Of course, customizing and combining the models for your needs and circumstances is critical—that's why we did the up-front brainstorming work in Chapters Five, Six, and Seven. But as a precursor to customization, pick the basic model or set of models from off the shelf. A future burst of inspiration might spark some innovator to propose an entirely new model, but this will be the exception. In most cases, it will be more straightforward to riff off of an existing template, as some models are already good enough and will match the experiences you want for students.

This chapter walks you through six questions to help you choose the best models for your needs from among those that are emerging most conspicuously across the country: Station Rotation, Lab Rotation, Flipped Classroom, Individual Rotation, Flex, A La Carte, and Enriched Virtual. If you've kept up with the earlier parts of the book, you likely have already contemplated these six questions:

1. What problem are you trying to solve?

2. What type of team do you need to solve the problem?

3. What do you want students to control?

4. What do you want the primary role of the teacher to be?

5. What physical space can you use?

6. How many internet-connected devices are available?

You will weigh other factors in making your decision, but these six questions— the answers to which likely emerged from the blank-slate brainstorming done in the previous chapters—top the list for helping teams home in on the options that are most likely to match their circumstances, constraints, and ideals. Table 8.7 and the table in Appendix 8.1 help bring together in one place all the ideas you have brainstormed to answer these questions and formulate your blended-learning model.

MATCH THE MODEL TO THE TYPE OF PROBLEM

The first question to ask is whether your team is tackling a problem related to mainstream students in core subjects or solving a nonconsumption gap. In Chapter Three we highlight examples of several core problems, including addressing, for example, the needs of kindergarteners who enter the district with wide disparities in reading skills, or insufficient funding for high school science labs. Nonconsumption problems include the need for credit recovery, access to courses outside the course catalog, or make-up options for absences—to name just a few.

In general today, sustaining models of blended learning are better matches for core problems, and disruptive models of blended learning are better matches for nonconsumption problems.[3] As online learning and the disruptive models of blended learning improve over time, this will begin to change, but when disruptive innovations begin, they are almost always best suited for either the problems for which there are no accessible solutions or the problems that are the *least* complicated.

Countless organizations and companies from other sectors have learned this lesson the hard way. In 1947, when scientists at AT&T's Bell Laboratories invented the transistor—a device that, in essence, controls the movement of electricity—it was disruptive relative to the prior technology, vacuum tubes. The transistor was smaller and more durable than a vacuum tube, but early transistors could not handle the power required for the consumer electronic products of the 1950s: tabletop radios and floor-standing televisions. The existing radio and television manufacturers were intrigued, though, so they invested hundreds of millions of dollars trying to make the transistor good enough to satisfy their core customers as a replacement for vacuum tubes. Despite all their investment, however, in those years it never made sense to swap in the transistor, given how much better the vacuum tube was.[4]

Such investment is typical of attempts to deploy disruptive technologies in existing, mainstream applications. But because disruptive technologies in their early form are ill-equipped to compete against the existing system, companies invest extraordinary money and time to try and make them good enough for their mainstream customers, yet they almost never see the payoff. They do not fail because of lack of investment; they fail because they try to cram the disruption into the largest and most obvious market, where customers will be happy only if the new technology is better than the established solution they were already using. That's a discouragingly high performance bar for a promising but new idea.

The easier way to leverage a disruptive innovation is to deploy it in areas of nonconsumption. In the case of the transistor, the first commercially successful application emerged from outside the mainstream consumer electronic market in the form of a hearing aid, an application that begged for something smaller than a fist-sized vacuum tube to provide its power. A few years later in 1955, Sony introduced the world's first battery-powered pocket transistor radio. Garbled by static, the pocket transistor radio could not compete against the elegant tabletop radios. But it found a successful commercial application among an overlooked group: teenagers, for whom the ability to take that rugged, compact, crackling transistor radio out of earshot of parents was of tremendous value. Over time, the transistor became good enough to handle the power that larger televisions and radios required, and within a few years, the vacuum tube–based businesses were out of business, despite their own investment in the transistor.

Targeting disruptive models of blended learning toward areas of nonconsumption works magic in two ways. First, because the school community's reference point is having no option at all with respect to the particular learning opportunity, it is much more likely to be delighted with the promising but new solution. The performance hurdle that the disruptive model has to clear therefore is relatively easy. In some cases, even a primitive online course is better than nothing at all. Core courses for mainstream students, on the other hand, present a much higher performance barrier to surmount because the school community will embrace the disruptive model only once it becomes superior to the best version of the traditional classroom.

Second, it's a shame *not* to use disruptive models to address nonconsumption. The education system has long suffered from lacking enough resources to meet an evolving and expanding list of societal demands. The traditional school architecture has stretched far over time to offer more social services, breakfasts, special education, and after-school care. Disruptive models of blended learning present a striking opportunity. At last schools can personalize learning, extend access, and rein in costs in ways that seemed impossible before the arrival of this innovation. To ignore the prospect of using disruptive innovation to resolve nonconsumption problems is to overlook a historic and long-awaited bright spot in an otherwise resource-constrained system.

In summary, the first question to ask when choosing the best blended-learning models to replicate is the following:

Question 1: What problem are you trying to solve?

A.   Core problem involving mainstream students

B.   Nonconsumption problem

If your answer is A, the easiest starting point is to choose a model or set of models that is sustaining to the traditional classroom, such as the Station Rotation, Lab Rotation, or Flipped Classroom. If your answer is B, you have a ripe opportunity to deploy disruptive models, such as the Individual Rotation, Flex, A La Carte, or Enriched Virtual models. Table 8.1 charts the models that are the best matches for option A versus option B.

Not every team chooses to match models to problems according to the recommendations in Table 8.1, and that is OK. For example, some schools opt to

Table 8.1   What Problem Are You Trying to Solve?

	Sustaining Models			Disruptive Models			
	Station Rotation	Lab Rotation	Flipped Class-room	Individual Rotation	Flex	A La Carte	Enriched Virtual
A. Core problem involving mainstream students	✓	✓	✓				
B. Noncon-sumption problem				✓	✓	✓	✓

redesign learning in their core subjects with a Flex model because it is inherently more suited for personalization and competency-based learning than is a Station Rotation model. Our only caution for schools making the decision to apply a sustaining model to a nonconsumption problem or a disruptive model to a core problem is that in either case, the implementation is likely to require more effort to explain to the school community and prepare for launch than if the school inverted that choice. Either is a viable option, however, and teams can make the decision to deprioritize this first question. Over time, disruptive models will become better and better at delighting even the mainstream and core. Some believe this is already coming to fruition. As the disruptive models continue to improve, Question 1 will become less relevant.

Table 8.7 at the end of this chapter provides a chart to keep a tally of the models that match your needs most closely for each of the six questions.

MATCH THE MODEL TO THE TYPE OF TEAM

The second question to ask when choosing which blended-learning model to implement is what type of team you have put together to solve the problem. Recall from Chapter Four that certain types of teams are suited to solving certain types of problems, which relates to the level of change an organization desires to make.

If you are using a functional or lightweight team to solve a problem, then the team will be unable to implement blended-learning models that require sweeping changes to school operations. Functional and lightweight teams do not have the power to create a truly transformative learning model on their own. By the same token, heavyweight and autonomous teams are inefficient, bureaucratic responses to problems that are narrow in scope. Hence the second question:

Question 2: What type of team do you need to solve the problem?

A. *Functional team.* The problem is a classroom, department, or grade-level problem only.

B. *Lightweight team.* The problem requires coordination with other parts of the school, outside of the classroom, department, or grade-level teachers.

C. *Heavyweight team.* The problem requires changing the architecture of the school.

D. *Autonomous team.* The problem requires a new education model entirely.

To answer this question, it may be helpful to review Chapter Four for specifics about the type of team that works best for different types of problems.

Table 8.2 lists the models that correspond to these choices. Functional teams (option A) are well-positioned to implement any Station Rotation or Flipped Classroom model that does not depend on resources from other parts of the school. Flipped Classrooms are especially compatible with functional teams. Many teachers flip their classrooms on their own with only a slight nod of approval from the administration and no help from a team at all. Sometimes these two models require other types of teams, however, which we discuss next.

Lightweight teams (option B) are well-suited to implement any Station Rotation, Lab Rotation, or Flipped Classroom that requires coordination across parts of the school but does not involve architectural changes, such as new schedules and staffing arrangements. A Lab Rotation needs at least a lightweight team, if not a heavyweight team, as it requires coordination between the computer lab and the classrooms, and sometimes with other parts of the organization as well. A Flipped Classroom can benefit from a lightweight team to provide professional development, technological support, and transition funds.

Heavyweight teams (option C) are the ideal organizational structure for implementing a Station Rotation or Lab Rotation model that requires an innovative configuration of classrooms, departments, and other components within the school. Flipped Classrooms rarely if ever require architectural changes at the

Table 8.2 What Type of Team Do You Need to Solve the Problem?

	Sustaining Models			Disruptive Models			
	Station Rotation	Lab Rotation	Flipped Class-room	Individual Rotation	Flex	A La Carte	Enriched Virtual
A. Functional team	✓		✓.				
B. Light - weight team	✓	✓	✓				
C. Heavy - weight team	✓	✓					
D. Autonomous team				✓	✓	✓	✓

school level, but many Station Rotation and Lab Rotation models aspire to develop new processes and breakthrough changes at the school and benefit from the leadership of a heavyweight team.

Autonomous teams (option D) are optimal for implementing the disruptive models. Leaders can best bring about disruptive change by creating an autonomous team, which has the freedom from the traditional classroom structure to rebuild the budget, staffing plan, facilities design, and curriculum from the ground up.

MATCH THE MODEL TO THE DESIRED STUDENT EXPERIENCE

The third question to ask when choosing models is how much control you want to give students over the time, place, path, and pace of their learning. Online learning opens the potential for students to chart a personal course that would have been impossible to manage in a traditional classroom with thirty students and one teacher. It facilitates student control of pace; they can pause, rewind, and skip forward depending on how quickly they're learning. It can allow for student control of pathway, both at the provider level ("Do I want to learn long division today through TenMarks, ST Math, Reasoning Mind, ALEKS, a textbook, or a small-group workshop?") and at the instructional level ("Do I want to watch a video lesson, try an interactive challenge, get a hint, or take an assessment?"). Online learning also facilitates student control of time and place. In the past, students could consume lectures only live and in person. Today they can access them—and many other educational experiences—24/7 from anywhere with an internet connection.

Educators face a choice in terms of how much and which types of control to cede to students. Some blended models allow students to control their pace and path for a portion of the course or subject, some let them control their pace and path throughout the entire course, and some not only let them set their pace and path but also give them leeway to skip in-person class altogether. This is the question to ask and the answers that are most typical:

Question 3: What do you want students to control?

A. Their pace and path during the online portion of the course

B. Their pace and path throughout almost all of the course

C. Their pace and path throughout almost all of the course, with the flexibility to skip in-person class at times

Table 8.3 lists the models that correspond to these choices. Most Rotation models allow for student control of pace and path during the online portion of the course (option A). The Flex model allows for student control of pace and path throughout almost all of the course, as does the Individual Rotation model, for the most part (option B). The A La Carte and Enriched Virtual models allow students not only to control pace and path throughout almost all of the course, but they also give students more flexibility in terms of whether they need to show up in person for class at all (option C).

Some more detail clarifies these guidelines, as well as the exceptions. The Station Rotation, Lab Rotation, and Flipped Classroom limit student control

Table 8.3 What Do You Want Students to Control?

	Sustaining Models			Disruptive Models			
	Station Rotation	Lab Rotation	Flipped Class-room	Individual Rotation	Flex	A La Carte	Enriched Virtual
A. Their pace and path during the online portion of the course	✓	✓	✓				
B. Their pace and path throughout almost all of the course				✓	✓		
C. Their pace and path throughout almost all of the course, with the flexibility to skip in-person class at times						✓	✓

to some extent. In the Station Rotation and Lab Rotation, students can move as fast as they want while they are sitting with their computers working on their own. But when the teacher calls for them to switch to the next station (or return to the classroom, in the case of the Lab Rotation), the students usually fall back in sync with the group pace and no longer have autonomy with respect to pace—even if they are grouped dynamically to be with students at a similar point in their learning. In the case of the Flipped Classroom, students can do their nightly online learning at whatever speed they choose. But the next day in class they often transition to a collective pace—or a set activity, even if that work is individualized to their level—pursuant to the face-to-face activities that the teacher has scheduled for that class period.

There are, of course, exceptions. Some teachers combine a Flipped Classroom with elements of a Flex model to allow students to move along their own path and pace during face-to-face project time, and some Station Rotations and Lab Rotations have multiple self-paced stations apart from the online-learning station. But our intent in making these characterizations is to provide a high-level observation about how most of these models have worked in practice to make it easier for teams to choose a basic template without having to visit examples of all of the different models in person. Despite exceptions, the pattern in general is that as a stand-alone model, most commonly the Station Rotation, Lab Rotation, and Flipped Classroom allow less student control of path and pace during face-to-face classroom time than the other models do.

Turning our attention to the disruptive models, we have observed that leaders who want to implement a disruptive model can choose among varying levels of student control. The Individual Rotation model is similar to the other Rotation models in the sense that it allows students to control their pace and path when they are at an online station, but then at fixed times they return to a group pace and path. At Carpe Diem, for example, students rotate to a new station every thirty-five minutes, regardless of where they are in the station or what they might prefer to do next. Because each student has an individualized schedule through the stations, however, the overall experience offers students far more control over the pace and path then does a Station Rotation or Lab Rotation model. In contrast, the Flex model dissolves the fixed schedule and allows each student to move through the content and transition between modalities in a more fluid way. At the Wichita Public Schools dropout recovery centers, students sit at individual workstations and control their pace as they work through Apex Learning courses. The on-site teachers pull them aside for group discussions and face-to-face tutoring, but these interactions occur based on need at the moment, not a set bell schedule.

The A La Carte and Enriched Virtual models are options for teams that want to give students control over time and place, in addition to path and pace. A La Carte courses do not necessarily require students to come to campus. And although not all A La Carte courses necessarily give students control over the path and pace of learning, particularly if they are fully synchronous, in general A La Carte courses move in this direction. This format tends to be a good fit for self-directed students who do not have time in their schedule to take another course during the regular school day, who are frequently absent because of extracurricular activities, or who for some other reason have difficulty taking a particular course on campus—perhaps because there is no teacher on the campus who can teach it. The Enriched Virtual model is similar, including the fact that students can, but don't necessarily, have control over their path and pace of learning. The key difference is that students are required to attend class in person at least some of the time, whether that's three days a week or three days a month. This model helps schools improve their facility utilization rates and can work well for self-directed students who prefer to undertake part of the course remote from the face-to-face teacher. These models are often a poor match for students who do not have a safe place with a nurturing parent or other learning coach to support and supervise them away from class.

MATCH THE MODEL TO THE ROLE OF THE TEACHER

Few people dispute that quality teachers are the single most important resource that schools can provide for students. Studies show that strong families and trauma-free childhoods are hugely beneficial, but in terms of the element that falls squarely on the shoulders of schools, nothing is more important than ensuring access to great teachers.

The arrival of online learning has brought seismic changes to the role of teachers and delineated the differences between the things students learn best through software, those they learn best with an online teacher, and those they learn best with a face-to-face teacher. Jon Bergmann spent twenty-four years delivering science lectures to middle and high school students before he realized that he could record his lectures on video, post them for students to watch from home, and then redesign classroom time to make it more learner centered, inquiry driven, and project based.

In certain circumstances, arguably the best thing a teacher can do for a student is deliver excellent face-to-face instruction. In other circumstances, when students are thriving with an online experience, the most helpful role for a teacher is to move away from the front of the classroom and instead help design each student's learning, provide support, mentor, tutor, facilitate discussions and projects, evaluate student work and mastery, and enrich. And at times the best role for teachers is to go online themselves and bring their expertise to a global audience as online teachers.

This leads to the fourth question for teams to consider when choosing the best blended-learning model:

Question 4: What do you want the primary role of the teacher to be?

A. Delivering face-to-face direct instruction

B. Providing face-to-face tutoring, guidance, and enrichment to supplement online lessons

C. Serving as an online teacher

Different teachers may take on different roles, but for the purpose of this exercise, consider only the lead teacher for the course or subject that you want to blend. What do you want the teacher's role to be within this course? As with the previous questions, no one model fits perfectly and exclusively with any of these answers. Many Rotation, Flex, A La Carte, and Enriched Virtual courses have teachers who wear more than one hat. Some schools are combining more than one model, which can cause teachers' roles to expand. But for the purpose of making a basic framework on which you can build, we have observed that the primary role of teachers tends to differ according to the pattern shown in Table 8.4.

Station Rotation and Lab Rotation teachers typically spend class time delivering face-to-face instruction in small groups or to the whole class (option A). They also monitor the other stations and modalities, but almost all of the Station Rotation and Lab Rotation instances in our research feature face-to-face instruction as a prominent element of the blended course or subject.

Table 8.4 What Do You Want the Primary Role of the Teacher to Be?

	Sustaining Models			Disruptive Models			
	Station Rotation	Lab Rotation	Flipped Class-room	Individual Rotation	Flex	A La Carte	Enriched Virtual
A. Delivering face-to-face instruction	✓	✓					
B. Providing face-to-face tutoring, guidance, and enrichment to supplement online lessons			✓	✓	✓		✓
C. Serving as the online teacher of record						✓	

In contrast, teachers in Flipped Classroom, Individual Rotation, Flex, and Enriched Virtual environments flip from being the primary source of lessons and content in person to being a face-to-face guide who helps students travel through the knowledge and abilities they develop preliminarily online (option B). After Aaron Sams of Woodland Park High School in Colorado flipped his classroom, although he continued to create online lessons for his students, he stopped lecturing during class time and instead facilitated group science experiments and inquiry-based projects. The in-class experience today looks completely different from the way it did before his flip when lecture was a significant part of each class period. Now students huddle in groups with lab goggles and experiment logs, and Sams's role has shifted to managing and orchestrating that more boisterous face-to-face session. At Carpe Diem, where an Individual Rotation model undergirds core academics and electives, students have access to fully online courses provided by Edgenuity. They rotate to face-to-face stations to support their online work with seminars and project-based learning, but not as the primary source of content and instruction.

Similarly, the Flex model for math, spelling, and grammar at Acton Academy relies on guides, instead of teachers, during core skills time. The guides' role is to help students (1) set weekly goals, (2) graph their own progress, and (3) maintain portfolios, and to ask helpful questions when students get "stuck." Teachers for Enriched Virtual courses typically play a similar role. They meet with students face-to-face to assist and enrich their online work, but not to deliver the daily, foundational lessons.

Finally, in some cases the best use of teachers is as online teachers delivering A La Carte courses (option C). For schools that do not have highly qualified teachers on hand for specific subjects or have other scheduling conflicts, their best alternative is often to find a reputable course and teacher online. Other schools choose this option because their students are begging for online courses and the schools prefer to build and staff their own rather than pay a third party. Quakertown trained its high school teachers to become online teachers because the teachers union strongly opposed hiring online teachers from outside.

MATCH THE MODEL TO THE PHYSICAL SPACE

One important constraint to consider as you select your blended-learning model is the reality of the available physical facility space. At the end of the 2012–13 school year at Summit Public Schools' Rainier campus, a charter school in San Jose, California, math teacher Zack Miller lamented, "My biggest struggle in last year's [2011–12] blended pilot was that while my students had such varying skill levels and learning gaps, I still had to teach to one pace. I kept thinking, 'If I could only break down the walls.'" He felt that the physical constraints of classroom walls and the egg-crate shape of the building impeded the flow of students necessary for a Flex model.

So that summer the school knocked down walls. When class resumed in the fall, students entered a seven-thousand-square-foot open-architecture learning facility that included individual workstations for two hundred students and four flexible spaces for small-group learning, one-on-one coaching, workshops, and seminars.[5]

In other cases, physical space presents an opportunity rather than a constraint. When John Murray, CEO of AdvancePath Academics, asks districts to let his company set up a dropout- and credit-recovery center on campus, his pitch is simple: "Give me three thousand square feet of space. I'll give you high school graduates." Districts find or make space in an underused facility, and Murray's team gets to work remodeling the space into a learning facility with four zones: a parent and visitor reception area, a technology computer lab, an offline reading and writing zone, and an area for small-group instruction with teachers.[6]

Whether leasing, building, remodeling, or making do with what's available, schools must respond to the realities of their physical facilities. This leads to the fifth question that helps teams choose the right blended model:

Question 5: What physical space can you use?

A. Existing classrooms

B. Existing classrooms and a computer lab

C. A large, open learning space

D. Any safe, supervised setting

Table 8.5 summarizes the physical spaces that each of the blended models typically inhabits. Most Station Rotations and Flipped Classrooms develop within existing classrooms (option A). They usually require furniture rearrangement and

Table 8.5 What Physical Space Can You Use?

	Sustaining Models			Disruptive Models			
	Station Rotation	Lab Rotation	Flipped Class-room	Individual Rotation	Flex	A La Carte	Enriched Virtual
A. Existing classrooms	✓		✓				
B. Existing classrooms and a computer lab		✓					
C. A large, open learning space				✓	✓		✓
D. Any safe, supervised setting						✓	

sometimes the installation of electrical outlets, but most commonly the existing floor plan of the traditional classroom can accommodate these Rotations. Most Lab Rotations rely on traditional classrooms as well for the more traditional face-to-face instruction component. But they require a computer or technology lab for the online-learning station (option B). Schools without that space will be hard-pressed to set up a Lab Rotation.

Individual Rotation, Flex, and Enriched Virtual courses benefit from a larger, open learning space instead of traditional classroom walls (option C). The value of an oversized classroom space is that it allows for students to flow among multiple formats and for guides to roam more easily among students at individual workstations, in learning teams, and in other breakout areas. Traditional classroom spaces can work in a pinch, but larger, flexible spaces are better fits for these models. A unique feature of the Enriched Virtual model is that it greatly reduces the demand among individual students for face-to-face time, which allows for innovative scheduling models that use existing space to serve more students.

The A La Carte model is the most adaptable to different space constraints. It can work equally well in traditional classrooms, computer labs, school libraries, or any safe, supervised on- or off-campus setting with a good internet connection (option D). The one exception is that when schools want to provide a comfortable, supervised setting for large numbers of students to engage in A La Carte courses together, they benefit from having a large enough room. In Chapter Three we discuss how Miami-Dade set up Virtual Learning Labs that house at least fifty students per site. Large rooms allow the district to supervise these students more efficiently as they complete A La Carte courses through the Florida Virtual School. Also, many A La Carte models feature cyber cafes in which students can learn among friends.

MATCH THE MODEL TO THE AVAILABILITY OF INTERNET-ENABLED DEVICES

Like physical facilities, the availability of internet-enabled computing devices can be the single determining factor when selecting blended-learning models, simply because at times it is the governing constraint. The less access students have to devices, the fewer models will work. Consequently, the sixth question to ask when selecting models is this:

Question 6: How many internet-enabled devices are available?

A. Enough for a fraction of the students

B. Enough for all students throughout the entire class period

C. Enough for all students to use in class and have at home or after school

Internet-enabled devices include desktops, laptops, tablets, or mobile phones. The problem with tablets and mobile phones, however, is that although they make for convenient consumption tools, they are lousy for production on their own. In other words, they are great for watching online videos and other media, but don't expect students to be able to compose essays or produce digital projects on them nearly as well as if they had a full-sized keyboard and screen. (We note that more and more schools are connecting physical keyboards to tablets to allow them to overcome this deficiency.)

Some models of blended learning work well in classrooms that do not have a one-to-one ratio of devices per students, whereas others require one device per child, not only in class but also at home. Table 8.6 summarizes the models that match each circumstance best.

One important finding is that many blended programs thrive even when students do not each have a personal device to use (option A). KIPP LA's Empower Academy and Comienza Community Prep both maintain a device-to-student ratio of roughly one-to-two.[7] This works because of their Station Rotation design, which generally requires that only students at the online-learning station have access to a computer.[8] Some schools set up Station Rotations that have as many as six stations, for example, which can further decrease the need for technology. Many schools are also able to get by without one-to-one device ratios for their Lab Rotation model. A school's learning lab might accommodate 130 students at any given time, and because of its Rotation model, this would be plenty for a school of roughly 600 students.[9]

In contrast, the Individual Rotation and Flex models require students to have access to a computer throughout the entire blended course or subject (option B).

Table 8.6 How Many Internet-Enabled Devices Are Available?

	Sustaining Models			Disruptive Models			
	Station Rotation	Lab Rotation	Flipped Class-room	Individual Rotation	Flex	A La Carte	Enriched Virtual
A. Enough for a fraction of the students	✓	✓					
B. Enough for all students throughout the entire class period				✓	✓		
C. Enough for all students to use in class and have at home or after school			✓			✓	✓

The Internet provides the backbone of student learning in both of these models, and students need to be able to access online content and instruction without waiting their turn.

Three models take the need for student access to devices a step farther. The Flipped Classroom, A La Carte, and Enriched Virtual models work best when students have access to a device both on campus throughout the entire blended block and off campus to complete their assigned online coursework (option C). In some cases schools expect students to complete A La Carte courses on campus using school computers, but this limits a student's ability to accelerate through a course during non-school hours. In general, the best device scenario for the Flipped Classroom, A La Carte, and Enriched Virtual models is for schools to ensure that every student has access to an internet-connected device at home and school.

PRIORITIZING OPTIONS AND MAKING THE SELECTION

If you've worked through the six questions and considered the analysis behind the options, your team is ready to choose a blended-learning model. Start by using Table 8.7 to prioritize the six questions we've analyzed. Which question matters most in your circumstance? What constraints are locked in? One group of Catholic schools we advised did not have a device for every student they wanted to include in the blended pilot. For them, Question 6 was the most important. A handful of schools in Pennsylvania faced significant community opposition to the idea of using online learning to replace the traditional classroom. Question 1 was a high-priority consideration for them. Another school in Rhode Island was constructing a new facility; it needed to give special consideration to Question 5.

Once you have prioritized the issues that matter most or are deal breakers, add up the total points for each model, based on your answers to Questions 1 through 6.[10] This gives you a sense of the number of ways each model fits across all six dimensions. The best models for your program are those that rise to the top relative to both criteria—they satisfy your top priorities and they correspond to your needs in the most ways. For further reference, Appendix 8.1 at the end of this chapter summarizes how the models compare in terms of each of the six questions.[11]

MOVING TOWARD MULTIPLE MODELS

There is a twist that can complicate model selection but also present an opportunity for lots of creativity. We are finding that many schools move beyond choosing only one model to create an ongoing process of selecting models as circumstances and needs present themselves. Da Vinci Schools in Hawthorne, California, combines the Flipped Classroom and Lab Rotation, for example. Teachers introduce students to new content online at home; at school the next day students rotate among small-group instruction, collaborative group work, advisory, internships, project labs, and online-learning lab time.[12]

Schools for the Future (SFF) in Detroit structures the day for entering students in an Individual Rotation; they cycle on a customized schedule among classes,

Table 8.7 Choose the Model That Fits Your Circumstances.

Give a point to the model(s) that match your needs for each question	Sustaining Models			Disruptive Models			
Question	Station Rotation	Lab Rotation	Flipped Class-room	Individual Rotation	Flex	A La Carte	Enriched Virtual
1. What problem are you trying to solve?							
2. What type of team do you need to solve the problem?							
3. What do you want students to control?							
4. What do you want the primary role of the teacher to be?							
5. What physical space can you use?							
6. How many internet-connected devices are available?							
Total points:							

individual work stations, internships, and community experiences. As they advance to SFF's upper levels, students gain greater independence and broader options about how, where, and what they learn. Their "limitless campus" includes a range of A La Carte high school and college courses.[13]

Danville Independent Schools, a district in Danville, Kentucky, relies on a Lab Rotation to help students complete a competency-based core curriculum. They demonstrate competency through standards-based assessments, performance tasks, or teacher recommendation. After mastering state-set college and career readiness benchmarks, students set forth on a personalized pathway with a self-selected area of focus for their learning and are free to engage in A La Carte courses.[14]

Perhaps the language of schools and classrooms is outdated. Educators are starting to speak of learning studios, learning plazas, and home bases to try to get at this notion of schools offering a portfolio of options pursuant to the needs of each learner.[15] To develop that full menu, the process of choosing models and building on them must be ongoing.

To Sum Up

- Rather than try to design a blended-learning model from scratch, leaders should choose one of the already established models— Station Rotation, Lab Rotation, Flipped Classroom, Individual Rotation, Flex, A La Carte, and Enriched Virtual—and then customize it.
- The first question to ask is, what problem are you trying to solve? Core problems involving mainstream students are the best match for sustaining models. Nonconsumption problems are fertile ground for disruptive models.
- The second question is, what type of team do you need to solve the problem? Disruptive models are most likely to be successful when you have an autonomous team, whereas there is more flexibility with the three sustaining models.
- The third question is, what do you want students to control? Three of the models allow students to control their pace and path during the online portion of the course. The other models grant students broader control.
- The fourth question is, what do you want the primary role of the teacher to be? Some models deploy the teacher as a guide or online teacher rather than as the source of face-to-face instruction.
- The fifth question is, what physical space can you use? All of the models except the Station Rotation and Flipped Classroom benefit from nontraditional classroom space.
- The sixth question is, how many internet-enabled devices are available? Station Rotations and Lab Rotations work well when only a fraction of students have access to a computer.
- Teams should choose a model by analyzing which models fit their needs in the most ways and in the highest-priority ways.
- Innovative schools repeat this process to develop a menu of models and options for students.

APPENDIX 8.1: WHICH BLENDED-LEARNING MODEL MATCHES YOUR CIRCUMSTANCES BEST?

Question	Station Rotation	Lab Rotation	Flipped Classroom	Individual Rotation	Flex	A La Carte	Enriched Virtual
What problem are you trying to solve?	Core problem involving mainstream students	Core problem involving mainstream students	Core problem involving mainstream students	Nonconsumption problem	Nonconsumption problem	Nonconsumption problem	Nonconsumption problem
What type of team do you need to solve the problem?	Functional, lightweight, or heavyweight	Lightweight or heavyweight	Functional or lightweight	Autonomous	Autonomous	Autonomous	Autonomous
What do you want students to control?	Their pace and path during the online portion of the course	Their pace and path during the online portion of the course	Their pace and path during the online portion of the course	Their pace and path throughout almost all of the course	Their pace and path throughout almost all of the course	Their pace and path throughout almost all of the course, with the flexibility to skip in-person class at times	Their pace and path throughout almost all of the course, with the flexibility to skip in-person class at times

Question	Station Rotation	Lab Rotation	Flipped Classroom	Individual Rotation	Flex	A La Carte	Enriched Virtual
What do you want the primary role of the teacher to be?	Delivering face-to-face instruction	Delivering face-to-face instruction	Providing face-to-face tutoring, guidance, and enrichment to supplement online lessons	Providing face-to-face tutoring, guidance, and enrichment to supplement online lessons	Providing face-to-face tutoring, guidance, and enrichment to supplement online lessons	Serving as the online teacher-of-record	Providing face-to-face tutoring, guidance, and enrichment to supplement online lessons
What physical space can you use?	Existing classrooms	Existing classrooms plus a computer lab	Existing classrooms	A large, open learning space	A large, open learning space	Any safe, supervised setting	A large, open learning space
How many internet-enabled devices are available?	Enough for a fraction of the students	Enough for a fraction of the students	Enough for all students to use in class and have at home or after school	Enough for all students throughout the entire class period	Enough for all students throughout the entire class period	Enough for all students to use in class and have at home or after school	Enough for all students to use in class and have at home or after school

NOTES

1. Nick DiNardo, "A Cross-Country Roadtrip to Design a School," EdSurge, January 14, 2014, https://www.edsurge.com/n/2014–01–14-a-cross-country-roadtrip-to-design-a-school (accessed January 17, 2014).

2. To learn about more models in operation, we recommend taking a look at the blended-learning profiles and case studies amassed in the Blended Learning Universe at the Clayton Christensen Institute at www.blendedlearning.org

3. We note that disruptive innovations are also well suited for problems where the existing solutions overshoot what users need to solve the problem and therefore those users are *overserved*. We also note that this can be a frustrating reality for some, as experts are generally concerned with the most intractable and challenging problems, which in the case of schools means serving students with the highest needs and most complicated problems, but successful disruptions usually tackle the less sophisticated challenges at the outset.

4. The story of the transistor is abridged from Christensen and Raynor, *The Innovator's Solution* (ch. 3, n. 15), pp. 103–107.

5. Diane Tavenner, "Embarking on Year Two: Moving Beyond Blended Learning," Blend My Learning, November 27, 2012, http://www.blendmylearning.com/2012/11/27/embarking-on-year-two-moving-beyond-blended-learning/ (accessed January 18, 2014).

6. Staker, "The Rise of K–12 Blended Learning" (introduction, n. 34).

7. Bernatek, Cohen, Hanlon, and Wilka, "Blended Learning in Practice" (introduction, n. 39), p. 18.

8. Students often rotate among two or three stations, only one of which is for online learning, which means that only one-half or one-third of students need a computer at any time during the rotation. Bernatek et al., "Blended Learning in Practice."

9. Ibid.

10. These questions will also help you think through your budget considerations as you construct your blended-learning model. The topic of budget and

financials to support blended learning is one into which we have chosen to not delve deeply in this book.

11. We also highly recommend that educators look to the Blended Learning Implementation Guide (ch. 1, n. 11) for assistance. The six questions and Appendix 8.1 offer a high-level way of thinking through these questions; the Guide looks closer at some of the operational questions that we leave untouched here.

12. "Da Vinci Schools: Da Vinci Communications," Next Generation Learning Challenges, http://net.educause.edu/ir/library/pdf/NG1205.pdf

13. "Schools for the Future: SFF Detroit," Next Generation Learning Challenges, http://net.educause.edu/ir/library/pdf/NG1215.pdf

14. "Danville Independent Schools: Bate Middle School and Danville High School," Next Generation Learning Challenges, http://net.educause.edu/ir/library/pdf/NGP1301.pdf

15. Pearlman, "Designing New Learning Environments to Support 21st Century Skills" (ch. 7, n. 33), p. 126.

Part 4

Implementing

Understanding → Mobilizing → Designing → **Implementing**

Chapter 9

Create the Culture

Have you ever walked into a school that on paper sounded amazing, but in practice just seemed "off"? The students weren't doing what they should be; the teachers looked tired; or maybe the facilities were messy. After all the brainstorming and designing that goes into creating an education innovation are over, execution still matters most. And when the culture isn't right or is uneven, the execution can fall apart.

Culture strikes many as a fuzzy topic to dedicate a chapter to in a book about designing and implementing blended learning on the ground. It's one of those things that people tend to talk about in oblique terms; they suggest that an organization's culture is just in the air of the place. "You know culture when you feel it," one might say.

But culture is a critical part of the success of any blended-learning program. A friend who works in blended schools once remarked to us, "Blended learning accelerates a good culture and makes it great, but it will also accelerate a bad culture and make it terrible."[1] Culture is especially useful—or toxic—in blended programs because blended learning goes hand in hand with giving students more control and flexibility. If students lack the processes and cultural norms to handle that agency, the shift toward a personalized environment can backfire.[2] To not address the topic of culture is to not address one of the most important parts of designing a blended-learning program—indeed, it is to overlook one of the most important parts of any school.

This means that even after a team designs every aspect of its blended model, from the student and teacher experiences to the physical and virtual environment, its work is not done. In fact, its efforts are sure to fall short if the team members fail to turn their attention to designing and creating strong cultural norms to cement their design together and make it run well. Regardless of whether the blended team that began the effort is functional, lightweight, heavyweight, or autonomous, it should see that effort through by attending to every detail of crafting the right culture.

If culture is so important yet is so ethereal as a concept, then how can teams control and shape it to maximize their chances of success? Understanding this begs the question of what is culture? And if it's so important to doing blended learning well, how do you create a "good" culture?

WHAT IS CULTURE?

Edgar Schein, a professor emeritus at MIT, is one of the leading scholars on organizational culture.[3] He defines organizational culture in these terms: "Culture is a way of working together toward common goals that have been followed so frequently and so successfully that people don't even think about trying to do things another way. If a culture has formed, people will autonomously do what they need to do to be successful."[4]

The instinct to work together toward common goals is not formed overnight. It develops gradually over time as people in an organization work together to solve problems and get things done. In every organization there is a first time when a problem arises. In a school, these problems may sound something like this:

"The teacher's lounge is a disaster—who's responsible for cleaning this place, anyway?"

"How do we deal with a parent's complaints?"

"John has already missed school ten times this year; what should we do about it?"

"How do we keep the cafeteria noise level under control?"

In each instance of a problem or task arising, the people responsible made a decision about what to do and how to do it. If their solution worked at least adequately, they are likely to resort to it again the next time a similar challenge arises. If it proved unsuccessful—the students rebelled, the teachers resisted, or the principal reprimanded, for example—those responsible for the solution will likely look for a different solution the next time. As this process of trial and error repeats itself, the people responsible refine their learning about what matters to the organization—the *priorities* of the organization—and how to execute them—the *processes*. They learn which behaviors the organization rewards and which it punishes.

Eventually the system is so internalized that these processes and priorities become reflex. As long as the routine keeps working well enough, why change it? A culture starts to coalesce around that behavior.

Schools have many processes and priorities that can coalesce over time into a shared culture. If high school administrators find that a process to create student schedules works well, then the next time they have to create schedules, they are likely to use the same process. Over time that becomes the culture for student scheduling, without having to think much about it. If teachers find that opening class discussions a certain way tends to engage students, they are likely to use that technique again. Over time that becomes part of the classroom culture.[5] If students learn that they are always complimented when they walk in the hallways and always reprimanded for running, then over time a cultural norm develops and students find it easier to self-regulate their hallway speed.

The power of culture is that as members of an organization reach a shared paradigm about how to work together to be successful, ultimately they don't have to stop to ask each other what to do. They just assume that they should keep doing what they've been doing because it works. In other words, it satisfies that particular organization's priorities and values. As a result, the organization becomes self-managing, as people autonomously do what they need to do to be successful.[6]

THE POWER OF CULTURE FOR CHILDREN

Organizations full of children are especially rewarded by an effort to help their young members become self-managing contributors toward the common good. A story from the Eyre family shows the power of strong culture in an organization with children.

Richard and Linda Eyre are the parents of nine children and have made a career of speaking and writing about how to build successful families.[7] They have appeared on *Oprah*, *The Today Show*, *Prime Time Live*, *60 Minutes*, and *Good Morning America*. In a book about teaching children responsibility, Linda told of a problem she faced when, as a young mother with three children at the time, she felt exasperated by her children's unwillingness to make their beds. Having a tidy house was a priority for her, and she wondered how to instill that in her children. At first she tried nagging and complaining each time she noticed an unmade bed. That process soon proved exasperating to both Linda and her children. She then tried ignoring the mess, hoping her children would grow out of it. Time passed, and that process failed, too. She tried the grin-and-bear-it approach and the get-angry method, but both were equally futile.

Finally she found a process that worked. First she had to teach her children how to make their beds. Each morning she took each child by the hand, once by one, and said, "Let's go make your bed." After establishing that skill, she and her husband called the family together and had a conversation about how working together on chores was important to each person's well-being. Then they asked the children to set their own goals about making their beds, cleaning their rooms, and brushing their teeth. The fourteen-year-old set the goal to make his bed every day for a week. Four days out of seven Linda went into his room to discover, to her amazement, that his bed was already made. On the other three days, just a few words to remind him of his goal brought immediate results.

Through trial, error, and a lot of thought, Linda found a process that worked for their family: first, teach the children *how*; then, let *them* set the goal. The Eyres repeated this process again and again, not only for beds but also for making breakfast, doing the dishes, and doing other chores. In time the routine developed into a strong family culture of working together on chores.[8]

THE POWER OF CULTURE IN SCHOOLS

Just as in companies and families, culture in schools is critical to smoothing the path for schools to achieve their mission. One friend told us about a school he started in San Francisco in the mid-1990s that needed a culture change. The school faced a problem that many schools face: after long days, the last thing teachers wanted to do was sit through a meeting. They were tired and had more work to do to get ready for school the next day. Home beckoned. A meeting seemed like a useless addition.

But meetings are important for communicating about school-wide activities and providing teachers time to coordinate on their lesson plans. The challenge was how to make them productive and keep teachers engaged.

The school decided to experiment with a new process to solve the problem. The process involved a method that Interaction Associates, a global leadership-development firm, created to improve how meetings are run. The method introduced a variety of structures to make a meeting more efficient, but in particular it introduced a technique to help make teachers excited about the meeting in the beginning so that it started off on the right foot. Meetings would begin with teachers sharing either a celebration or a "connection" reflection. As our friend said:

> The celebration is based on research that shows that teachers—and anyone for that matter—will meet more productively if they feel celebrated and appreciated by or connected with their coworkers. Celebrations change the tone and feeling of the meeting from a useless distraction to something worth valuing. The celebration can be of a colleague, a student, a family member, or anything. No one has to speak up. We usually give three to five minutes for sharing of quick celebrations. It really works and changes the way meetings work. A connection is used when something bad happened or sometimes—like after 9/11 or a suicide or something—where a celebration just doesn't seem right, and then the prompt is "What do you feel connected to?"

The process worked so well that the school used this meeting technique again and again, until it became embedded as the culture. Our friend eventually left the school to start another one. Twelve years later he returned to visit the school.

What he saw amazed him. The staff and teachers were still doing celebrations in all of their meetings. When he asked why they did them, no one there knew. It was just the way things were done. The culture had long survived his departure. The implication is that not only is culture powerful, but it's also durable. Proceed with caution when managing culture because it is long lasting.

HOW TO SHAPE CULTURE

Both the Eyre household and the celebrations tradition attest to the fact that leaders can shape the culture of their organization. With regard to schools, in some cases a culture already exists, but it's not working. Students are not on track, teachers are overwhelmed—something about the culture is off-kilter. The knee-jerk reaction for many leaders at this point is to attack the culture itself and call for cultural change. But simply talking about culture is not effective. Other leaders, particularly some urban superintendents in recent years, have tried to shock their district into changing its culture by creating a "change or perish" crisis, only to be met with fierce resistance and little change to show for it.[9] The good news, though, is that leaders do not need to wait for—or force—a crisis that's powerful enough to cause a change. They can change culture through a more managed process.

Educators can deliberately build a culture by following a set of rules. The first is this: Start by defining a problem or task—one that recurs again and again. Set aside the school's existing pattern of response to the problem. The idea here is to try something new that will work better.

Next, pull a group out of the organization and appoint it to figure out how to solve the problem. If the group fails, that's OK. Ask it to try again with a different process. Then once the group has succeeded, don't disperse the team. Instead, ask the same team to solve the problem every time it recurs—over and over again. The more times they solve the problem the same way and find success, the more instinctive it becomes. Culture is formed through repetition. All too often when problems crop up, if a solution works, the discussion ends and the team disbands. If the solution doesn't work, the leader changes or reprimands the team. Neither of these approaches works for creating a deliberate culture.[10]

Once a culture has been shown to work, write it down and talk about it as often as possible. Many school leaders see the value in having a written artifact of their culture that they can promote. Jeff and Laura Sandefer at Acton Academy are religious about defining and promoting the key aspects of the Acton Academy culture — one that may not suit everybody, but one that works in their community. Some of these include:

> Everyone can serve as a learner and a Guide. Coaching duties spread throughout the community in a voluntary system of change, where the greatest gifts and needs can be matched to each other.

- The quality of work is judged by peers, often against a world-class example, or rated by visitors at a studio exhibition. The best work is captured in electronic and hard-copy portfolios and will be used when students pitch for apprenticeships.

- Guides serve students and parents as if they were valued partners; anonymous weekly customer-satisfaction surveys are sent to students and parents, and the results are published.[11]

But merely writing and talking about the culture is not enough. Leaders must make decisions that are entirely aligned to it. Consider what happens in a family if the parents simply decree "This is the way our family behaves," but then do not follow that up with consistent rewards, punishments, and leading by example. Communication is important, but it is even more important to hold to that communication and follow through with it.

You can tell the health of an organization's culture by asking, "When faced with a choice of how to do something, do members of the organization make the decision that the culture 'wanted' them to make? And was the feedback they received consistent with that?"

The rules for changing a bad culture and for shaping a culture from scratch are identical. Identify and define the problems that need to be solved in the new organization and then solve them. If the solutions are successful, then repeat until the processes and priorities become reflex within the organization's culture.

The following list summarizes the essential rules for creating or changing culture.

How to shape culture

✓ Define a problem or task that recurs again and again.

✓ Appoint a group to solve the problem.

- ✓ If they fail, ask them to try again with a different process.
- ✓ If they succeed, ask the same group to repeat the process every time the problem recurs.
- ✓ Write down and promote your culture.
- ✓ Live in a way that is consistent with the culture.

THE POWER OF CULTURE IN BLENDED-LEARNING IMPLEMENTATIONS

Shaping culture is critical in any school, but particularly one with blended learning. Oliver Sicat stated the following when he was six months into his tenure as CEO of USC Hybrid High School:

> If there was only one thing we learned in charters v.1.0, it is that culture matters. And I am not talking about culture in the sense that everyone is walking in single-file lines. I am talking about holding students to high expectations for behavior and having rewards and consequences for every positive and negative behavior we don't tolerate, without excuses. This is even more important if you are building for open-learning environments. How do we plan, model, train, and hold students and staff accountable for the culture we want to create? We needed to prioritize this so learning could happen.[12]

That about sums it up. But here are three examples to drive the point home.

 WATCH CLIP 19: USC Hybrid High School shifts the teacher role and creates a deliberate culture to deliver its Flex model.

www.wiley.com/go/blended19

Anacostia High School

In profiling Anacostia High School, a 697-student Title I school in Washington, D.C., that has long been one of the district's most underperforming schools, a report by the American Enterprise Institute highlighted the school's efforts to move to a blended-learning environment. The authors wrote about how the students used netbooks with an online portal that gave them access to an array of multimedia tools for learning and on-demand assessments that provided immediate feedback. The report talked about how students could log in with unique passwords so that teachers could track each student's individual progress.

And yet, the authors wrote, as they were observing a class, they saw that students logged in not with their unique ID but with a generic one. Some students struggled even with that, and it took them up to five minutes to enter the password. Rather than use the online assessment capabilities, the teacher used paper worksheets. And when one student struggled to understand a word, rather than use the computer's dictionary or Google, she walked over to a bookshelf and took her time flipping through a dictionary for help.[13]

This represents a classic example of a program where leaders have left culture to chance, rather than aggressively shaping it. The school was not intentional about (1) identifying the range of problems and tasks that students, teachers, and staff would confront in a blended setting; (2) appointing a team to find successful ways to solve or address those problems or tasks; and then (3) asking them to solve those same problems repeatedly in that way to build and then reinforce the culture. As a result, it was considered OK for students to take five minutes to log into the online portal at the beginning of class, to not use their unique ID, or to use their scarce learning time by sauntering over to look up a word in a physical dictionary, rather than use an online one. No one had crafted the right processes up front, and as a result, the de facto culture was chaotic.

Gilroy Prep School

Contrast Anacostia High School to Gilroy Prep School, a charter school in Gilroy, California, that uses a Lab Rotation model. Here students know that once they walk into the traditional classroom, they must be in their seats within twelve seconds and working on the "Do Now" activity that is on the board. When students are in the computer lab, they have fifteen seconds from when they walk in the door to put their headphones on and log into their software program. As a result, students know that when they are in a learning environment, there should be no down time. Instead, when students rotate between different groupings five or six times during the day, that's when they take mini recesses to relax, reset, and get ready for the next task. Although Gilroy Prep's culture may not suit everybody, the intentionality behind that culture has worked for the school, as Gilroy Prep achieved the highest API score—978—in California for a first-year charter school in 2011–12.[14]

 WATCH CLIP 20: Gilroy Prep students experience a Lab Rotation as a central feature of their daily schedule.

www.wiley.com/go/blended20

Carpe Diem

Culture is key to the success of Carpe Diem, a blended-learning school we introduce in Chapter One. Carpe Diem's founder, Rick Ogston, spent considerable time working with the school's staff, teachers, and students on how to respond to recurring challenges or situations to develop successful processes—or routines—that prioritize learning and respect students' needs. In Carpe Diem's model, students rotate to their next activity every thirty-five minutes. Having students move efficiently between activities and from nonlearning activities into learning ones was therefore of vital importance so that students would not waste time once they arrived at their next activity and lose precious minutes of learning. Ogston developed a successful process for students to learn how to move from activity to activity. One observer of Carpe Diem recalled to us how Ogston showed his students how to march into school in the morning and then made his students march in again and again at the beginning of the school year, even if it was 100 degrees outside, because his culture was "sacred." Getting the processes right was paramount. There was no detail too small to ensure that his students behaved well and knew what routines to use in different circumstances.

This focus extended to teachers and staff as well. When visiting Carpe Diem, we saw a couple of students briefly put their heads down on their desks and take what appeared to be a nap. We asked Ogston whether a teacher was going to come over and do something, only to have him ask us a couple of questions in return: Haven't you ever needed a break at work—a quick nap? If your supervisor came over and reprimanded you, would that be helpful to your productivity? He told us that just like in work, sometimes students need a brief break, and that is OK. What he has worked on with his teachers is knowing when a break has gone too long and then going over and checking with the student just to be sure everything is fine. Depending on the response, and assuming everything is OK, the teacher might even tell the student to take more time to rest before getting back to work. Sure enough, as we watched, the students who had put their heads down popped back up only a minute or two later and resumed their learning.

Ogston had also helped his students understand their responsibilities and what processes were and were not acceptable in response to challenges they would face as blended learners. The very process of helping the students develop their own culture of success signaled to them that Carpe Diem was a place that respected them and wanted them to succeed.

Often, one of the biggest shifts in a blended-learning environment is that students in the same studio will be engaged in different modalities and working on a variety of skills. This climate requires that the culture support this flexibility. The imperative for blended-learning teachers in this new environment is to be able to shape the culture into one of high expectations and of student ownership of their own learning. When that culture is in place, a teacher is not necessarily alarmed at seeing students conferring with peers during personalized-learning time. Although it may appear chaotic, if teachers invest in creating a strong culture up front, with clear norms and expectations, then the culture will in fact be quite structured, with clear methods to the madness. The key is not that schools should always be quiet or always be boisterous, but that they should be silent when students need to be silent to maximize their learning and boisterous when noise and collaboration are in order.

IT'S NOT TOO LATE

Some who read this may throw their hands up in despair and wonder if it's too late. The culture at their schools is already set—and it's not pretty.

The good news is that reshaping culture does not start with worrying about how to change a big, dysfunctional mess of a culture. As we wrote, shaping culture begins one task at a time. How should students enter the building? Appoint a few people (it could even be a team of students) to figure out a process that works, repeat it over and over, and then hold people to it. Now move on to the next task.

A school we visited in California discovered the importance of shaping culture, but not without a stumble first. Although it was a Flex model, the school had in many ways modeled itself after Carpe Diem's design. But after a year of operations, it was clear that the students had not done well. What had gone wrong? The school had opened so quickly over the summer that the staff had not taken the time to design the kinds of processes that it needed to handle a challenging population in a large open-learning environment. As a result, teachers, staff, and students developed their own processes. Because the organization had not agreed on priorities set clearly around student success, these ad hoc processes that solved problems helped students and staff get by but didn't always promote academic success. In many cases, staff and students fell back on processes familiar to their old schooling environments that were not suited for success in a blended-learning environment. By not being intentional about shaping its culture up front, the school was left with a group of students who had fallen behind for an entire year of their schooling.

The effort required to turn around the culture for the next year was significant but not insurmountable. The principal assigned teams to think through every daily interaction, activity, and challenge; what the school expected behavior-wise; the systems for tracking the desired behavior; how to train the students in that expected behavior; how to incentivize that behavior and disincentivize other behaviors; and how to make sure that the teachers and staff bought into the processes and priorities the school sought to instill. This meant looking at every challenge students might face in a given day, including what to do if they were late, needed to go to the bathroom, had a computer problem, needed access to a website that was blocked, or had a question.

The processes that the school established were not always predictable. For certain problems, the school developed hand signals so that the staff would not need to create a disturbance by walking across the room to solve a problem. For students with questions about academic work, the school taught them to seek out the answer online or from a peer before going to the teacher. When teachers did receive a question, they in turn were trained to ask students another question that invited students to own their learning and do further research on the question, rather than provide "the answer" and allow students to escape the hard work necessary to realize genuine success. The attention to culture paid off, as the school boosted its results dramatically, although it is still overcoming the legacy of its bad start.

The lesson from that school is that culture is a strong force for good or evil. Harnessing it is one of the most powerful things leaders can do to implement a blended-learning program in which people will autonomously do what they need to do to be successful.

To Sum Up

- Creating the right culture is critical for a blended-learning model to be successful.
- Edgar Schein defines culture as "a way of working together toward common goals that have been followed so frequently and so successfully that people don't even think about trying to do things another way."
- Culture is contained in an organization's processes—or ways of working together—and priorities—or shared criteria for decision making.
- To shape culture, define the problems that must be solved and then allow a team of people to solve them, one by one. If the team is unsuccessful in solving a problem, let it try again. Once the team is successful, let it solve the problem with that process repeatedly until it becomes ingrained in the culture. Write down and reinforce the culture, and live in a way that is consistent with it.
- There are myriad recurring activities or problems in blended-learning settings. Being intentional about what processes are used to solve these problems and the priorities of the organization is critical in creating a culture that leads to student success.

(continued)

(continued)

- Reshaping a culture does not start with worrying about how to change a big, dysfunctional mess of a culture. Shaping a culture begins one task at a time. It's not too late to start creating better processes and priorities.

NOTES

1. We thank Anthony Kim, founder of Education Elements, which helps districts implement blended learning, for his help in articulating the importance of a school's culture over the years, as well as Mark Kushner, the founder of Flex Public Schools, a set of blended-learning schools rolling out across the nation, for helping us understand more deeply how culture works in schools and how important it is to get culture right. Also, former Secretary of Education Rod Paige gave further voice to this idea in an op-ed in the *Houston Chronicle*: "Another component that separates ed tech success stories from false starts is the 'secret sauce' all successful schools share: culture and values." See Rod Paige, "Paige: Digital Classrooms Are Reshaping Education," *Houston Chronicle*, February 8, 2014 (http://www.chron.com/opinion/outlook/article/Paige-Digital-classrooms-are-reshaping-education-5217202.php?cmpid=opedhphcat).

2. Brian Greenberg, the CEO of Silicon Schools Fund, made this important point in a June 2013 email update about the progress of the schools in his fund's portfolio.

3. This section is adapted and simplified from the published note by Clayton M. Christensen, "What Is an Organization's Culture?" Harvard Business School, August 2, 2006 (9–399–104). That note itself draws heavily from the concepts explained in the first three chapters of the following book: Edgar Schein, *Organizational Culture and Leadership* (San Francisco: Jossey-Bass Publishers, 1988). In addition, this section draws heavily from Clayton M. Christensen, Karen Dillon, and James Allworth, *How Will You Measure Your Life?* (New York: HarperCollins, 2012), Ch. 9.

4. Schein (ibid.) also uses a more formal definition for organizational culture; he describes it as "a pattern of basic assumptions—invented, discovered, or developed by a given group as it learns to cope with its problems of external adaptation and internal integration—that has worked well enough to be considered valid and, therefore, to be taught to new members as the correct way to perceive, think, and feel in relation to those problems" ("What Is an Organization's Culture," p. 2).

5. This raises an important point. Given the classroom structure of the majority of today's schools, depending on a school's philosophy or how it's led or managed, the school may have a strong and coherent internal culture across the organization. By this we mean that teachers and staff together will have a strong set of common learning experiences across a range of problems. On the other hand, although the school may have tackled certain problems as a whole organization, such that the school has a culture, certain problems may have been tackled only within each individual classroom and therefore each classroom will have its own distinct culture as well because it has operated, to a certain extent, as its own organization. Each classroom teacher will handle certain challenges in different ways as a result.

6. Many will often label a culture in which employees wear casual clothes rather than dressy ones and work sporadic hours rather than predictable shifts an "informal" culture as opposed to a "formal" one. But how people dress doesn't truly tell us what the culture of a place is. How people dress is just an artifact of culture. Instead, we must observe the processes and priorities that people employ instinctively when solving problems and making decisions. A group that wears casual clothes might actually be quite rigid and hierarchical in the way people work together. Would that still be an "informal" culture? In other words, it is important not to confuse the artifacts that are manifestations of a culture with the culture itself.

7. One of the Eyres' daughters, Charity Eyre, also was formerly a colleague of ours at the Clayton Christensen Institute.

8. Linda and Richard Eyre, *Teaching Children Responsibility* (Salt Lake City, UT: Deseret Book Company, 1982), pp. 57–59.

9. Michelle Rhee's tenure as superintendent in Washington, D.C., was marked with tension and fights as she sought to shock the district schools to change their culture. Although arguably she did succeed in changing the culture within the district organization itself, many of the traditional public schools resisted the cultural shifts she attempted to bring about during her tenure.

10. Christensen, Dillon, and Allworth, *How Will You Measure Your Life?*

11. Jeff Sandefer, "Learner-Driven Communities: Preparing Young American Heroes for Lifelong Learning in the Twenty-First Century" (unpublished).

12. Oliver Sicat, "Initial Conclusions of Hybrid High's First Year," Blend My Learning, October 13, 2013 http://www.blendmylearning.com/2013/10/31/initial-conclusions-hybrid-high-first-yea/ (accessed April 15, 2014).

13. Daniel K. Lautzenheiser and Taryn Hochleitner, "Blended Learning in DC Public Schools: How One District Is Reinventing Its Classrooms," American Enterprise Institute, January 30, 2014, http://www.aei.org/papers/education/k-12/blended-learning-in-dc-public-schools-how-one-district-is-reinventing-its-classrooms/

14. 2012–13 Accountability Progress Reporting (APR), http://api.cde.ca.gov/Acnt2013/2012BaseSch.aspx?allcds=43694840123760; Brian Greenberg, Rob Schwartz, and Michael Horn, "Blended Learning: Personalizing Education for Students," Coursera, Week 3, Video 6: Shifting Teacher Mindsets, https://class.coursera.org/blendedlearning-001. In 2013 Gilroy Prep's API score was 942 on a 1000-point scale. That placed Gilroy Prep among the top-performing schools in the state of California. http://schools.latimes.com/2013-api-scores/ranking/page/1/

Chapter 10

Discover Your Way to Success

Leaders often express concern about undertaking innovation when children are involved. Innovation implies experimentation and uncertainty. Isn't disruptive innovation, as well as breakthrough sustaining innovation, too risky to pursue in schools, given that the well-being of children is at stake? As the poet Robert Burns observed, "The best-laid plans of mice and men often go awry."[1] And educators know that rarely do bold new plans survive implementation with actual students.

In some cases, of course, the risk of getting it wrong is low, and leaders can move forward with swift action to deploy the innovation across the entire school. But that's true only when three conditions are satisfied:[2]

- First, you must have a plan that addresses all of the important details required for success, with a high degree of confidence that the assumptions being made are correct, and those responsible for the implementation must understand each important detail.

- Second, the plan must make as much sense to all members of the organization as they view the world from their own context as it does to the person making the plan, so that everyone will act appropriately and consistently.

- Third, outside forces—such as the reaction of the community and students or the impact of other schools, programs, or technology—must be reasonably stable and predictable as the plan unfolds.

If all three of these are true, then go for it! But in most cases, teams implementing a blended-learning program, particularly for the first time, need a very different implementation process.

DISCOVERY-DRIVEN PLANNING

When launching something that is unfamiliar and unpredictable, with a low ratio of knowledge to hypotheses, educators need to change the planning and design process. A standard planning process—making a plan, looking at the projected outcomes from the plan, and then, assuming those outcomes look desirable, implementing it—will not work, because the assumptions, both implicit and explicit, on which the outcomes rest are often wrong.[3] This is why bold new plans—be they disruptive or sustaining—typically do not survive long beyond their point of initiation.

Even some of the most successful schools or examples of blended learning about which we've written in this book have made significant adjustments to their original plans as they have operated. One key to their success has been their ability to test their hypotheses and continue to iterate on their plans as they gain more information.

Summit Public Schools, for example, uses what is called the lean-startup method, a way of rapidly iterating toward success, to guide the development of its blended-learning model. The school network first experimented with a Station Rotation model that used the Khan Academy for its content in its math classes. After a year, it concluded that the model did not give students enough personalization and ownership over their learning, so the following year it piloted a Flex model in math in two of its schools. Throughout the year, Summit iterated on the model by examining the data and using input from student focus groups. Armed with this information, Summit made dramatic changes to the physical structure of the learning environment, how it guided students, and the interaction between content knowledge and project-based learning. A year later it unveiled a very different-looking Flex model for all subjects in all of its schools, based on what it had learned. Summit continues to evolve its blended-learning model as it gathers more data and experience.

Rocketship Education, famous for its Lab Rotation model, moved temporarily away from that model to deploy online learning alongside students' core teachers, rather than in learning labs, to see if that would strengthen the connection between what students were doing with teachers and what they were doing online. USC Hybrid High, a blended-learning charter school in Los Angeles, dramatically altered its model after its first year. Carpe Diem has continued to change its physical space and tweak its exact rotational schedule throughout its existence. It turns out that it's hard to know in advance what will and won't work when launching something new. Being flexible by updating your assumptions inherent in the model is key.

This isn't true only when working with children in schools. Research suggests that even among new companies that are successful, 90 percent succeeded with a strategy that was different from the one that the founder had originally deliberately planned.[4]

Therefore, when educators are creating something new and different from what they have always done previously, they need a different way to create a plan—particularly if the tolerance for failure is low and the need for caution is high, as is so often the case when innovating in education with children.

A process called "discovery-driven planning"—first introduced by Rita Gunther McGrath, a professor at Columbia Business School, and Ian C. MacMillan, a professor at the Wharton School of the University of Pennsylvania—is the one that we have found most useful for planning in this circumstance.[5] Discovery-driven planning bears a strong resemblance to the newer design methodology called "lean start-up," an approach that Steve Blank first conceptualized in 2003 based in part on the concept of discovery-driven planning. Because most schools are not start-ups seeking to "acquire" students—rather, they are already working with students, parents, and teachers who have existing expectations for their school—we think the discovery-driven planning framework, which helps reduce the risks of innovation, makes the most sense for most school leaders and teachers designing blended-learning models.

In a discovery-driven planning process, the key is to start with the desired outcome in mind. From there, the crucial next step is to list all of the assumptions that must prove true in order to realize the desired outcomes. With the assumptions in hand, the next step is to implement a plan to learn — as a way to test, as quickly and cheaply as possible, whether the critical assumptions are reasonable. If the assumptions prove true, then organizations can invest in executing the strategy. If assumptions prove false or uncertain, then organizations can change accordingly or continue to test before they have gone too far. The order of these steps, which we elaborate on next, mirrors the structure of this book in many ways. Exhibit 10.1 summarizes the steps.

Exhibit 10.1 Discovery-Driven Planning Process

Step 1: List desired outcomes.

Step 2: Determine what assumptions must prove true for outcomes to be realized.

Step 3: Implement a plan to learn to test whether the critical assumptions are reasonable.

Step 4: Implement the strategy when key assumptions prove true.

When should you use this process? When you are implementing something that is unfamiliar and unpredictable.

START WITH THE OUTCOMES

First, start with the desired outcomes, or projections, up front. If everybody knows what the outcomes must look like for the innovation to be worthwhile, then there is no sense in playing a game of Texas Hold 'Em.[6] Just lay the cards out on the table at the outset. What does the final state of the innovation need to do? What are you trying to accomplish? And how will you know you have been successful? The key is to make sure you have a SMART goal and can measure these outcomes so you know whether you have achieved your goals, as we explain in Chapter Three.

Summit Public Schools' goal, for example, is to dramatically increase its six-year college graduation rate, from 55 percent to preparing 100 percent of students to succeed in college. FirstLine Public Schools in Louisiana — the charter network we met in Chapter Three that raised student scores in low-performing schools from around the 25th percentile to between the 50th to 60th — wanted to aim even higher.[7] Quakertown, the school district in Pennsylvania that we met in Chapter One, innovated to win back students who had left the district for full-time cyber charter schools.

CREATE AN ASSUMPTIONS CHECKLIST

The second step is where the real work begins. With the desired goals and outcomes identified, compile an assumptions checklist. List all of the assumptions being made that must prove true in order for the desired outcomes to materialize. Be exhaustive in this stage. All of the assumptions that schools make implicitly should also be on the table, including the use of time and school schedules, space, and staffing. One way to capture the full range of these assumptions is to go section by section through this book and lay out all of the design elements being put in place, including the type of team implementing the innovation and who is on the team; the student experience; the teacher experience; the software, hardware, infrastructure, and facilities; the blended-learning model and where it is being implemented (whether in a core academic area or area of nonconsumption); and the culture. By cataloging all of these — and their implicit underlying components — you will assemble a comprehensive list of assumptions. That means everything from "this math software will be rigorous enough" to "our teachers will have the data they need to intervene in the right ways," to "the time we give students to learn is enough for them to master the curriculum."

Summit Public Schools, for example, assumed originally that a Station Rotation model would give students enough personalization and agency over their learning to prepare them to succeed in college. The network soon concluded that it had to do something more dramatic. If we imagine that the school model that Summit has implemented is still just a plan that we had designed in the course of reading this book and not yet a reality, we can brainstorm several assumptions that it is making about how its blended schools will work. At a high level, Summit assumes many things about the student experience, including the following:

- Its students can handle the self-pacing.
- Project-based learning will best develop students' deeper-thinking and cognitive skills and fulfill their "job to be done" of feeling successful.

- Summit can more effectively build its own learning management system, Activate, in partnership with a for-profit company, Illuminate, rather than buying something off the shelf.

- Ten minutes of dedicated mentorship time for each student each Friday will be enough.

Summit's teacher experience makes several assumptions, including that (1) the student expeditions that occur four times a year, coupled with other professional development activities, will be enough for teachers to shift to new roles focused on reading student data and developing students' cognitive and noncognitive skills, and (2) having teachers meet twice per week as a team will give them the right amount of time to review and make decisions with student data. In Summit's physical environment it is making several assumptions, including that (1) an open environment without walls that does away with the classroom will work in this new learning model, and (2) providing one-to-one Chromebooks for school use only is the right technology for its model. As one final example, it has also assumed in its culture that student focus groups will yield valuable information to iterate and improve.

FirstLine's schools also have several assumptions that must prove true in order to realize its goals. Initially, for example, FirstLine assumed that its online learning labs would be the best way for its students to learn English/Language Arts, but soon it decided to shift away from a blended-learning model for that subject. If the school had not yet been created but was still just a plan, another assumption in the FirstLine model concerning the student experience would be that sixty minutes of online time for kindergarten through third graders and one hundred minutes online for students in grades 4 through 8 would be the right amount to accomplish their learning goals—and would not have other unintended effects, such as those stemming from too much time in front of a computer screen. In its teacher experience, some assumptions behind FirstLine's model are that the paraprofessionals who staff the learning lab do not need deep content knowledge, but must have motivational skills, and that 120 minutes of professional development on Fridays with the director of blended learning and a blended-learning project manager is the right amount. Initially, FirstLine also assumed that providing teachers professional development with the learning lab software via a webinar would be effective, but it soon learned that this was not effective, so it shifted to investing money in having the software program representatives come monthly. In its physical environment, FirstLine assumed initially that it could use laptops on rolling laptop carts, but it soon learned that the laptops carted around in this manner were easily damaged.

FirstLine, like all schools, also made financial assumptions. Although this is an area we have not discussed much in the book, every school needs to be able to deliver on its plan in a financially sustainable manner. The key is to start with the total available budget and then reverse-engineer the financials accordingly. For example, FirstLine has a set budget to implement blended learning, so it needed to start with that number. Three assumptions in its plan were that it could afford a certain number of computers for the school, that it would not have to increase the class size, and that it could reduce support staff instead—which is not only a financial assumption but also one about the viability of the learning model itself.

Similarly, Quakertown made the following assumptions about the skills of its teachers and the transferability of face-to-face skills to the online medium:

- Teachers would know how to create good online courses.

- Just one mentor would be sufficient in each school to keep students on track.

- One person could take on the dual role of technology and professional development support staffer.

- Teachers could teach in both face-to-face classes and online at the same time.

- Teachers would not have to spend significant extra time preparing for their online courses because they could use the same content from their face-to-face courses.

This last assumption had financial implications. Once the assumption proved false, Quakertown encountered an embedded assumption: that it would not have to pay teachers extra for their course development time, which in turn proved false.

This process of listing out assumptions should take a day or two, and it is time well spent. Sometimes the list of assumptions at this stage will number more than one hundred! We also recommend having people at the table in this brainstorming exercise who represent a variety of departments and perspectives, so that the assumptions list will be exhaustive and help the leader understand where people within an organization do and do not agree. In Figure 10.1 we have provided a chart of some of the assumptions to consider as you brainstorm.

Figure 10.1 Be Expansive about the Assumptions

TEAM
- Are the right people at the table?
- Does the team leader have the right level of authority?
- Do we have enough senior leader support?

STUDENT EXPERIENCE
- Do some of our students need different experiences to be successful?
- Are there enough opportunities for them to have fun with friends in the course of working?

TEACHER EXPERIENCE
- Are we asking teachers to do things for which they are not trained?
- Are teachers matched to the right roles where they can feel success?

SOFTWARE
- Does the software have enough instructional minutes?
- Is the content rigorous enough?
- Will it provide actionable, easily understood data?

HARDWARE
- Is the hardware durable enough?
- Do we have enough Wi-Fi?
- Can we afford upgrades?
- Do we have enough backup equipment if things break?

FACILITY
- Do we have enough electrical outlets?
- Does the furniture match the experiences for students?
- Does the space reinforce the desired culture?

LEARNING MODEL
- Are we asking students to stay in rotations for too long?
- Does this model provide opportunities that match the experiences we want to offer students?

CULTURE
- Will the process for switching between modalities work for students?
- Is implementing blended learning a priority for the team members?
- Do we have the right norms in place for students?

Once you are done compiling all of the assumptions, the next job is to rank the assumptions from the most to the least crucial. We have found that having the same group of individuals ask two questions about each assumption is the best way to accomplish this.[8]

First, ask what could happen if you are wrong about an assumption. In other words, which of these assumptions, if proved untrue, would most seriously derail the success of the project? If the assumption is wrong, will it be catastrophic to the project? Will it require a major overhaul of the plan? Is the impact just minor and does it require only a few tweaks? Or is being wrong no big deal, as it will have no impact on the plan? If being wrong will be catastrophic to the project, assign it a priority value of 1; if it's no big deal, assign it a 3. A rank of 2 is in between.

Second, ask how confident you are that each assumption is correct. A fun test of how confident people are is to see if they are willing to give up one year's salary if they are wrong—meaning they have a high degree of confidence that they know the answer. Perhaps they are willing to give up only one week's salary if they are wrong? Or one day's worth? Or maybe they aren't willing to bet any of their salary because they have no sense of whether the assumption is correct. Assign a value based on the confidence. A rank of 3 signals real confidence, whereas a rank of 1 means no confidence at all that the assumption is correct.

After ranking all of the assumptions, map them on the graph in Figure 10.2 based on their assigned point value. This forms the assumptions checklist.

IMPLEMENT A PLAN — TO LEARN MORE

With the prioritized assumptions checklist in hand, the next step is to implement a plan to test the validity of the assumptions. Plan to check the most important assumptions—those in Zone 1—first because those are the assumptions with the least confidence behind them that are also the most crucial to the project's success.

In the initial stages of planning, the tests should be as simple, cheap, and quick as possible—they should simply directionally validate or invalidate information about the most critical assumptions. For example, it is a good idea to look at other schools—like the ones written about in this book—to see whether the assumptions hold water before going too far down a road. Reading the existing

Figure 10.2 Prioritizing Assumptions and Risks

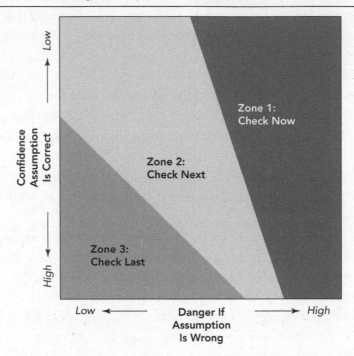

research, having early conversations, or making quick mock-ups or prototypes makes sense. A prototype is anything that helps communicate the idea for what you are doing, which can mean everything from mock-ups and models to simulations and role-playing experiences. It is often helpful to create what people call the "minimum viable product"; this means slapping together the simplest product or prototype that allows the testing of the salient assumptions as quickly as possible. More concretely, perhaps a key assumption being made concerns the rigor of a math program. To test its rigor, after talking to others who use it and reading about it, a school could ask for one license for the math program so that its teachers can poke around and see if it passes their own smell test for being rigorous enough. The school might then find a place—such as in summer school or after school—to pilot the math program for a couple of weeks before buying it and using it for all of its students for an entire year. And it might do this for a couple of other programs as well. We have included in Exhibit 10.2 some more ways to creatively and quickly test the assumptions.

Exhibit 10.2 Test Creatively

Keep it simple, keep it cheap
- Create a rapid, "good enough" prototype.
- Talk to students and parents.
- Talk to internal resources.
- Talk to other schools doing something similar.
- Visit other schools.
- Look to your history.
- Read the research.
- Identify early milestones.
- Talk to the business manager to make sure it is sustainable.
- Talk to experts in the field.
- Conduct a focus group.
- Launch a pilot, perhaps in the summer or after school.

As the team moves closer and closer to launch, the tests should become more comprehensive and precise—and perhaps more costly. But the important thing is to not invest a lot of time and resources early before knowing whether the assumptions are proving true—or at least are in the right ballpark. To create a rhythm for the tests and to know when it's time to get more precise with them, create checkpoints to systematically test the assumptions.[9] The checkpoints are specific dates when tests of several assumptions should be completed, so that the team can come together and evaluate what it has learned, as we discuss in the next step.

The period leading up to the first checkpoint could last one month and be designed to give team members time to study other blended-learning schools and test some (but not all) of the assumptions at a high level. A second checkpoint might occur a month after that and include an analysis of the software market. In the intervening month, the team could talk to other school leaders to test assumptions yet again—often including many of the same ones that were tested in the last step but at a more precise level, so that the plan is refined continually as the team gains more information. Further down the line a checkpoint might include a working prototype or pilot of the blended-learning model, and then the launch of the blended-learning model itself.

After the model is launched, there should be ongoing checkpoints to allow the team to step back and see what it has learned and might want to adjust, so that continuous improvement becomes baked into the team's DNA. Once the innovation is implemented, though, there is a risk in innovating too fast and furiously. For example, making dramatic changes every week risks confusing the school community and undermining the trust of students, parents, and teachers. One reason for designing and executing tests before rolling out the whole plan is to try to figure things out before going too far down the road with an implementation. Following this process helps schools avoid expensive, high-profile failures, as checkpoints become opportunities to decide whether to move forward—the last step in the process.

SHOULD WE GO FORWARD, CHANGE, OR SHELVE THE PLAN?

The last step is the decision whether to continue implementing the strategy. Each time a checkpoint passes, there is a set of choices that must be made, rather than blindly moving forward regardless of the results.

If your assumptions are proving true, then keep moving forward to the next checkpoint.

If they are not—as will more than likely be the case—you have a few options. Perhaps you can tweak the plan to keep moving forward; for example, maybe the math software an educator had planned to use will be good for only twenty minutes of instruction a day rather than thirty minutes; this means the rotation schedule will have to be adjusted.

Alternatively, there may need to be bigger adjustments. Perhaps the blended-learning model needs to be implemented by a different team in an area of nonconsumption where there will be more time to fine-tune the innovation before it must be scaled to the entire school to show that it is successful.

Or finally, perhaps the assumptions underlying the success of the plan are wildly unrealistic, and the plan just won't work. If this is the case, then there is an opportunity to shelve the plan before too much money has been invested and the stakes have become too high to abandon the idea.

At each checkpoint the team will gain new information. An assumption that seemed like it was right in a previous checkpoint may be revealed to be more complex than it was originally thought to be. That's OK. And if the team learns that ultimately the assumptions are unrealistic and it won't be able to pull off the program, that is not a reason for despair. Fast failure is a success; the team learned that the idea would not work before wasting a lot of time and money implementing something that wouldn't work. The key is to celebrate each time a decision is made. Rather than have people feel like they have to defend a pet idea, the victory is learning more about an assumption, not proving that someone is right or wrong.

Ultimately, as the team makes adjustments and iterates, it may find that it is going down a path with assumptions that are proving true. Even though the plan that is emerging and gradually being implemented is different from the one that was foreseen originally, if it will be successful in realizing the desired outcomes, then that's a resounding success—and the ultimate value of the discovery-driven process.

To Sum Up

- When launching something unfamiliar and unpredictable, for which the ratio of knowledge to hypotheses is low, educators need to change the planning and design process. Discovery-driven planning is the method that we have found most useful for planning in this circumstance.
- Discovery-driven planning has four steps. It is designed to reduce the risk of innovation. By encouraging fast failure, it helps avoid expensive, high-profile failures.
- First, start with the desired outcomes, or projections. Have a SMART goal.
- Second, with the desired goals and outcomes identified, compile an assumptions checklist. List all of the assumptions being made that must be proven true in order for the desired outcomes to materialize. Then rank the assumptions by how confident you are that each assumption is correct and how dangerous it is to the project's success if you are wrong.

(continued)

(continued)

- Third, implement a plan to learn more, to test whether the critical assumptions are reasonable.
- Fourth, at predetermined checkpoints, based on the results from the tests, decide whether to implement the innovation, change the innovation, or shelve it.

NOTES

1. The line from the Robert Burns poem "To a Mouse, on Turning Her Up in Her Nest with the Plough," reads "The best-laid schemes o' mice an' men / Gang aft agley," but is often paraphrased in English the way we have here.

2. Much of the thinking behind this circumstance-based theory for strategic planning has been adapted from Clayton M. Christensen and Michael Raynor, *The Innovator's Solution* (Boston: Harvard Business Press, 2003), Chapter Eight. The following sections borrow from these ideas.

3. The standard planning process works well in a circumstance in which the ratio of knowledge to hypotheses is high. That means there is a high degree of confidence that the assumptions being made are correct because you've done it so often in the past in a similar circumstance. Often this process will work well, for example, in a world of familiar sustaining innovations—precisely because that world is so familiar and predictable. Many experienced educators, for example, who have delivered Social Studies lessons or offered Social Studies projects for many years don't find it too difficult to plan a new lesson or project that will work in the classroom reasonably closely to how they envision it. Similarly, those who have opened several new schools that were similar to each other—and successful—don't find it that hard to plan for opening yet another new school that will also be similar—in its methodology, grade levels, and students and community that it serves—and to achieve success with that initial plan.

4. Christensen and Raynor, *The Innovator's Solution*, Chapter Eight (Kindle Locations 2677–2678).

5. We highly recommend Rita Gunther McGrath and Ian C. MacMillan's book *Discovery-Driven Growth: A Breakthrough Process to Reduce Risk and Seize Opportunity* (Boston: Harvard Business Press, 2009).

6. When people use a standard planning process rather than a discovery-driven one in an uncertain circumstance, they often play a game with their assumptions at the heart of their plan by continually drumming them up to make the outcomes look better and better so that the plan will be approved.

7. As mentioned in Chapter Three, FirstLine could have had a goal that was more precise. The same is true for Quakertown.

8. We thank Innosight, LLC, a consulting firm that uses the theories of disruptive innovation to drive new growth for clients, for their insight into this process. Much of this section is taken from their original work; for those who want to go deeper, we recommend a book that helpfully lays out their findings. See Scott D. Anthony, Mark W. Johnson, Joseph V. Sinfield, and Elizabeth J. Altman, *The Innovator's Guide to Growth: Putting Disruptive Innovation to Work* (Boston: Harvard Business Press, 2008), Chapter Seven.

9. For more on how to select checkpoints, see McGrath and MacMillan, *Discovery-Driven Growth*, Chapter Seven.

Chapter 11

Conclusion

Innovating is a process, not an event.

In this book we have sought first to show the unprecedented opportunities that innovating with the emerging set of online learning tools offers to students, teachers, schools, and society, and then to describe a process to realize those benefits.

But following this process once—even for innovations outside of blended learning—doesn't constitute the end of the journey. As Chapter Ten notes, instilling an ethos of continuous improvement—always seeking to learn and do better—is important. Making progress and never standing still is a hallmark of a healthy society and healthy schools, and it models the capacity for lifelong learning that we seek to instill in students. We hope that the ideas from this book will propel you—and educators around the world—to develop a steady rhythm of innovation.

Adopting this innovation mindset will be critical to achieving success. Although blended learning offers enormous potential to personalize learning for each student's distinct learning needs and to free up student and teacher time to focus on many of the activities that are critical to student success but too often receive short shrift today, it's still early days. True, there are great success stories in the field—we have profiled several of them in this book—and there are some clear pathways forward. But both the online tools and the blended-learning models themselves are continuing to evolve. Teachers have no trouble pointing to their wish lists for how the available technologies need to improve. Innovative educators are mixing and matching models to create designs that work in their school buildings with their students. But blended learning, at this point in its evolution, is not a walk in the park.

IMPLEMENT OVER TIME

The good news is that you don't need to rush and do everything at once.

First, give yourself time to plan and implement prudently. For its first blended pilot, Oakland Unified School District selected the schools in January and started planning in February, and the programs began at the start of the school year in August and September.[1] Montessori For All, a blended public school in Austin, Texas, took more than a year of planning before opening its doors.[2] This is not an overnight process. A healthy planning time frame for schools that are adding a blended component to their existing model is six months at a minimum; for those that are launching a new model, twelve to eighteen months is more normal.[3] Although you should feel some urgency about the work, allow yourself a reasonable amount of time commensurate with the level of change being made and resources available to plan and implement the change.

Second, the innovation should happen in phases. One way to do this is to focus on a narrow problem or goal before tackling a different or broader rallying cry the next year. Summer school is often an attractive proving ground. Some schools or school systems choose to start blended learning for one grade of students and then expand it by one more grade level each year. Others start with teachers in a particular subject discipline. Districts and charter-school networks sometimes blend school by school. Still others choose to wet their feet with one model and then evolve their innovation over time. For example, Summit Public Schools first dipped its toes into blended learning by piloting a basic Station Rotation in its math classes in two of its schools. A year later it experimented with a Flex model in place of the Station Rotation for those math classes. The year after that, in 2013–14, it moved to a full-blown Flex model for all of its subjects in all of its schools. Many will choose some combination of these approaches.

If you work in phases, start with an overall plan with the sequence of stages and time frame in mind, but treat this as a discovery-driven plan as well. Adjust as you learn. As school community members see blended learning in action, their appetite for more innovation often grows. Also, when you move in a phased approach, inevitably there will be different team structures along the way and people will play different roles. Setting clear expectations and goals for administrators, teachers, students, and parents is important, as is making sure that people have a clear understanding of their role in the innovation and how it will evolve.

BLENDED LEARNING IS A TEAM SPORT

Everyone has a role to play in blended learning.

Teachers can start innovating right away and boost learning by flipping their classrooms or implementing a Station Rotation. As teachers engage in their own innovations within their functional teams, they can start to generate excitement about what they are doing among others in the schooling community to spur more change. And they can lead other teachers to organize in teams to plan broader changes.

School administrators can support bottom-up approaches from teachers by encouraging and facilitating their efforts to innovate. Helping teachers have time to plan and learn, providing professional development opportunities for them, and clearing obstacles that are in their way, such as technological barriers, is vital. By the same token, school leaders can be proactive in forming teams and inviting teachers to join those teams to respond to a variety of rallying cries.

Parents should be involved in any innovation effort. If parents don't understand what is going on and why it will benefit their children, they can quickly and understandably become barriers to change. But they can also be the biggest advocates of all. At Rocketship Education, the schools cultivate the parental community—through such efforts as daily morning meetings that parents can attend, a parent volunteer policy, and public recognition of parents' efforts.[4] The parents in turn help the broader community understand the power of

Rocketship's education model. Parent demand can be a powerful force as well for creating change. In some communities, schools are shifting to personalized learning in response to parent requests. In others, such as in the Los Altos School District in California, the parental community is also a critical player in helping raise funds to support the transition to a blended-learning environment.

Superintendents, school network heads, and other system-wide leaders have important roles to play, as the discussion in Chapter Four on the importance of autonomous and heavyweight teams makes clear. For these actors, taking a portfolio approach—empowering different schools to create different innovations that solve problems in different circumstances—is important. Similarly, all leaders should adopt a split-screen strategy and solve both core problems with sustaining innovations like Station Rotation models and nonconsumption problems with disruptive innovations like Flex and A La Carte models. There is no single best model, but there is a need to institute a comprehensive innovation process that encourages both types of innovation and that specifically shelters and protects disruptive innovations from being subsumed by an organization's traditional processes.

These leaders should also play an active role in making sure there is infrastructure that allows the innovation to occur. Ensuring adequate internet access is a must; determining the right role for the central authority in device acquisition, licensing software, and technology support is trickier, as different schools and teachers have different needs. Determining what to centralize versus what to empower others to lead is a balancing act that demands careful thought. For example, allowing schools to pick software from a menu of curated options might be a reasonable balance, but allowing each school in a network to use a different student information system likely makes less sense.

School boards, policymakers, and other leaders need to stay involved to support action, on both the sustaining and disruptive fronts, with the power of the purse, and to ask questions that propel the innovators to take prudent steps with an aligned mission of student success. But they should also be wary of top-down actions that could stifle innovation.

Networks or clusters of innovators provide important opportunities for leaders and teachers to talk with others engaged in similar work to troubleshoot, learn from techniques and designs that worked in similar circumstances, have candid discussions about opportunities and pitfalls, and aggregate smart demand to encourage vendors to be more responsive. Leading can be a lonely endeavor. Being part of a network of innovators or leading within a cluster has big benefits for accessing information, technology, and needed institutions to smooth the process of innovation.[5] Regional clusters involved with next-generation, blended-learning models are emerging in Silicon Valley; Washington, D.C.; Chicago; and elsewhere for just these purposes.

Finally, remember to include *students* on the team. If the role of school is to help students become successful lifelong learners, then helping them own their learning—developing student agency—is critical. As they progress through their schooling from kindergarten through twelfth grade, schools should help them have increasing levels of control over the time, place, path, and pace of their learning. Not only that, but students can also assist in teaching and tutoring. Summit Public Schools, as we wrote earlier, even uses student focus groups to inform the design and evolution of their schools.

UNDERSTAND, MOBILIZE, DESIGN, IMPLEMENT

Don't innovate for the sake of innovating, any more than you would implement technology for technology's sake.

Start with a rallying cry and a SMART goal that will allow you to know whether you've been successful in innovating.

Assemble the right team, one that is appropriate to the scope of the challenge.

Understand your students' jobs to be done, and design the right set of student experiences. Learner experience should infuse all that you do.

Design the right teaching experience to deliver on the goal and the desired student experience.

Only then should you think about the technology—software, hardware, and infrastructure—and the facilities design. What can you change and what do you need to work with that will modify your existing plans?

Then choose your model and customize it in ways that make sense for your circumstances.

Be intentional about the culture you want to see, and actively shape the organization's processes and priorities to be successful.

Lastly, follow a discovery-driven process to help you be successful and avoid high-profile failures. With the outcomes for success captured in your SMART goal and your preliminary plan in place, identify the assumptions you're making, rank them, implement a plan to learn which assumptions are right and which need tweaking, and then set up intentional checkpoints to see whether and how to proceed.

This book offers not a playbook of what every school should do, but a playbook to help find the right approach for *you* in *your* circumstances. Just as there is no one-size-fits-all way to educate all students, there is no one-size-fits-all school, blended-learning model, software, or even way to innovate. Figure 11.1 summarizes the blueprint for developing and implementing a blended-learning strategy that we offer in this book.

Blended learning holds enormous potential to transform our factory-model education system into a student-centered design that captures the benefits of personalization, equity and access, and cost control. Although it is not a panacea, for increasingly antiquated schools—and the students in those schools—it's an essential piece of the puzzle.

With this knowledge and expertise in hand, it's time to roll up our sleeves and build the future of learning. Teachers, school and community leaders, parents, and students all have a role to play to help all students prepare for the complex and promising future that awaits them.

Figure 11.1 Blueprint for Blended Learning

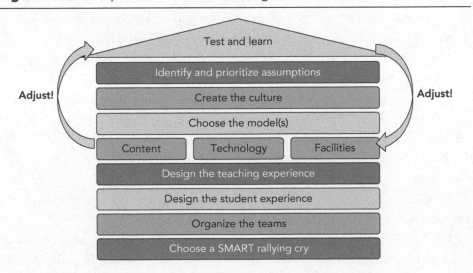

NOTES

1. Interview with Carrie Douglas, chief strategy officer, CEE-Trust, June 6, 2014.

2. In fact, the founders worked on the plan for 3.5 years, but they began planning on a full-time, salaried basis ten months before the launch date. Interview with Sara Cotner, founder and executive director, Montessori For All, June 6, 2014.

3. Interview with Andy Calkins, deputy director, Next Generation Learning Challenges, Educause, April 6, 2014.

4. Rebecca Kisner, "The Parent Engagement Continuum in High-Performing Charter Schools: A Guide for Schools," Donnell-Kay Foundation, May 2013, p. 5.

5. Harvard Business School Professor Michael Porter has written, "The enduring competitive advantages in a global economy lie increasingly in local things—knowledge, relationships, motivation—that distant rivals cannot match." Michael E. Porter, "Clusters and the New Economics of Competition," Harvard Business Review, November- December 1998, p. 78. Although the idea expressed here relates to commercial value networks, the principles have value for educators as well. Porter also writes, "Being part of a cluster allows companies to operate more productively in sourcing inputs; accessing information, technology, and needed institutions; coordinating with related companies; and measuring and motivating improvement" (p. 81).

Appendix: Questions for Discussion

The following questions may help to facilitate your reflections on *Blended*. They may also be used to stimulate discussion of *Blended* in a Professional Learning Community, staff development workshop, or teacher education course.

CHAPTER 1

1. Imagine that you are back in class as a middle school student. Would you prefer technology-rich instruction or blended learning? For you as a middle school student, what would be the advantages and disadvantages of each type?

2. What is the best use of face-to-face time? Jon Bergmann, one of the founders of the Flipped Classroom, found that for his students, "It was not me standing in front of my students yakking. That was not the correct answer; the correct answer was hands-on activities [and] inquiry- and project-based learning." On a scale of 1 to 5, with 1 representing "true in all cases" and 5 "never true," to what extent do you think that Bergmann's answer is true for all students?

3. What are the opportunities and drawbacks of the Flex model? In what circumstances can you imagine Flex working well, and in which do you think it is unlikely to be successful?

4. If tomorrow you were to start learning a foreign language through blended learning, what model or combination of models would you want to use?

CHAPTER 2

1. Do you agree that schools will continue to exist but that high school classrooms will not? Why?

2. In your opinion, of the four broad sets of activities described by the authors—deeper learning, safe care, wraparound services, and fun with friends and extracurricular activities—that schools could start to embrace with the emergence of online learning, which is the most important for your community? Rank them from the most important to the least. Why have you chosen this order?

3. Are there critical activities that schools should shift to doing more of that the authors have not included? Name them and explain why they are important.

CHAPTER 3

1. If you could use blended learning to solve one budget shortfall in your school(s), what would it be and why?

2. The authors list several goals that other schools have set prior to embarking on blended learning, including to personalize learning and thereby improve test scores, to endow students with greater agency and control, and to improve teacher training. Make the case for why one of these is the most important in your community.

3. If you had to choose between (a) improving the traditional classroom with a sustaining innovation that serves mainstream students in core classes and (b) introducing a disruptive model to bring a new solution to an area of nonconsumption, which would you choose? Why?

CHAPTER 4

1. In your present circumstances, what level of problem is most urgent to solve and why? What type of team would you need in order to solve it? Who would you place on the team, and who would lead it?

2. Consider New York City's attempts to innovate through the use of multiple teams. Do you think they will be successful with the approach they have taken? In your own circumstances, if you thought regulatory relief was important, what type of team would you need to deploy and why?

3. Would you personally rather serve on a heavyweight or a functional team? Why?

CHAPTER 5

1. On a scale of 1 to 5, with 1 representing very important and 5 representing not at all important, how critical do you think it is to design school so that students find learning joyful and intrinsically motivating? Discuss.

2. Think of a recent time when you purchased a product. Analyze that purchase using the jobs-to-be-done theory. What job were you "hiring" that product to do in your life at the moment? How well did the vendor deliver all the right experiences associated with your purchasing and using the product to help you fulfill the job you were trying to do? What other experiences should the vendor have offered?

3. Summit delivers eight experiences that help students to feel successful and have fun with friends: student agency, individual mastery, access to actionable data and rapid feedback, transparency in learning goals, sustained periods of solitary reading time, meaningful work experiences, mentoring experiences, and positive group experiences. Which one or two of these do you find most important from a student's jobs-to-be-done perspective?

4. Brainstorm ideas for experiences that could help students in your community feel successful and have fun with friends, given the specific circumstances they face.

CHAPTER 6

1. On a scale of 1 to 5, with 1 representing very important and 5 representing not at all important, how important do you think being a mentor is in a teacher's job? In your own community, do you think there is a growing need for children to have positive role models and mentors? Why?

2. Name two jobs to be done that most teachers have in their lives. Why are those their most important jobs?

3. Do you agree with the authors that teachers are motivated by recognition for their achievements and would be pleased to stop working in a solitary environment and move to team-based teaching? Why?

4. Sketch out your ideal teaching model. Would there be one teacher or multiple teachers? What would their roles be?

CHAPTER 7

1. Discuss ways that modularity has allowed for more flexibility and customization in any aspect of your life.

2. The authors say that for some students, the fully integrated, interdependent model is more than adequate in terms of offering comprehensive functionality, and now the greater need is for choice, flexibility, and the opportunity to customize. Do you think this is true yet for any students in your community?

3. If you had to choose between having schools develop all their own online content or having them use a facilitated network, which would you prefer? Why?

4. In terms of the physical architecture of school buildings, if you had to choose between traditional, egg-crate classrooms and open, flexible learning studios, which would you choose? What are the pros and cons of each, in your opinion?

CHAPTER 8

1. What problem are you trying to solve?

2. What type of team do you need to solve the problem?

3. What do you want students to control?

4. What do you want the teacher's primary role to be?

5. What physical space can you use?

6. How many internet-connected devices are available?

7. Which of these questions is the most important in your circumstances or opinion?

8. For which of these questions is the answer one that you do not have the authority or power to change?

CHAPTER 9

1. Name one process or routine that has coalesced into a healthy aspect of your organization's culture. What do you like about that cultural norm?

2. Name one process or routine in your organization's culture that you think is unsuccessful or harmful. What different process that might work better could you test instead?

3. What is one new process that you would like to test to see if it helps make your blended model successful?

CHAPTER 10

1. Name a high-profile failure in education, business, or government. What major assumptions do you think were made that, had they been tested before the launch, could have prevented the failure?

2. Imagine if you were part of the initial team that designed Summit Public Schools' model. What assumptions about the design do you think are the riskiest?

3. What simple, cheap, and quick tests would you want to put in place to test those assumptions?

CONCLUSION

1. In your opinion, which of the following groups in your community needs to take action first to mobilize the transformation toward student-centered learning: teachers, school administrators, parents, superintendents, school network heads and other system-wide leaders, school boards and policymakers, networks of innovators, or students?

2. Review the blended-learning blueprint (see Figure 11.1). What have you learned by reading about and discussing its layers? What are your biggest takeaways?

Index

on education, 2; pattern of disruptive innovation in, 3–5; roots of blended learning in, 32–33; technological innovations fueling, 4; using Khan Academy for, 5–6. *See also* Online content
Operating systems, 203–205
Organizing teams, 115, 121, 124–126, 130–131; applying team framework to schools, 120–129; autonomous teams, 115, 118–120, 121, 126–129, 130–131, 132; heavyweight teams, 115, 117–118, 121, 124–126, 130–131, 132; to initiate blended learning, 113–114; lightweight teams, 115, 116–117, 121, 123–124, 131; overview, 131–132; pros/cons of teams, 130–131; types of teams and tasks, 114–115; using functional teams, 115–116, 120–123; using multiple types of teams, 129
Osborne Executive, 189
Outside content providers, 197–199
Oversold and Underused (Cuban), 96–97

P

Parents, 283–284
Personal computers: changes in architecture, 192–193; number in schools, 96; one-to-one computer programs at K–12, 96–97
Personalized learning: about, 9; integrating into blended learning, 157; need for, 11; as part of student-centered learning, 8; Rose's innovative programs in, 12–14
Peters, Brooke, 219
Phasing in blended learning, 282–283
Physical activity, 150–151
Pilot programs, 273–276
Planning. *See* Discovery-driven planning
Processes, 268
Products: architecture of, 190; failure to produce successful, 139–142; interdependent and modular architecture of, 191–192; unsuccessful ColorMatch innovation, 176–177

Project-based learning, 55
Prototype tests, 273–276

Q

Quakertown Community School District, 99–100, 269, 271
Questions: for choosing blended learning models, 220–221, 223–236, 240; discussion, 289–293

R

Ratey, John, 150
Reading: making time for student, 149, 154; READ 180 program outcomes, 31, 39
Reed, Lanita, 173
Replicating blended learning successes, 220, 240
Response-to-Intervention (RTI) method, 100
Ridge Middle School, 208
Right Denied, A, 1
Riley, Bob, 14
Rocketship Education, 41, 42, 267
Rogers Family Foundation, 104
Rose, Joel, 12–14, 45
Rosenstock, Larry, 32
Rosetta Stone, 32
Rotation model: about, 38, 55; Flex vs., 47; Flipped Classroom, 42–44, 55, 58; hybrid solutions of, 72, 73–75, 85; Individual Rotation, 45–46, 55–56, 58; Lab Rotation, 38, 41–42, 55, 57; Station Rotation, 39–41, 55, 56; table of options, 242–243. *See also specific types of Rotation models*

S

Sams, Aaron, 231
San Francisco Flex Academy, 48
Sandefer, Jeff and Laura, 101, 254–255
Schein, Edgar, 250, 261
Scholastic performance: of children of divorced parents, 173; disruptive innovations and, 3; Individual Rotation and, 46; measuring KIPP's, 16–19; READ 180, 39; redefining for Flipped Classroom, 75